EDUCATION STUDIES

Written by educational specialists and including over fifty interdisciplinary entries, this essential compendium offers accessible, detailed definitions of the core concepts typically explored on undergraduate Education Studies courses.

Its interactive design clarifies topics at an introductory, intermediate and advanced level, supporting students across the three years of their undergraduate study. The history and evolution of each concept is outlined with concepts practically grouped around four interrelated key educational categories – the personal, philosophy, practice and power. Key academic debates and points of contest are explored, reference to real-life educational examples are offered, and reflective questions and further reading scaffold critical engagement.

Education Studies: The Key Concepts is a bookshelf must-have, moving readers towards a coherent stance based on theory and research. It is an easy-to-use resource for anyone looking to better understand education. It is also useful for those researching education at postgraduate level to broaden their educational knowledge base outside their specific foci.

Dave Trotman is Professor of Education Policy, Newman University, Birmingham, UK.

Helen E. Lees is Reader in Alternative Education Studies, Newman University, Birmingham, UK.

Roger Willoughby is Senior Lecturer in Education and Professional Studies, Newman University, Birmingham, UK.

EDUCATION STUDIES

The Key Concepts

Edited by Dave Trotman,
Helen E. Lees and Roger Willoughby

Routledge
Taylor & Francis Group

LONDON AND NEW YORK

First published 2018
by Routledge
2 Park Square, Milton Park, Abingdon, Oxon OX14 4RN

and by Routledge
711 Third Avenue, New York, NY 10017

Routledge is an imprint of the Taylor & Francis Group, an informa business

British Library Cataloguing-in-Publication Data
A catalogue record for this book is available from the British Library

Library of Congress Cataloging-in-Publication Data
A catalog record for this book has been requested

ISBN: 978-1-138-95777-0 (hbk)
ISBN: 978-1-138-95782-4 (pbk)
ISBN: 978-1-315-66150-6 (ebk)

Typeset in Bembo
by Cenveo Publisher Services

Printed and bound by CPI Group (UK) Ltd, Croydon, CR0 4YY

CONTENTS

INTRODUCTION AND GUIDE TO USING THE BOOK

This book is aimed chiefly at undergraduate **Education Studies** students. It is, however, useful for anyone studying or wishing to better understand education. It offers an accessible format designed to both introduce and support increasingly sophisticated understandings of educational issues; involving a wide range of key concepts central to the subject.

Beginning with its origins and current usage, each concept entry provides students with a succinct background explanation and its significance for education. In doing this, each concept is developed at three levels, increasing in complexity and mirroring important lines of intellectual progression inherent in undergraduate study. Levels four, five and six of the three-year degree are represented by an introductory 'starting' symbol ⏻ followed by engagement ✿ and ultimately moving towards a degree of fluency ☺ .

Cross-referencing between entries is important to extend understanding. Each entry will typically have several such cross-references, indicated by the word being both printed in bold and underlined (e.g., **power**). This indicates the book holds an entire separate entry for that concept. If a word is printed in bold, without being underlined (e.g., **relationality**), this signals it is in the glossary at the back of the book, with a brief explanation.

The format of this book allows readers, through its concept-specific reference lists, to identify further relevant and accessible materials (articles, books and websites). Within each of these lists we have highlighted in bold three particularly recommended readings. It is anticipated that undergraduate education students will encounter most, if not all, of the concepts here, with some more significantly grasped than others, depending on individual interests. Those researching education at postgraduate level can use this book to supplement their specialist knowledge in areas which have remained outside of their specific foci, enabling a broader knowledge base of educational interests.

Our decision has been not to present concepts in simple alphabetical order but, rather, to organise them around four interrelated key educational categories of the personal, philosophy, practice and power. In order of appearance, the personal has been placed first, as this is often the first significant educational theme an education studies course might address and reflects the profound and deeply personal effects that education can have upon the individual. Power has been positioned as the final category so that it mirrors something of the educational journey—from appreciating the personal to critically understanding the presence and effects of socio-political forces in education. Between these philosophy and practice recognise the development of a personal philosophy of education informed by theoretical ideas about the nature of education and practice as informed action for the common good.

The book is written by educational specialists working in the UK. It therefore often draws on UK examples. Each concept has been written, however, with the aim of the text being as relevant as possible to an international audience. Some concepts such as **law, policy, politics** and others are more country-specific than, say, **hegemony, power** or **pedagogy**, which are more international in scope. The task is made more challenging by the local nature of education. Nevertheless, a concept is a concept and interpretations are a part of the interactive design of this book. This dialogic approach includes, at the end of the level texts, some questions for students to consider. We see this book as a creative exchange between the writers and the readers who are warmly encouraged to debate, problematise and reconsider what is written here in a process of ongoing critical engagement with education as contested terrain.

Do we need a book like this? In bringing this text together, we have been heartened by how edifying having each concept explained has been for ourselves as university **teacher**s as well as for our students. Students find these concise introductions to the key concepts of education useful.

The study of education at degree level is a highly popular choice for a broad range of students, many of whom come to the subject with varying educational interests and career ambitions. It is this **diversity** of student profiles and for each their **motivation** to study education which we hope this book serves.

The growth of **Education Studies** as a degree subject has been complemented by a number of informative texts devoted to the study of education as an **interdisciplinary** or thematic field of enquiry. Involving aspects of education that include economics, history, philosophy, psychology and sociology, among others, approaches to the subject have frequently involved the exploration of key issues, debates and themes.

The approach we take in this text is of course different. For many students new to the study of education, terminology and ideas they may not have encountered before are likely to come thick and fast, some of which will be more difficult to grasp than others. Some will be more elusive and prone to mis-understanding and assumption. Recognising these challenges, we have drawn on the expertise of each of the contributors, through their experience of **teaching** key aspects of Education Studies, to create a primer for Education Studies not just from an interdisciplinary or thematic perspective but, fundamentally, from a *conceptual* perspective.

Concepts are, however, tricky things. Our understanding and interpretation of them is inevitably positioned by our disciplinary backgrounds, political stances, **gender**, **ethnicity**, personality and other influences. Educational concepts are, as we emphasise throughout this book, evolving and essentially dynamic entities. Such evolution can, at times, be dramatic and concepts at particular points in time are subject to revision or replacement, even to the point of substantial shifts in collective thinking.

Our choice of concepts, here, represents then our current collective understanding of what are, or should be, key concepts in the study of education. Inevitably, our **selection**s will be controversial—for some readers—over what is and is not included.

Such a project would not have been possible without enlisting the support, help and guidance of our colleagues and other experienced academics in their respective fields of expertise. We owe our contributors a significant debt of gratitude. In this undertaking, as the reader might anticipate, the text reflects a range of educational standpoints, positions and **voices**. We hope this book helps you to better understand, shape and enjoy your study of education.

Dave Trotman, Helen E. Lees and Roger Willoughby

PERSONAL

KEY CONCEPT: ADULT EDUCATION

Peter Harris

Concept origins

Savicevic (1999) suggests that the origins of adult education can be traced back to Greek, Romantic and humanistic philosophers who all maintained that **learning** extends, and should extend, beyond **childhood**. This understanding of education as an aspect of everyday life, continuing throughout the lifespan can also be viewed as broadly derivative of John Dewey's critique of traditional education and his notion of a 'progressive' education (1944). Different traditions of adult education have evolved globally and over time. In North America and the UK, the related notion of 'andragogy'—the art and science of helping adults to learn—was popularised by Eduard Lindeman in 1926 and then Malcolm Knowles (1950) and others (Bruner, 1959; Kidd, 1973). Parallel movements developed in Europe, such as in France with 'education permanente' (Conseil de l'Europe, 1970); in Scandinavia, with the Folk High **School** Movement founded in Denmark by Nikolai Grundtvig, as well as in Africa (Kabuga, 1977) and South America (Freire, 1970).

Current status and usage

Today, adult education is conceived as the work of certain historical organisations, social movements and institutions, or as education orientated to and for adults as students. Merriam and Brockett define adult education as 'activities intentionally designed to bring about **learning** among those whose age, social roles, or self-perception define them as adults' (Merriam and Brockett, 1996, p.8). Common themes retained within current usage include a concern with social reform, the educational possibilities of everyday life, the removal of external tokens of learning and an emphasis on informal rather than formal pedagogical methods. More recently, the speed of advancement in information **technology** is impacting on adult learning experiences. The concepts of adult education and andragogy are increasingly being usurped by the notions of *lifelong learning* and *heutagogy* (Hase and Kenyon, 2000). Heutagogical approaches to education emphasise learner **creativity**, flexibility, and capability and argue that in the 21st century it is no longer realistic to define the purpose of education as transmitting what is known. The main purpose of adult education must therefore be to develop skills of inquiry.

How can adult education be described and delineated? Elias and Merriam (1980) identify several broad philosophical strands of adult education, each with related but distinct emphases. *Liberal* adult education is focused in distinct subject **disciplines**, and is concerned with the intellectual, spiritual and moral development of the individual person (see also Jarvis, 1995). Typically, it often incorporates the cultivation of artistic and aesthetic sensibility, thereby 'liberating' the adult learner from ignorance. An example of a Liberal adult education programme would be the Great Books Program in Chicago (1947). *Progressive* adult education is more concerned with social reform and the progression of mutual interests through democracy. Engagement in democratic processes in wider **society** is promoted through a relationship between **teacher** and the adult learner, which places the learner and their experiences at the centre of educational concern. The emphasis of the *Humanistic* adult educator is in the development of individual potential or 'self-actualisation' (Maslow, 1954), but often through supportive peer group work processes designed to encourage self-evaluation and discovery (Rogers, 1973). Proponents of *Radical* adult education (Freire, 1970) see it as a force for social and economic change via the raising of political awareness within oppressed groups, which then leads them to take personal and political action to challenge that oppression.

Demarcating the multiple notions of adult education involves negotiating the question of how adulthood itself is defined. Should this be on the basis of biology? e.g., the age we can reproduce; or legality?, e.g., when we can vote. Does it equate to the performance of certain social roles, such as living independently from parents? Knowles (2015) suggests it might be more fruitful to focus on the psychological characteristics of 'adult' learners and what differentiates them from children.

3

Adults, as a result of human processes of psychological development and maturation, have a different self-concept in that they need to be seen and treated by others as people who are capable of *self-direction*. This produces a distinctive orientation to **learning**. Adults need to know *why* they need to learn something before undertaking to learn it. Adult learning is thus more self-directed in that individuals seek to diagnose their own learning needs and goals, identify resources, implement strategies and evaluate outcomes. As adults tend to bring more, and different, experiences to their education, this provides adult educators with an opportunity to tap into those experiences within the educative process. In turn, this has important implications for their participation in wider **society**. As Hayes suggests, 'When we fail to take control of our education, we fail to take control of our lives. Self-directed inquiry, the process of taking control of your own education is the lifeblood of democracy' (Hayes, 1998, p.xiv).

In order to locate adult education in a more contemporary environment we need to examine how conditions of late modernity (Baumann, 1992) impact upon it (see Lovett, 1988 for a radical take). Arguably, traditional concepts of adult education fitted more squarely into ideas circulating during and after the 1970s, for example, Ivan Illich's **deschooling educational theory** (1976). Economic, social and cultural changes mean that many adults now live in a **society** that has strong individualising tendencies and a requirement for permanent **learning**. The growth of service sector employment, **globalisation**, flexible labour markets and new forms of communication and information **technology** has produced a demand for a multi-skilled work force and a workplace where adaptability and innovation are key (Usher and Edwards, 1994). In some countries such as the UK, this has drawn **policy** makers to the rhetoric of *lifelong learning* (DfEE, 1998). In this context, communitarian values (such as a stress on the collective pursuit of a common good) can become reconfigured and devalued within an increasing emphasis on individual, rather than collective, learning experience. Moreover, within late modern societies the whole notion of a pre-existent, bounded and coherent self with an inherent potential and the goal of personal **autonomy** gives way to a playfulness where **identity** is constantly formed, reformed or 'tried on'. In such a context adult education's hitherto guiding **paradigm**s (whether **liberal**, progressive, humanistic or radical) might prove to be inadequate in a world where consumption becomes a way of signifying difference and individual choice and even knowledge itself becomes marketised in *performative* terms (Ball, 2003; Biesta, 2006). Within such

4

societies, if collective advancement is emphasised it is often with regard to maintaining or gaining economic advantage and learning becomes oriented to employer or consumer interests. For adult education, this has two detrimental consequences, namely: the erosion of opportunities for adults to learn without the intrusion of vocational and **instrumental** goals, and the constraint of adult educators' desire to promote community, democracy and social change.

Questions to consider

1. Can adult education be distinguished from education in general?
2. Are andragogy and heutagogy the antithesis of **pedagogy**?
3. In what ways are adult learners different to child learners?
4. Does becoming an adult mean becoming more educationally self-directed?
5. How does adult education operate within a late modern context?

References (with recommended readings in bold)

Ball, S. (2003) 'The teacher's soul and the terrors of performativity', *Journal of Education Policy,* 18 (2), pp.215–228.

Baumann, Z. (1992) *Intimations of postmodernity.* London: Routledge.

Biesta, G.J.J. (2006) 'What's the point of lifelong learning if lifelong learning has no point? On the democratic deficit of policies for lifelong learning', *European Educational Research Journal,* 5 (3–4), pp.169–180.

Bruner, E.S. (1959) *An overview of adult education research.* Chicago, IL: Adult Education Association.

Conseil de l'Europe (1970) *Education permanente.* The Hague: Martinus Nijhoff.

Dewey, J. (1944) *Democracy and education.* New York: Free Press.

DfEE (1998) *The learning age: A renaissance for Britain.* London: HMSO.

Elias, J. and Merriam, S. (1980) *Philosophical foundations of adult education.* Malabar, FL: Robert Krieger.

Freire, P. (1970) *Pedagogy of the oppressed.* Harmondsworth: Penguin.

Hase, S. and Kenyon, C. (2000) 'From andragogy to heutagogy'. Ultibase Articles, 5, pp.1–10. Available at: www.psy.gla.ac.uk/~steve/pr/Heutagogy.html (accessed 26 October 2016).

Hayes, C. (1998) *Beyond the American dream: Lifelong learning and the search for meaning in a postmodern world.* Wasilla, AK: Autodidactic Press.

Illich, I. (1976) *De-schooling society.* London: Penguin.

Jarvis, P. (1995) *Adult and continuing education: Theory and practice,* 2nd edn. London: Routledge.

Kabuga, C. (1977) 'Why andragogy?', *Adult Education and Development: Journal for Adult Education in Africa, Asia, and Latin America,* 9, pp.1–3. Reprinted in Knowles, M.S. (1990) *The adult learner: A neglected species,* 4th edn. Houston, TX: Gulf Publishing Company, pp.233–239.

Kidd, J.R. (1973) *How adults learn.* New York: Association Press.

Knowles, M. (1950) *Informal adult education.* New York: Association Press.

Knowles, M. (2015) *The adult learner: The definitive classic in adult education and human resource development.* London: Routledge.

Lindeman, E.C. (1926) *The meaning of adult education.* New York: New Republic. New edn. Norman, OK: The Oklahoma Research Center for Continuing Professional and Higher Education, 1989.

Lovett, T. (ed.) (1988) *Radical approaches to adult education.* London: Hutchinson.

Maslow, A.H. (1954) *Motivation and personality.* New York: Harper and Row.

Merriam, S.B. and Brockett, R.G. (1996) *The profession and practice of adult education.* San Francisco: Jossey-Bass.

Rogers, C. (1973) *Encounter groups.* Harmondsworth: Penguin.

Savicevic, D.M. (1999) *Adult education: From practice to theory building.* Frankfurt am Main: Peter Lang.

Usher, R. and Edwards, R. (1994) *Post modernism and education,* London: Routledge.

KEY CONCEPT: ATTACHMENT

Roger Willoughby

Concept origins

Developed by John Bowlby, attachment theory emerged gradually during the two decades following the Second World War. Drawing on **psychoanalysis**, ethology, developmental and **cognitive** psychology, cybernetics and information processing (Bretherton, 1992), Bowlby's (1944, 1951) early studies of the negative impact of parent–child separation on the subsequent emotional health of children were groundbreaking and controversial. By the end of the 1950s Bowlby (1958, 1959, 1960) gave his initial articulation of attachment theory as the growing child's tie to its mother forming the basis for relational security, confidence, morale, curiosity and love. At its simplest, an infant's attachment **behaviour** promoted closeness to the attachment figure, which—from an evolutionary perspective—increased chances of survival. This served a protective function *and* as a secure base for exploration of the environment. Numerous other researchers joined Bowlby in investigating and refining attachment theory. Patterns that Mary Ainsworth and others observed in 'Strange Situation' (Ainsworth and Wittig, 1969) encounters initially resulted in attachment being broadly classified as either secure, insecure avoidant, or insecure ambivalent (Ainsworth and Bell, 1970; Ainsworth *et al.*, 1978). This classification was later further refined. The opening period of work on attachment theory was summarised in Bowlby's (1969, 1973, 1980) *Attachment and Loss* trilogy. By this time the body of this work was already significantly impacting not only on psychological therapy with children, but far more broadly on the management and **care** of children in nurseries and other early years settings, hospitals, and within educational provision; helping **teachers** and other stakeholders understand and better utilise the human affective dimensions of their practice.

Current status and usage

In developing Ainsworth's attachment classification, Main and Solomon (1990) identified a disorganised type, thus making four broad categories: this type came to be particularly associated with significant maternal psychological dysfunction. The latest research, from the mid 1990s onwards, has included increasing efforts to explore the neuro-psycho-biological underpinnings of attachment theory and chart the impact of environmental and attachment experiences on neurological structures (Schore, 2012; Schore, 2017). An understanding of attachment theory has much to offer educational specialists, especially, but by no means exclusively, in early years contexts and with children in and from **care** systems. Building on the attachment template established within the infant during its first two years, when the brain growth spurt occurs (the brain doubling in size), **teachers** are increasingly drawing on these ideas to promote both academic and psychosocial outcomes (e.g., Bombèr, 2007; Bergin and Bergin, 2009; Cozolino, 2013; Parker *et al.*, 2016).

In approaching the concept of attachment (Bowlby, 1988) it is useful to consider it as a key way of understanding **relationships**; their function, strengths, problems and joys and how these evolve across the lifespan and within different **culture**s. Attachment theory does not stop at children and their parental relations—it has been applied to couples, between grand-children and grand-parents, between **teachers** and students and elsewhere. Experimental studies offer useful evidence to support this work: Lorenz (1935) on imprinting in newly hatched goslings and that of Harlow (1961; Harlow and Zimmermann, 1958; *cf.* van der Horst *et al.*, 2008) on the impact of maternal deprivation on rhesus monkeys being particularly illustrative. Taking just the latter, Harlow highlighted a number of phenomena, including: (1) infant monkeys seeking safety with their mothers when faced with danger; (2) the negative effects of being raised in isolation, effects which increased and would become more enduring the longer the privation continued; and (3) their preference for surrogate cloth mothers (to which they could cling and obtain comfort) over simple wire models (that would provide food). The notion of critical periods, optimal for the creation of attachment bonds and after which their construction is impaired, derived from such studies and was further supported by research on so-called feral children. This type of approach raises obvious questions, such as the extent to which results from animal studies can be generalised to humans and the ethically problematic nature of some of the research. These are important points of access into beginning to critically consider this work.

In deepening one's understanding of attachment an extensive body of literature may be considered. In an earlier survey of the field, Steele (2002) highlighted among other things the utility of attachment in investigating the role of the father on a child's development (thus underlining the relationship-specific nature of the concept); its relevance in considering the impact of parental divorce and separation; and the impact and **politics** of day-**care**. In the course of this, Steele stressed the relevance of the Adult Attachment Interview (AAI), developed by Main and Goldwyn (1987), as a **qualitative** interview method of assessing accounts adults gave of both their own **childhood** experiences with their parents and their contemporary understanding of these experiences. The resultant classification of these AAI (and similar) accounts enabled reasonably reliable predictions to be made of parental sensitivity and patterns of attachment security across generations (Grossmann et al., 2005). With effective interventions available, such **assessment** can be very useful as a step towards helping parents-to-be and those with childcare responsibilities to better resolve their own emotional **relationships** to their formative attachment figures. If we see early years workers and subsequent **teachers** as important secondary attachment figures for infants, students and young people, and we take the affective and **pastoral** dimensions of **teaching** seriously, this opens up possibilities for further developing reflective practice during teacher training and in ongoing CPD. Such an approach could have significant benefits for both teachers and students (Bombèr, 2007; Parker et al., 2016).

Attachment was a controversial concept when it emerged, challenging then existing orthodoxies. It has come to be challenged itself as it has grown into a dominant **paradigm**. Part of the challenge comes from the **neoliberal** critique of the affective dimension and therapeutic education (e.g., Ecclestone and Hayes, 2009). More interestingly perhaps, implicit social **class** and patriarchal assumptions within the language of attachment theorising, several feminist critics claim, perpetuate **essentialist** views of women and obscures the exploitative circumstances under which most women mother, naturalising the heterosexual nuclear

family (Birns, 1999; Franzblau, 1999 and 2002; Wendt, 2016). These are important questions both about the socio-historical context of the concept and its derivative practices, about its integrity, its **politics**, and about its validity and credibility (Duschinsky *et al.*, 2015). In engaging with such questions, it is vital to consider the key points at issue and the manner in which this (just as any other) dynamic theory has changed over time in response to challenging new data (Feyerabend, 1975). Thus, while initial formulations of attachment clearly privileged infant–mother relations (monotropy), this gave way to a modern emphasis on an array of attachment figures (Schaffer and Emerson, 1964; Rutter, 1981), each with their own relationship-specific characteristics, while still recognising the biopsychosocial specificity of the mother and maternal function. Following earlier work by Ainsworth (1963), Otto and Keller (2014) have presented interesting work on the cultural variations in attachment across the world. From another vertex, critics' assumptions may themselves be scrutinised, something Liss and Erchull (2012) did in an **empirical** study which found that feminist mothers are in practice more supportive of attachment parenting that their non-feminist counterparts. Such findings are useful in evaluating these inevitably complex debates.

Questions to consider

1. Are **teachers** aware of attachment theory and should they be? Why?
2. Physical contact experiences with parents offer reassurance and promote security, so should teachers do this across the various phases of education?
3. Attachment theory uses technical terms (e.g., 'affectional bonds' for 'love'): discuss the advantages and shortcomings of such subject specific vocabulary.
4. What are the differences between Bowlby's ideas on attachment **relationships**, Piaget's notion of schemas, Vygotsky's ZPD, and psychoanalytic object relations theory?

References (with recommended readings in bold)

Ainsworth, M.D.S. (1963) 'The development of infant–mother interaction among the Ganda', in Foss, B.M. (ed.) *Determinants of infant behavior*, vol. 2. New York: Wiley, pp.67–104.

Ainsworth, M.D.S. and Bell, S.M. (1970) 'Attachment, exploration, and separation: Illustrated by the behavior of one-year-olds in a strange situation', *Child Development*, 41, pp.49–67.

Ainsworth, M.D.S. and Wittig, B.A. (1969) 'Attachment and the exploratory behaviour of one-year-olds in a strange situation', in Foss, B.M. (ed.) *Determinants of infant behaviour*, vol. 4. London: Methuen, pp.113–136.

Ainsworth, M.D.S., Blehar, M.C., Waters, E. and Wall, S.N. (1978) *Patterns of attachment: A psychological study of the Strange Situation*. Hillsdale, NJ: Erlbaum.

Bergin, C. and Bergin, D. (2009) 'Attachment in the classroom', *Educational Psychology Review*, 21, pp.141–170.

Birns, B. (1999) 'Attachment theory revisited: Challenging conceptual and methodological sacred cows', *Feminism & Psychology*, 9, pp.10–21.

Bombèr, L.H. (2007) *Inside I'm hurting: Practical strategies for supporting children with attachment difficulties in schools*. London: Worth Publishing.

Bowlby, J. (1944) 'Forty-four juvenile thieves: Their characters and home lives', *International Journal of Psychoanalysis*, 25, pp.19–52.

Bowlby, J. (1951) *Maternal care and mental health*. Geneva: World Health Organization.

Bowlby, J. (1958) 'The nature of the child's tie to his mother', *International Journal of Psychoanalysis*, 39, pp.1–23.

Bowlby, J. (1959) 'Separation anxiety', *International Journal of Psychoanalysis*, 41, pp.1–25.

Bowlby, J. (1960) 'Grief and mourning in infancy and early childhood', *The Psychoanalytic Study of the Child*, 15, pp.9–52.

Bowlby, J. (1969) *Attachment and loss: Attachment*. London: Hogarth Press.

Bowlby, J. (1973) *Attachment and loss: Separation, anxiety and anger*. London: Hogarth Press.

Bowlby, J. (1980) *Attachment and loss: Loss, sadness and depression*. London: Hogarth Press.

Bowlby, J. (1988) *A secure base: Parent–child attachment and healthy human development*. **London: Tavistock.**

Bretherton, I. (1992) 'The origins of attachment theory: John Bowlby and Mary Ainsworth', *Developmental Psychology*, 28, pp.759–775.

Cozolino, L. (2013) *The social neuroscience of education: Optimizing attachment and learning in the classroom*. **London: Norton.**

Duschinsky, R., Greco, M. and Solomon, J. (2015) 'The politics of attachment: Lines of flight with Bowlby, Deleuze and Guattari', *Theory, Culture & Society*, 32, pp.173–195.

Ecclestone, K. and Hayes, D. (2009) *The dangerous rise of therapeutic education*. London: Routledge.

Feyerabend, P. (1975) *Against method*. London: New Left Books.

Franzblau, S.H. (1999) 'Historicizing attachment theory: Binding the ties that bind', *Feminism & Psychology*, 9, pp.22–31.

Franzblau, S.H. (2002) 'Deconstructing attachment theory: Naturalizing the politics of motherhood', in Collins, L.H., Dunlap, M.R. and Chrisleer, J.C. (eds) *Charting a new course for feminist psychology*. Westport, CT: Praeger, pp.93–110.

Grossmann, K.E., Grossmann, K. and Waters, E. (eds) (2005) *Attachment from infancy to adulthood: The major longitudinal studies*. New York: Guilford Press.

Harlow, H.F. (1961) 'The development of affectional patterns in infant monkeys', in Foss, B.M. (ed.) *Determinants of infant behaviour*. London: Methuen, pp.75–97.

Harlow, H.F. and Zimmermann, R.R. (1958) 'The development of affective responsiveness in infant monkeys', *Proceedings of the American Philosophical Society*, 102, pp.501–509.

Liss, M. and Erchull, M.J. (2012) 'Feminism and attachment parenting: Attitudes, stereotypes, and misperceptions', *Sex Roles*, 67, pp.131–142.

Lorenz, K.Z. (1935) 'Der Kumpan in der Umwelt des Vogels' [The companion in the bird's world], *Journal für Ornithologie*, 83, pp.137–213.

Main, M. and Goldwyn, R. (1987) *Adult Attachment Interview rating and classification system*. Unpublished manual, Berkeley: University of California.

Main, M. and Solomon, J. (1990) 'Procedures for identifying infants as disorganized/disoriented during the Ainsworth Strange Situation', in Greenberg, M.T., Cicchetti, D. and Cummings, E.M. (eds) *Attachment in the preschool years*. Chicago, University of Chicago Press, pp.121–160.

Otto, H. and Keller, H. (eds) (2014) *Different faces of attachment: Cultural variations on a universal human need*. Cambridge: Cambridge University Press.

Parker, R., Rose, J. and Gilbert, L. (2016) 'Attachment aware schools: An alternative to behaviourism in supporting children's behaviour?', in Lees, H.E. and Noddings, N. (eds) *The Palgrave international handbook of alternative education*. London: Palgrave, pp.463–483.

Rutter, M. (1981) *Maternal deprivation reassessed*, 2nd edn. Harmondsworth: Penguin.

Schaffer, H.R. and Emerson, P.F. (1964) 'The development of social attachments in infancy', *Monographs of the Society for Research in Child Development*, 29 (Serial 94).

Schore, A.N. (2012) 'Bowlby's environment of evolutionary adaptiveness: Recent studies on the interpersonal neurobiology of attachment and emotional development', in Narvaez, D., Panksepp, J., Schore, A. and Gleason, T. (eds) *Evolution, early experience, and human development: From research to practice and policy.* New York: Oxford University Press, 2012, pp.31–67.

Schore, A.N. (2017) 'Modern attachment theory', in Gold, S.N. (ed.) *APA handbook of trauma psychology*, volume 1. Washington, DC: American Psychological Association, vol. 1, pp.389–406.

Steele, H. (2002) 'State of the art: Attachment', *The Psychologist*, 15 (10), pp.518–522.

van der Horst, F.C.P., LeRoy, H.A. and van der Veer, R. (2008) 'When strangers meet: John Bowlby and Harry Harlow on attachment behavior', *Integrative Psychological and Behavioral Science*, 42, pp.370–388.

Wendt, S. (2016) 'Conversations about theory: Feminism and social work', in Wendt, S. and Moulding, N. (eds) *Contemporary feminisms in social work practice.* London: Routledge, pp.11–23.

KEY CONCEPT: BEHAVIOUR

Roger Willoughby

Concept origins

Behaviour refers to observable actions which are classified and understood in relation to commonly accepted standards and norms. The adaptation of behaviour in relation to environmental demands (Darwin, 1859, 1871), can be seen as one of the distinguishing features of early hominids, our early bipedal human ancestors, along with tool making, rudimentary language development, and art (Catania, 1985; Potts, 2002). In philosophy, Plato in 380BC depicted adaptation to one's appropriate position within **society** and playing one's 'proper' function as conducive to a good life (2008). Similar precursors to **functionalism** are evident, particularly in the **ethics**-led naturalism of Hobbes (1651), who argued that human behaviour in the 'state of nature' would involve incessant conflict, the pursuit of **power** and individual interests. Life as a result would be 'solitary, poor, nasty, brutish, and short' (Hobbes, 1994, p.76). Behaviour, Hobbes argued, was only held in check through a form of social contract, supported by authority through **politics**. More optimistic views of human nature and behaviour were articulated by David Hume (1751), among others, whose emphasis on sympathy or fellow-feeling, what we would now refer to as empathy, he saw as driving action (1998). Such divergent views on our underlying human nature and its expression in behaviour inevitably pulled education **policy** and **praxis** in competing directions.

Current status and usage

Understanding human behaviour in Darwinian evolutionary terms, such that its adaptation facilitated the survival and reproduction of its practitioners, has resulted in contemporary reworkings of these theories in sociobiology (Dawkins, 1976; Wilson,

---

2000) and in a more nuanced way in evolutionary psychology (Wright, 1994; *cf.* Cziko, 2000). Evolutionary psychology, in particular, gives greater recognition to environmental influences on behaviour and to human flexibility. More generally, behaviour as a conceptual entity is commonly associated—in a rather reductive fashion—with **behaviourism** in psychology. However, other **school**s of psychological thought (from **attachment** theory through **psychoanalysis** to **constructivism**), have substantial interest in behaviour, generally seeing its external observable manifestations as mediated responses to external or internal stimuli, including unconscious sources. In view of the tendency to evaluate behaviour in relation to societal norms, schools and other social institutions are commonly charged with its policing and regulation. Education approaches this through a wide variety of means, including **pedagogy**, behaviour and discipline policies, **school** culture, and the **hidden curriculum**. Psychologically informed techniques are typically employed in these contexts in efforts to promote desired and minimise unwanted behaviour. Occasionally, where biological factors are thought to be implicated, medication can have a role; attention-deficit/hyperactivity disorder (ADHD) being perhaps the best known such case (Long *et al.*, 2011). Such control of persons is inevitably problematic, with the norms appealed to for its justification being variously disputed, fragmentary or fictional. In this critical context, Foucault's (1978–1986) work on biopower and control of **society** has influenced many.

Control of behaviour is commonly sought through various types of psycho-social manipulation, such as threats or promises, in an effort to steer individual or group behaviour in a socio-culturally desired direction. With education and the **school** placed at the forefront of this 'civilising' process, the stakes are very high. Societal anxieties about children and young people (deMause, 2002), of liveliness, and of aggression, have fuelled educational **policy** and practice that can entail the repression of spontaneity and even the creation of emotional inhibitions, as **psychoanalysis** has long argued (Freud, 1907). Education can thus form not just scaffolding to support behavioural and emotional growth, but can become a straight-jacket that restricts freedom in relation to many key areas, from **gender** and **sexuality** through **politics,** to intellectual endeavour. With behaviour at the forefront of many schools' and **teachers'** concerns, and poor student behaviour being implicated in the high attrition rate among (especially newly qualified) teachers (Aloe *et al.*, 2014), further training and advice on the topic is high on the wish-lists of many in education. Texts such as Sue Cowley's *Getting the Buggers to Behave* (2014) have become understandably popular in such contexts.

Positioning behaviour as either a 'problem' or more severely as a 'disorder' typically involves judgements about its persistency and frequency and the degree to which it violates social norms or impairs an individual's functioning. However, the capacity to engineer behaviour change in response to such **labelling** through social experience and **learning** varies according to factors such as the degree of **plasticity** inherent in the behaviour: high plasticity leaves ample room for change, whereas low levels involve inflexible behaviour patterns. Let us take so-called anti-social behaviour as one example to illustrate this. Moffitt (1993) distinguished two groups who exhibit antisocial behaviour – one where the behaviour is life-course persistent and another where it is largely limited to adolescence. Neuropsychological and adverse environmental factors typify the former group, whereas Moffitt saw the latter group's behaviour as virtually normative and attributable to peer processes and an experienced maturity gap between biological and social maturity (*cf.* Erikson, 1968). Subsequent studies, summarised by Fairchild *et al.* (2013), while corroborating Moffitt's view of the life-course persistent group, suggested that anti-social behaviour emerging in adolescence can run into adulthood and can be associated with neuropsychological and neurochemical patterns similar to those found in the former group. This challenges any clear-cut distinction between intervention strategies specifically tailored to one or other group. Bullying is another example. This is perhaps the highest profile of the problem behaviours encountered in **school**s. Its management is challenging, with recent research highlighting significant declines in anti-bullying programme effectiveness with older adolescents (Long *et al.*, 2011; Yeager, *et al.*, 2015). Again, careful study of the phenomena, distinguishing its various sub-types, the causal factors of each, and appropriate interventions is likely to lead to better outcomes.

As with other concepts, behaviour is a site of contest. Traditional conceptualisations of disruptive behaviour, often drawing on social **learning** theory and disease models, depicted such behaviour as a result of exposure to environmental models. More recent longitudinal research, usefully summarised by Tremblay (2010), suggests that disruptive behaviours are a much more universal phenomenon during early **childhood** and that these give way to pro-social behaviours, which are themselves learned from environmental sources. Failure to acquire alternative behaviours congruent with social norms typically leads to varieties of formal and informal **labelling**. Given the differing and complex genetic, epigenetic and environmental influences on such behaviour formation (Morgado and Vale-Dias, 2013), intervention and prevention strategies unsurprisingly range from the psycho-social to the extreme bio-medical. Questioning of both social norms against which behaviour is judged and the control strategies deployed to shape it has drawn on a range of critical **discourses**. Gramsci's (1971) concept of **hegemony**, through which engineered 'consent' for the shaping of **society**—and thus of behaviour—by the dominant group occurs, is particularly helpful. So too is Foucault's (1978–1986) emphasis on surveillance, **power** and biopower, particularly in helping question restrictive agendas on crucial areas such as **sexuality** and **gender**. In this context, the work of Butler (1990, 1993) occupies an interesting though questionable position, particularly in her deconstructive critique of such identities as substantially fictive social constructions, their apparent reality deriving from iterative doing (behaviour), thus aligning it with **performativity**. Concerns over the potentially repressive and alienating consequences of the educational establishment's efforts to manage behaviour, has for some time resulted in resistance from various quarters, articulated most notably through Illich's (1972) ideas on **deschooling**, Freire's (1970) on **democratic education**, and Holt's (1977) on **unschooling**. These trends have been furthered by broader questioning of both the reductive and potentially alienating impact of a narrow focus on behaviour. This has led in some quarters to a renewed emphasis on **relationships** and a more **holistic** approach; one such initiative is Parker *et al.*'s (2016) **attachment** based approach to supporting children's behaviour in **school**. While attachment theory is not free itself from criticism (e.g., around supposed essentialising and naturalising tendencies), such initiatives helpfully challenge the prevailing orthodoxies around behaviour, opening up space for greater critical thinking.

Questions to consider

1. Are people more than their behaviour?
2. If left to our own devices, would life be 'solitary, poor, nasty, brutish, and short'?
3. What are the benefits of restraint on our behaviour over the lifespan?
4. To what extent should **school**s be in the business of shaping behaviour?
5. Why is some people's objectionable behaviour tolerated more than others?

References (with recommended readings in bold)

Aloe, A.M., Amo, L.C. and Shanahan, M.E. (2014) 'Classroom management self-efficacy and burnout multivariate meta-analysis', *Educational Psychology Review*, 26 (1), pp.101–126.

Butler, J. (1990) *Gender trouble: Feminism and the subversion of identity.* New York: Routledge.

Butler, J. (1993) *Bodies that matter: On the discursive limits of sex.* New York: Routledge.

Catania, A.C. (1985) 'Rule-governed behaviour and the origins of language', in Lowe, C.F., Richelle, M., Blackman, D.E. and Bradshaw, C.M. (eds) *Behaviour analysis and contemporary psychology.* London: Lawrence Erlbaum, pp.135–156.

Cowley, S. (2014) *Getting the buggers to behave*, 5th edn. London: Bloomsbury.

Cziko, G. (2000) *The things we do: Using the lessons of Bernard and Darwin to understand the what, how, and why of our behavior.* Cambridge, MA: MIT Press.

Darwin, C. (1859) *On the origin of species by means of natural selection, or the preservation of favoured races in the struggle for life.* London: John Murray.

Darwin, C. (1871) *The descent of man, and selection in relation to sex.* London: John Murray.

Dawkins, R. (1976) *The selfish gene.* Oxford: Oxford University Press.

deMause, L. (2002) *The emotional life of nations.* New York: Karnac.

Erikson, E.H. (1968) *Identity, youth and crisis.* New York: Norton.

Fairchild, G., van Goozen, S.H.M., Calder, A.J. and Goodyer, I.M. (2013) 'Research review evaluating and reformulating the developmental taxonomic theory of antisocial behaviour', *The Journal of Child Psychology and Psychiatry*, 54 (9), pp.924–940.

Foucault, M. (1978–1986) *The history of sexuality.* **Translated by R. Hurley, 3 vols. New York: Pantheon.**

Freire, P. (1970) *Pedagogy of the oppressed.* Harmondsworth: Penguin.

Freud, S. (1907) 'The sexual enlightenment of children (an open letter to Dr M Furst)', in Strachey, J. (ed.) *The standard edition of the complete psychological works of Sigmund Freud*, vol. 9. London: Hogarth Press, 1959, pp.131–139.

Gramsci, A. (1971) *Selections from the prison notebooks of Antonio Gramsci.* Translated and edited by Quintin Hoare and Geoffrey Norwell-Smith. London: Lawrence and Wishart.

Hobbes, T. (1994 [1651]) *Leviathan.* Edited by Edwin Curley. Indianapolis, IN: Hackett Publishing Company.

Holt, J. (1977) *How children fail.* Harmondsworth: Penguin.

Hume, D. (1998 [1751]) *An enquiry concerning the principles of morals.* Edited by T.L. Beauchamp. Oxford: Oxford University Press, 1998.

Illich, I. (1972) *Deschooling society.* New York: Marion Boyar.

Long, M., Wood, C., Littleton, K., Passenger, T. and Sheehy, K. (2011) *The psychology of education*, **2nd edn. Abingdon: Routledge.**

Moffitt, T.E. (1993) 'Adolescence-limited and life-course-persistent antisocial behavior: A developmental taxonomy', *Psychological Review*, 100, pp.674–701.

Morgado, A.M. and Vale-Dias, M.D.L. (2013) 'The antisocial phenomenon in adolescence: What is literature telling us?', *Aggression and Violent Behavior*, 18 (4), pp.436–443.

Parker, R., Rose, J. and Gilbert, L. (2016) 'Attachment aware schools: An alternative to behaviourism in supporting children's behaviour?', in Lees, H.E. and Noddings, N. (eds) *The Palgrave international handbook of alternative education.* London: Palgrave Macmillan, pp.463–483.

Plato (2008 [380BC]) *Republic.* Translated by R. Waterfield. Oxford: Oxford University Press.

Potts, R. (2002) 'Complexity and adaptability in human evolution', in Goodman, M. and Moffat, A.M. (eds) *Probing human origins.* Cambridge, MA: American Academy of Arts and Sciences, pp.33–57.

Tremblay, R.E. (2010) 'Developmental origins of disruptive behaviour problems: The "original sin" hypothesis, epigenetics and their consequences for prevention', *The Journal of Child Psychology and Psychiatry*, 51 (4), pp.341–367.

Wilson E.O. (2000) *Sociobiology: The new synthesis.* Cambridge, MA: Belknap Press.

Wright, R. (1994) *The moral animal: Evolutionary psychology and everyday life*. New York: Pantheon.

Yeager, D.S., Fong, C.J., Lee, H.Y. and Espelage, D.L. (2015) 'Declines in efficacy of anti-bullying programs among older adolescents: Theory and a three-level meta-analysis', *Journal of Applied Developmental Psychology*, 37, pp.36–51.

KEY CONCEPT: CHILDHOOD

Leoarna Mathias

Concept origins

An understanding of the term 'childhood', as defining young human beings prior to the onset of puberty, was established in the late Old English period (11th century). Some 500 years later in 1550, Thomas Becon, an English cleric and Protestant reformer, asks within his writings 'What is a child, or to be a child?' (cited in Cunningham, 2006, p.12). In posing such a question, Becon hints at the challenges of defining the concept of childhood, and in particular, the binary nature of the term; children live real lives in real time, childhoods are theoretical and endure beyond individual experiences (Corsaro, 2011). The Greeks had no word for childhood, though they developed clear philosophical ideas about education which centred on preparing young citizens for their future role in **society** (Postman, 1982). Plato and his contemporaries, in emphasising only this preparatory nature of our earliest years, underpin the work of Aries (1962) and Cunningham (2006) who have argued persuasively that childhood, as an acknowledged and distinct stage in the human life-span, did not exist prior to the 17th century. Defining the nature of childhood remains difficult as debates about when childhood starts or ends, what it should contain, and what it should not, are far from settled, because we are 'heirs to so many conflicting views of childhood from the past' (Cunningham, 2006, p.14).

Current status and usage

During the 20th century, the United Nations definition of a 'child' as a 'human being below 18 years of age' generally held sway in legal, **policy**, social and cultural terms. Others argue that at this 21st-century juncture, we can only understand childhood as a relational concept, one that is persistently intertwined with notions of the state, the market and of history (Balagopalan,

2014). Some have current fears of the commodification of childhood (Schor, 2003). Others fear more the extent to which we
control childhood, through mechanisms such as **school** attendance, as they facilitate the 'production of children's conformity'
(James and James, 2012, p.108). This control is increasingly seen
as a constraint on children's physical and mental wellbeing. For
example, according to Unicef, UK children score consistently
poorly on measures of six dimensions of wellbeing in comparison to the children of other wealthy nations (2007, 2011, 2013).
Thus, debates continue to focus upon what childhood is for and
should contain.

 Childhood is, and has been, 'eulogised for qualities … sorely missing
in adults' (Bauman 2006, p.8). It was romanticised by Rousseau, in his
educational treatise *Emile* (1762; see Kelly and Bloom, 2010), for having value on its own terms. Yet a survey of the lives of children in any
part of the globe presents the student of **education studies** with a
rich source of contrary perspectives (Penn, 2005). A variety of news
media informs us daily of the many ways in which children and their
families are suffering, are denied chances to meet their own basic needs,
or assert their rights. In theorising the hierarchy of needs, Maslow in
1943 gave us a way of understanding human need; the 20th century
saw a reconfiguration of these needs as enforceable rights. In 1989,
the United Nations established the Convention on the Rights of the
Child (UNCRC), the third such iteration of rights for children to be
produced during the 20th century at a global level. Yet the UNCRC's
(1989) description of children as having (merely) an 'evolving capacity'
to enforce their rights allows adults to limit children's opportunities
to experience childhood at many turns. We may agree that children
have a right to food, shelter, bodily integrity, nurture within a familial
context, education and more in principle, and that these are all possible
elements of what we might term a childhood. Yet, today, the realities
faced by young British children excluded from **school**, or by Syrian
children travelling unaccompanied and seeking asylum in Europe, or
by young females in sub-Saharan Africa who become subject to female
genital mutilation, collide head on with any insistence that such rights
are being upheld (Loreman, 2009). We are again reminded that there is
a 'degree of tension between… perceptions of what childhood could
and should be, and [children's] lived experiences' (Smith, 2010, p.201).

The opportunities that children have to lead lives in which they fulfil the potential accorded to them by the UNCRC vary enormously. This happens at a global level (compare 5-year-old child labourers in Bangladesh or Pakistan to a similar aged cohort attending Forest School settings in Scandinavia), and at a local level (consider 17-year-olds in Scotland, who were allowed to vote in the recent Scottish independence referendum but then denied a similar vote by the British government in the referendum on membership of the European Union). Thus 'the problem ... lies not with individual children and their families, but with the structural inequalities that mark their lives' (Wells, 2009, p.184), and in turn, such inequalities shape our ongoing understanding of the nature of childhood.

As indicated above a plethora of perspectives on the nature of childhood inform current thinking (Cunningham, 2006). Some of these perspectives, or **discourses**, are rooted in historical and religious traditions reaching back centuries. Thus a puritanical discourse of childhood, in which children are seen as born 'in sin', or evil, was commonplace during Thomas Becon's time, but can still be discerned in David Cameron's description of 'feckless, fatherless' rioters in the UK in 2011 (Levitas, 2012). The philosopher John Locke, in 1689, adopted a more generous tone in describing childhood as a period of 'tabula rasa' or blank slate. For him, the role of **society** was to educate and fill up the young, empty mind with the discernible truth (1977). Locke's perspective is taken further by Rousseau (1762), as he maps out for us the distinctive nature of childhood and the adult role in preserving that distinctiveness (Kelly and Bloom, 2010). Rousseau-ian Romanticism as a discourse shapes our view of childhood in the 21st century; consider the sympathy and sadness felt innately by many in response to pleas for funds by large charities, such as Unicef, in the wake of natural disasters or armed conflict. Such emotions are perhaps driven by a belief in the 'specialness' of childhood (Postman, 1982, p.7). The 20th century also witnessed the rise of psychological developmental **discourse**, first fully outlined by Jean Piaget (1896–1980), though we might see the work of Freud (1856–1939) as a genuine precursor. Piaget set out to understand the stages of human development as they occur chronologically, and in doing so offers a view of children as needing to be supported by adults as they progress through childhood in almost linear fashion. While other **discourses**, variably described as Jesuit, Utilitarian, Marxist or Bowlbian (see **attachment**) are present in the literature, we turn now to two final perspectives that are heavily intertwined. A **neoliberal** discourse has become visible in the latter part of the 20th century that determines children's lives as both producers and consumers, but no more; children are valuable only for the potential of their human capital once they reach maturity. This perspective leads Bauman to argue that childhood has 'become merely a preparatory stage for the selling of the self' (2006, p.9), and Waters to suggest that children are now 'the currency for [**school**s] rather than the beneficiaries of education' (2013, p.u.). Postman (1982), Buckingham (2007) and others take this argument further by warning of the disappearance or death of childhood, as children access knowledge through unmediated platforms, and take on adult ways of operating at ever earlier ages, particularly through the conduit of information **technology**.

 As with all social studies, the study of childhood requires us to be aware of the inherent limitations of adopting any single perspective, to be cautious in our attempt to assert a position of objective truth. Our knowledge of children is at all times understood through both our own experience of having been a child, and our now adult standpoint. We have also seen that any number of **discourses** of childhood can run in parallel with each other, and often contradict the realities of being a child in any given geography or time frame. Thus, some commentators have called on us to deconstruct such **discourses** in order to challenge taken for granted 'truths' (Prout, 2005; Smith, 2010), or as Foucault suggests, problematise such 'regimes' (1975). Rather, we are asked to recognise that childhood is no more than a 'shifting set of ideas' (Cunningham, 1995, p.1, cited in Smith, 2010, p.12), and to focus instead upon children's lived experience. Others argue that we have grounded our 'global model of childhood on a Western middle class ideal' and that, as such, our understanding lacks nuance (Ansell, 2016, p.45). In this we risk **labelling** children as 'victims' or 'beneficiaries' of whatever occurs and might be either done to or with them (Cunningham 2006, p.16). Thus, we may, as adults, be prone to (however unwittingly) denying their role as 'active agents' in their own lives, capable of 'making meaning for themselves' (Hyde *et al.*, 2010, p.1). In debating the concept of childhood we may need to recognise that our personally held beliefs will in turn determine what we feel it is right for us to do for children. While we might agree that global **politics** and economics have 'imposed a particular kind of rule' over some childhoods (Penn, 2005, p.174) the construction of the UNCRC and the rights contained therein position adults as 'rescuers' or 'rights-defenders', but less so as 'liberators' capable of allowing children a genuine degree of self-determination of the kind Illich (1971) described in *Deschooling*

Society (Postman, 1982, p.139—see **alternative education**, **power** and **unschooling**). While we can respond positively to the progress that both the Millennium Development Goals (2000–2015) and latterly the Sustainable Development Goals (2016–2030)—both UN initiatives—may have brought about in terms of increasing access to primary schooling or improving maternal health, among other challenges, this should not prevent us from being mindful of our preoccupation with narrowing 'the gap between deficit and normal childhoods at national and global levels' (Wyness, 2015, p.170). Such configurations of childhood as either normal, or in deficit, are ultimately value-laden. When it comes to education, these configurations imply that **pedagogy** is also value-laden.

Questions to consider

1. Why, until recently, was childhood not recognised as a stage in its own right?
2. Which **discourses** dominate our understanding of the nature of childhood in the 21st century?
3. What problems arise with an **instrumental** approach to appreciating children's potential?
4. Is it true we view all childhoods through a Western, middle-**class** normative ideal?
5. How can we support children to become active agents in their own lives?

References (with recommended readings in bold)

Ansell, N. (2016) *Children, youth and development*. London: Routledge.

Aries, P. (1962) *Centuries of childhood*. London: Jonathan Cape.

Balagopalan, S. (2014) *Inhabiting childhood: Children, labour and schooling in postcolonial India*. London: Palgrave Macmillan.

Bauman, Z. (2006) 'Children make you happier … and poorer', *International Journal of Children's Spirituality* 11 (1) pp.5–10.

Buckingham, D. (2007) *Beyond technology: Children's learning in the age of digital culture*. Cambridge: Polity.

Corsaro, W. (2011) *The sociology of childhood*, 3rd edn. Thousand Oaks, CA: Pine Forge Press.

Cunningham, H. (1995) *Children and childhood in western society since 1500*. London: Pearson.

Cunningham, H. (2006) *The invention of childhood.* **London: BBC Books.**

Foucault, M. (1975) *Discipline and punish.* London: Penguin Social Sciences.

Hyde, B., Youst, K.M. and Ota, C. (2010) 'Defining childhood at the beginning of the twenty-first century: Children as agents', *International Journal of Children's Spirituality*, 15 (1), pp.1–3.

Illich, I. (1971) *Deschooling society.* London: Marion Boyars.

James, A. and James, A. (2012) *Key concepts for childhood studies.* London: Sage.

Kelly, C. and Bloom, A. (ed.) (2010) *Rousseau: Emile, or on education.* Dartmouth, NH: Dartmouth College Press.

Levitas, R. (2012) *There may be trouble ahead: What we know about those 120,000 'troubled families'.* Bristol: Poverty and Social Exclusion in the UK. Available at: www.poverty.ac.uk/policy-response-working-papers-families-social-policy-life-chances-children-parenting-uk-government (accessed 28 November 2016).

Locke, J. (1689) *Some thoughts concerning education.* London: Awnsham and John Churchill.

Locke, J. (1977) *An essay concerning human understanding.* London: J.M. Dent & Son.

Loreman, T. (2009) *Respecting childhood.* London: Continuum International.

Maslow, A.H. (2012) *A theory of human motivation.* New York: Start Publishing.

Penn, H. (2005) *Unequal childhoods.* London: Routledge.

Postman, N. (1982) *The disappearance of childhood.* New York: Random House.

Prout, A. (2005) *The future of childhood.* London: Routledge.

Schor, J. (2003) 'The commodification of childhood: Tales from the advertising frontlines', *Hedgehog Review*, 5 (2), pp.7–23.

Smith, R. (2010) *A universal child?* London: Palgrave Macmillan.

Unicef (2007) 'Child poverty in perspective: An overview of wellbeing in rich countries', *Report Card 7*, Florence: Innocenti Research Centre.

Unicef (2011) *Children's wellbeing in UK, Sweden and Spain: The role of inequality and materialism.* London: Ipsos Mori Social Research Institute.

Unicef (2013) 'Fairness for children: A league table of inequality and wellbeing in rich countries', *Report Card 13*, Florence: Innocenti Research Centre.

UNCRC (1989) *Convention on the rights of the child.* New York: United Nations. Available at: http://353ld710iigr2n4po7k4kgvv-wpengine.netdna-ssl.com/wp-content/uploads/2010/05/UNCRC_PRESS200910web.pdf (accessed 28 November 2016).

Waters, M. (2013) *Thinking allowed: On schooling.* London: Independent Thinking Press (pages unnumbered).

Wells, K. (2009) ***Childhood in a global perspective.*** **Cambridge: Polity.**

Wyness, M. (2015) *Childhood.* Cambridge: Polity.

KEY CONCEPT: CONSENT

Helen E. Lees

Concept origins

Consent is a *word* from Old French 'consentir,' and Latin 'consentīre' meaning 'to feel together, agree' (Collins Dictionary). As an educational concept, consent is found historically in the work of Rousseau and Dewey where consensus is valued (Dewey, 1916; Bertram, 2012). Education **policy**—which affects **school**s—has historically used the illusion of 'compulsory education' in **law** as signifying school attendance (see **elective home education**) to justify particular educational methods, **pedagogy** and **assessment**s as normal and required, when greater choice is in fact possible if not pursued (Lees, 2014). Nevertheless, the long social history of co-operative working—consensual co-operation—has translated into more than 850 co-operative schools in the UK alone and a global co-operative higher education movement (see e.g., www.co-operativeschools. coop; Facer *et al.*, 2012; Neary and Winn, 2016). In the lives of **teachers** wishing to express their **child-centred** pedagogy, consent in education started perhaps with their sense of vocation for the **profession** and their own **educational theory**.

Current status and usage

Under the umbrella of 'education as good' not consulting for consent is entirely normal practice in some **school**s. Some call that leadership or **profession**, while others dislike it although this is often left in **silence**, unexpressed. School councils involving students aim to increase consent-led decision making (see **democratic education**) although this is not universal practice (Trafford, 2003). Some commentators suggest non-consensual pedagogic acts in **school** are appropriate and helpful and fit children for **society** (Tsabar, 2014). In a world without much consideration of consent, this may be right as a preparatory education.

Despite this **hegemony**, consent-filled education—represented often by **alternative education** of various kinds—asks students what they want to learn, how, why and when. It reports some benefits such as a sense of community and self-esteem (Lees, 2016; Miedema, 2016), but it continues to be controversial to have **equality** of **power** between adults and children. Interesting developments of organised, mass but non-formalised democracy can these days be seen in 'people' movements such as the 'occupy' movement, 'not in my name' and change.org where seeing non-consensual **law** making as open to challenge is called for through **technology**. On the other hand, technology is 'manufacturing consent' (see Herman and Chomsky, 1988), as seen in the US presidential election of 2016, where the result was attributed in part to false Facebook news feeds (Solon, 2016). Whatever may be true, consent is currently important as a concept linked to **ontology** and **epistemology** and especially so in and for education perhaps, given its close links to society and its reality. For example, concerned about a lack of *informed* consent, the Irish president called after the US election for the debating techniques inherent in philosophy lessons to be available in schools 'to discriminate between truthful language and illusory rhetoric' (Humphreys, 2016).

As research in various disciplines shows, people struggle to understand the concept of consent (e.g., Hirschman, 1970; Belenky *et al.*, 1997; Barker, 2013). This is *particularly* so in education, due to children's place in this domain (Carlen *et al.*, 1992; Yoneyama, 1999; Lewis, 2010). It is thus apt to wonder why a book of *key* concepts in **education studies** might choose to include a little known concept. Apart from political times needing knowledge of consent for **social justice**, the answer lies in the relative *invisibility* of consent in systems of **schooling** as professional practice in the face of **policy**. Indeed, it is possible to say that economies of consent are operating in **school**s but subversively, which educational literature signals (Willis, 1977; Carlen *et al.*, 1992). What impact has this had on our young people as they move into adulthood? **Curriculum** attempts in school education to inculcate or **teach** forms of mutual social engagement—from environmental awareness to **citizenship** lessons for social responsibility and activity—have not yet been well understood. Some suggest this is on account of disparities between rhetoric and truth: students have no experience of **power** or consent on offer in these lessons to enact as lived practice to match what is being taught (Harber, 2009; Smyth, 2016). Levels of consent unawareness extend of course among young people into their personal lives. Attitudinal surveys (Powell, 2010), for example, show that young people neither know nor can identify what sexual consent is for themselves, let alone act upon it properly and consistently with others for their sakes. In every aspect of young people's lives consent features: work, **sexuality**, **family**, friends, community. Consent is an especially interesting issue when it comes to **pedagogy** and **power** in relation to **learning**.

✿ Given that most children attend **school** to get an education to fit them for **society**, there are interesting concerns in many of these settings with consent (or lack of it) around their appearance. While considering this does not take account of issues of control, uniformity of image and branding, compliance, **fascism**, behavioural regulation, the **hidden curriculum** and so on, the matter of school rules about what to wear is a classic example of lack of consent in education. While some might deem deciding what to wear or how to do one's hair is the micro-**politics** of a young person's life, for some young people such matters can be the fundamental building blocks of personal **identity**. A number of cases of personal expression of appearance have been in the news over the past decade in England: from a student sent home for wearing corn-rows in their hair to another excluded for insisting on wearing the Sikh Kara bangle. In both cases, the parents took the school to court and the school lost on **human rights** grounds: the corn-rows were judged an expression of Afro-Caribbean cultural heritage, not an extreme hairstyle, and the Kara bangle was adjudicated as a legitimate religious piece of jewellery, not a fashion bangle (Lipsett, 2008; Agencies, 2011). In this sense, consent is a battleground for the most intimate aspects of a person with some **school** settings seeking to avoid consent protocols in favour of rules, regulations and 'standards'. Such micro-issues are at the crux of debates about what is allowed and allowable in educational settings. In Googling 'hair sent home school', 6 million hits register, including one English report of a girl sent home for 'facially displaying a level of attractiveness that could be inappropriate with so many male students in the school' (Chief Reporter, 2016). The questions here then around consent in school are linked to more than consent and/or education. They include social mores, traditions, generation gaps, sexism, conservatism, **sexuality**, negativity,

power, freedom, a lack of common-sense and questions about human control. Do such examples tell us something about the modern school in line with Flint and Peim's (2012) assertion that **schooling** is becoming or has become a foreclosing of possibilities of self and selving?

:' At the heart of education lies a lot of **silence** about consent. Is it ever discussed whether young people are free to lie down in assemblies if tired, or simply in the mood to do so? Why not? Is it ever debated whether swearing is an acceptable part of **school** settings communication. If not, why not? Turning up late is not allowed. Why not? These examples lead us to understand that much of the school and of its educational practices are 'given'—and often governmentally through **policy**—rather than locally *negotiated* to suit individuals. This is, of course, a particular view and does not take into account nuances concerning developmental issues around boundaries and boundary testing. Indeed, these matters could arguably represent **mainstream** sites of interpersonal, intergenerational and inter-group contest, through which status, **power**, authority, **identity**, etc., are negotiated. Nevertheless, it is assumed widely that certain social ideas are educational in and of themselves. This might not be true. Perhaps having bodily freedom while **learning** is appropriate? One example was a pilot study (now being pursued by Oxford University) by then head teacher Dr Paul Kelley at Monkseaton High School in North Tyneside in 2009, which found 'starting an hour later improved grades in core subjects by 19 per cent' (Knapton, 2014). It is suggested (see Barnett, 2015) that this bodily rhythm of sleep would enable them to learn better overall. It is not clear whether a later school day start time itself results in better learning or the cause is happier, more relaxed (less coerced?) students. In some university and school locations in Denmark, students are offered a sense of freedom in terms of time and relation to place-space. One student reported:

> I would describe it as different, I'd describe it as freedom … it's a really good school, I like it a lot, because you're not really … when the rooms are open and it's like your mind is more open also (female student, aged 15).
>
> (Montgomery and Hope, 2016, p.312)

Thus we could feasibly ask: If a student felt more freedom (with consent seeking in place to allow for this), could education be improved?

Questions to consider

1. Who has the right to curtail personal consent in education?
2. What is consent?
3. Is consent educationally important?
4. What is the relationship of **schooling** to consent negotiations at the level of **learning**, personal appearance and interpersonal communication style?
5. What would education be if consent-seeking protocols (see **democratic education**) were the means of creating educational organisation?

References (with recommended readings in bold)

Agencies (2011) 'School's refusal to let boy wear cornrow braids is ruled racial discrimination', *Guardian*, 17 June.

Barker, M. (2013) 'Consent is a grey area? A comparison of understandings of consent in *Fifty Shades of Grey* and on the BDSM blogosphere', *Sexualities*, 16 (8), pp.896–914.

Barnett, D. (2015) 'Start school day at 11am to let students sleep in, says expert', *Guardian*, 8 September.

Belenky, M., Clinchy, B., Goldberger, N. and Tarule, J. (1997) *Women's ways of knowing: The development of self, voice, and mind*. 10th edn. New York: Basic Books.

Bertram, C. (2012) 'Jean Jacques Rousseau', *The Stanford encyclopedia of philosophy* (Winter 2014 Edition). Available at: http://plato.stanford.edu/archives/win2012/entries/rousseau (accessed 28 November 2016).

Carlen, P., Gleeson, D. and Wardhaugh, J. (1992) *Truancy: The politics of compulsory schooling*. Buckingham: Open University Press.

Chief Reporter (2016) 'Outrage at Southend school after girl is sent home for looking too pretty in uniform', *Southend News Network*, 18 March. Available at: http://tinyurl.com/hwkzstt (accessed 28 November 2016).

Dewey, J. (1916) *Democracy and education: An introduction to the philosophy of education*. New York: Macmillan.

Facer, K., Thorpe, J. and Shaw, L. (2012) 'Co-operative education and schools: An old idea for new times?', *Power and Education*, 4 (3), pp.327–341.

Flint, K.J. and Peim, N. (2012) *Rethinking the education improvement agenda: A critical philosophical approach*. London: Continuum.

Harber, C. (2009) '"Revolution, what revolution?": Contextual issues in citizenship education in schools in England', *Citizenship, Social and Economics Education*, 8 (1), pp.42–53.

Herman, E.S. and Chomsky, N. (1988) *Manufacturing consent: The political economy of the mass media*. New York: Pantheon Books.

Hirschman, A.O. (1970) *Exit, voice, and loyalty*. Cambridge, MA: Harvard University Press.

Humphreys, J. (2016) 'Teach philosophy to heal our "post-truth" society, says President Higgins', *Irish Times*, 19 November.

Knapton, S. (2014) 'Teenagers to start school at 10am in Oxford University sleep experiment', *The Telegraph*, 9 October.

Lees, H.E. (2014) *Education without schools: Discovering alternatives*. Bristol: Policy Press.

Lees, H.E. (2016) 'Educational mutuality', in Lees, H.E. and Noddings, N. (eds) *The Palgrave international handbook of alternative education*. London: Palgrave Macmillan, pp.159–175.

Lewis, A. (2010) 'Silence in the context of "child voice"', *Children & Society*, 24, pp.14–23.

Lipsett, A. (2008) 'Sikh schoolgirl wins bangle court case', *Guardian*, 29 July.

Miedema, E.L. (2016) 'Exploring moral character in everyday life: Former democratic school student's understandings and school experiences', unpublished MPhil thesis, University of Brighton, Brighton.

Montgomery, C. and Hope, M. (2016) 'Creating spaces for autonomy: The architecture of learning and thinking in Danish schools and universities', in Lees, H.E. and Noddings, N. (eds) *The Palgrave international handbook of alternative education*. London: Palgrave Macmillan, pp.305–319.

Neary, M. and Winn, J. (2016) 'Beyond public and private: A framework for co-operative higher education', *Co-operative education conference*, Manchester, 21–22 April.

Powell, A. (2010) *Sex, power and consent: Youth culture and the unwritten rules*. Cambridge: Cambridge University Press.

Smyth, J. (2016) 'Geographies of trust: A politics of resistance for an alternative education', in Lees, H.E. and Noddings, N. (eds) *The Palgrave international handbook of alternative education*. London: Palgrave Macmillan, pp.385–400.

Solon, O. (2016) 'Facebook's failure: Did fake news and polarized politics get Trump elected?', *Guardian*, 10 November.

Trafford, B. (2003) *School councils, school democracy, school improvement: Why, what, how?* Leicester: Secondary Heads Association.

Tsabar, B. (2014) 'Resistance and imperfection as educational work: Going against the "harmony" of individualistic ideology', *Other Education*, 3 (1), pp.23–40.

Willis, P.E. (1977) *Learning to labor: How working class kids get working class jobs.* New York: Columbia University Press.

Yoneyama, S. (1999) *The Japanese high school: Silence and resistance.* London: Routledge.

KEY CONCEPT: CREATIVITY

Dave Trotman

Concept origins

From the Latin *Creare* (to make or produce), creativity is one of the more recent concepts to appear in the lexicon of education, although its origins can be traced to early Eastern and Western philosophies (Albert and Runco, 1999, p.18). While the early Greeks regarded creativity as nothing more than imitation (see Plato's *The Republic*, Book X), Confucian and Hindu philosophies have long regarded creativity as an aspect of individual cultivation and spiritual expression (Lubart, 1999, p.340; Leong, 2011, p.54). Associated with the idea of the artistic genius of the eighteenth century, by the mid-twentieth century, creativity was to become the subject of increasing interest for researchers working in the field of psychology, particularly in North America, from whence much of the early research on creativity has emerged.

Current status and usage

In UK **school**s, creativity is often unhelpfully used as a 'catch-all' to describe various aspects of the **curriculum**. This can encompass the arts (art, creative writing, dance, drama, media, music), aspects of **culture**, **play**, thinking skills, problem-solving, philosophy or simply anything that can be regarded as unconventional. When applied to **teaching**, it frequently implies the adoption of methods that give children and young people greater **autonomy** and responsibility for their own **learning**—something that has been strongly associated with progressive education. Beyond UK shores, creativity has become of increasing interest to Pacific Rim countries, which, while performing well in conventional measurements of education, are concerned that their education systems do less well in promoting creativity. In

> this regard, it frequently stands problematically for capitalist-oriented innovation, problem-solving and entrepreneurialism in the manufacture of new commodities (Craft, 2008, p.17). In its most current usage, creativity is typically seen as a positive force for good in relation to personal, cultural and societal development.

Creativity is one of the 'slippery' concepts in education where a simple single definition is best avoided—despite attempts by some people to do just that. Rather, it is better to consider aspects of creativity that are commonly referred to when describing someone, something, or a particular enterprise as being 'creative'. In discussing 'what is creativity?' these aspects are likely to include: **play** and experimentation; risk-taking; problem-solving; imaginative and divergent thinking; innovation and originality; self-expression and personal growth. These commonly cited aspects of creativity will, however, be subject to different emphases, depending on the particular orientation a person or group has to creativity. An *entrepreneurial* view of creativity, in the world of business, commodities and market competition is likely to emphasise innovation and calculated risk-taking in order to generate new products for consumers. A *person-centred* view of creativity, in contrast, is more likely to be concerned with creativity as a process that nourishes the interior world of the individual or collective **imagination**, feeling and personal expression. This underscores one of the common binary arguments about creativity: whether it is about products and outcomes that can be publicly assessed and agreed upon, or the nurturing of a personal internal process, where public outcomes have less importance than the creative fulfilment of the creator.

One of the earliest modern insights into the process of creativity comes from British academic Graham Wallas, who, in his 1926 work, *The art of thought*, proposes a five-stage model of creativity, involving preparation, incubation, intimation, illumination and verification. Each stage of the model marks a particular phase in the process—from the stimulus of initial ideas to the completion and reflection on the creative outcome. More recent attempts to understand this process can be found in the work of the American social psychologist Mihaly Csik-szentmihalyi. In his work on creativity, Csikszentmihalyi (1996) reports the positive qualities of the state of 'flow', experienced by participants when immersed in a range of creative projects. While flow is a largely positive quality, creativity, particularly at the stage of incubation, can be a restless, frustrating and nerve-wracking process—see, for example, John Tusa's (2003) accounts of the creative process among professional artists. Other scholars working in the field argue that creativity can be categorised into four specific stages using a 'four-c' model (Kaufman and Beghetto, 2009). This view of creativity begins with the 'min-c' of personal interpretation of experience in the formative years of **childhood**, progressing to the 'little c' of everyday creative experimentation and exploration. 'Pro-C' creativity is that demonstrated at expert level, such as that of the professional composer, film-maker or artist, which, in turn, may lead in exceptional circumstances to the 'Big C' of the creative genius.

Much of this assumes that there is a general agreement on creativity from a largely Western perspective. Hence, a further dimension of the tricky nature of creativity is that it is also contingent upon the *socio-cultural perspective* or 'lenses' through which phenomena and practices are deemed to be creative. Matsunobu (2011), for example, cautions that what might be considered legitimate creative acts in some **cultures** could be unacceptable or inappropriate in others. Broad distinctions between Western and Eastern standpoints, for instance, have been reported by Lubart (1999), who notes that Eastern traditions have much less preoccupation with innovative problem-solving than the West and, instead, place greater emphasis on spiritual expression and self-realisation. The rapid growth of digital technologies has also created new challenges for thinking about creativity. For example, the term 'vernacular creativity' has been used by those researching the use of participative digital media to describe innovative reconfigurations of aspects of culture as non-elitist, social and collaborative (Buckingham, 2009). Although much of the current use of the term creativity frames it as a good thing, Cropley *et al.* (2010) caution that there is also a dark side. Instruments of torture, weapons of war and criminal activity all involve degrees of **imagination**, experimentation and ingenuity—key characteristics of creativity, but in malevolent form. Hence, we would be mistaken if we simply consider creativity as a force for good.

Questions to consider

1. Can creativity be taught?
2. What things might we point to as examples of creativity in action?
3. Can creativity be assessed?
4. How might an entrepreneurial view of creativity differ from one that sees creativity as promoting personal wellbeing?
5. How can we develop creativity in children and young people without promoting it in a future malevolent form?

References (with recommended readings in bold)

Albert, R.S. and Runco, M.A. (1999) 'A history of research on creativity', in Sternberg, R.J. (ed.) *Handbook of creativity*. New York: Cambridge University Press, pp.16–31.

Buckingham, D. (2009) 'A common place art? Understanding amateur media production', in Buckingham, D. and Willett, R. (eds) *Video cultures: Media technology and everyday creativity*. Basingstoke: Palgrave Macmillan.

Craft, A. (2008) 'Tensions in creativity and education: Enter wisdom and trusteeship', in Craft, A., Gardner, H. and Claxton, G. *Creativity, wisdom and trusteeship: Exploring the role of education*. Thousand Oaks, CA: Corwin Press, pp.16-34.

Cropley, D., Cropley, A.J., Kaufman J.C. and Runco, M.A. (2010) *The dark side of creativity*. Cambridge: Cambridge University Press.

Csikszentmihalyi, M. (1996) *Creativity: Flow and the psychology of discovery and invention*. New York: HarperCollins.

Kaufman, J.C. and Beghetto, R.A. (2009) 'Beyond big and little: The four C model of creativity', *Review of General Psychology*, 13 (1), pp.1–12.

Leong, S. (2011) 'Creativity and the arts in Chinese societies', in Sefton-Green, J., Thomson, P., Green, K. and Bresler, L. *The Routledge international handbook of creative learning*. Abingdon: Routledge, pp.54–62.

Lubart, T.I. (1999) 'Creativity across cultures', in Sternberg, R.J. (ed.) *Handbook of creativity*. New York: Cambridge University Press, pp.339–350.

Matsunobu, K. (2011) 'Creativity of formulaic learning: Pedagogy of imitation and repetition', in Sefton-Green, J., Thomson, P., Green,

K. and Bresler, L. *The Routledge international handbook of creative learning*. London: Routledge, pp.45–53.

Tusa, J. (2003) *On creativity: Interviews exploring the process.* **London: Methuen Books.**

Wallas, G. (1926) *The art of thought*. London: Jonathan Cape.

KEY CONCEPT: FAMILY

Allison Tatton and Roger Willoughby

Concept origins

From the Latin *familia*—family servants, domestics collectively, the servants in a household. The word family first referred to 'the household' and later to the descendents and servants of a common ancestor. The original Latin meaning is rarely used explicitly in its present usage which most often describes parents and their children. In the English language, in the 15th century, it related to a collective body of people living under the protection of one head of a household. This might have included parents, children and servants and, additionally, any lodgers or boarders. From the 17th century, its usage shifted towards the more recent notion of family, wherein it came to represent people closely related by blood or marriage, including aunts, uncles, cousins, etc. (Slee, 2002).

Current status and usage

The term 'family' is one with which everyone is familiar, yet it can be surprisingly difficult to define as it means different things to different people and in different **culture**s (Allan and Crow, 2001; Wharton, 2012). Two traditional western views of the family centre around (1) the 'nuclear family', which includes two married people, one male and one female, and their biological children and (2) the 'extended family', which includes the wider networks such as aunts, uncles, cousins, grandparents, etc. The 20th century brought an acknowledgement of an increasing number and **diversity** in **family** types, such as: same-sex **relationships**, single-parent families, kinship networks, post-divorce reconfiguration of families (Chambers, 2012), cohabitation, living apart, adoptive families, fostering families and surrogacy. This diversity is further complicated with new reproductive technologies, such as sperm or egg donation and in vitro fertilisation (IVF) by donor. Families are usually formed in one of three ways: (1) biologically, through having a blood connection; (2) legally, through marriage and related forms of State recognition such as adoption or the formalisation of fostering; or (3) socially, with neighbours, godparents, and friends (Hutchison, 2012).

The family is often portrayed as the 'fundamental unit of **society**' (Loveless and Holman, 2007; Newman, 2009), with parents seen as the child's 'first and most enduring educator' (DCFS, 2007). Particularly since Victorian times, there has been an idealised notion of the family, usually involving a heterosexual married couple and their offspring, all living in the same household (Erera, 2002). This idealisation culminated in the 1950s' and 1960s' fictional portrayals in film, television and print of harmonious family lives that reflected and reinforced this model. Changes in this perceived 'norm' are often viewed as having a detrimental impact on society, including on educational attainment (Carolan and Wasserman, 2015). However, in reality, families have always come in various forms. Death, divorce and separation have meant the loss of one or more partner from the household, with the resultant joining of two or more families if new **relationships** are established. In England and Wales, by 2013, 47% of children were born into non-traditional nuclear families, albeit 84% were born to cohabiting couples (ONS, 2014). There are also an increasing number of families with three or more generations living in the same household due to cultural or economic decisions (ONS, 2015). All of these factors indicate a shifting of normative family frameworks (Silva and Bennett, 2004; Ingoldsby and Smith, 2006).

While the family is regarded as one of the basic building blocks of **society**, it also exists in tension with the State, the traditional privacy of the former conflicting to varying degrees with monitoring and managerial tendencies of the latter. Comparing life outcomes for children brought up in families with those raised in **institutional** settings, average families clearly confer important educational and other life advantages on their members (Li and Mumford, 2009; McLanahan and Garfinkel, 2012). Taking just one example to illustrate a mechanism underlying this, Newson (1978) argued that it is the infant's experience of 'unreasonable **care**', the sense the infant has that her parent considers her especially valuable, that is important for the child's development of a positive sense of self. Newson thus argued that 'partiality' is a necessary characteristic of the care-giving role for the child and contrasts with the **ethics** of impartiality that can undermine **institutional** care. Recognition of such developmental, pro-social and educational benefits has traditionally encouraged varying degrees of State support for families and at the same time inhibited State interference. While, ideologically, such a stance can prop up patriarchy and dominant or hegemonic **discourses** that preserve **power** structures (Gramsci, 1971; Foucault, 1980, 1995), they may also obscure genuine risks within families, such as of abuse and neglect. **School**s can act as a check on these more serious risks, as well as serving to mitigate family shortcomings more generally, and offer children a bridge beyond the family towards independence. Of course, such roles are problematic. Positioning the child in relation to the family, the school and the wider community has been important within education and the other human sciences (Meltzer, 1976; Bronfenbrenner, 1979). There are various approaches to conceptualising this. Bronfenbrenner's (1979) work is the most influential here, with its depiction of the nested layers of influence on the child and the family helping to promote multi-disciplinary and multi-agency thinking, as well as representing the complexity of forces on them.

As with other concepts, the notion of family is a site of contest. It is disputed territory. Historically, the rise of urban living—particularly in Westernised countries—has often been accompanied by a shift from extended families and allied patterns of kinship towards nuclear family units. Economically and ideologically driven, such shifts, Althusser (1971) and other Marxists argue, situate families as instruments of social control, with **instrumental** shaping of the thinking and **behaviour** of their members into line with 'authority' and reproducing the status quo. **School** is a further extension of this and the degree of cooperation and alignment of aims between the school and family extend the grip of a potentially false consciousness further. **Psychoanalyis** has approaches to the family which share in this deconstructive critique, seeing the family not so much as a harmonious setting, but as the site in which desire is activated initially within the mother–infant dyad, and then its satisfaction restricted to the parental couple. This essential Oedipal situation optimally facilitates a promise of future fulfilment for the child beyond the family, while fantasies act as a patch to cover the conflict (Lacan 2003). These unresolved tensions are thus brought directly to the school, where again both the **cognitive** and affective dimensions of educational work are catalysed and challenged (Dowling and Osborne, 2003). Both Marxist and psychoanalytic arguments have influenced feminist critiques of the family, within which women and children are figured as relatively disempowered, oppressed and economically unrecognised (Wharton, 2012; Brown, 2012, 2014). Foucault's work on the family depicts it as a continually contested fiction (Taylor, 2012). Here, biopolitics, sexualisation, and family dynamics may be seen as existing at the crossroads between kinship, **sexuality** and the state, with other factors—such as **ethnicity**—inevitably complicating this. The challenge, here as elsewhere, is to both recognise the very real benefits of families for educational outcomes and at the same time consider the various problematics of this dynamic evolving institution.

Questions to consider

1. What 'families' on TV, film, print or other media stand out in your mind and why?
2. Why are some families more fragile than others?
3. Should **school**s **teach** relationship and sex/**sexuality** education to include matters of the family?
4. To what extent are (and should) schools be *in loco parentis*?
5. What do you think of **power** dynamics and **voice** in family life?

References (with recommended readings in bold)

Allan, G. and Crow, G. (2001) *Families, households and society.* **Basingstoke: Palgrave Macmillan.**

Althusser, L. (1971) 'Ideology and ideological state apparatus', in Althusser, L. (ed.) *Lenin and philosophy and other essays.* New York: Monthly Review Press, pp.127–186.

Bronfenbrenner, U. (1979) *The ecology of human development: Experiments by nature and design.* Cambridge, MA: Harvard University Press.

Brown, H.A. (2012) *Marx on gender and the family: A critical study.* Leiden: Brill.

Brown, H.A. (2014) 'Marx on gender and the family: A summary', *Monthly Review,* 66 (2), pp.48–57. Available at: http://monthlyreview.org/2014/06/01/marx-on-gender-and-the-family-a-summary (accessed 26 October 2016).

Carolan, B.V. and Wasserman, S.J. (2015) 'Does parenting style matter? Concerted cultivation, educational expectations, and the transmission of educational advantage', *Sociological Perspectives*, 58 (2), pp.168–187.

Chambers, D. (2012) *A sociology of family life: Change and diversity in intimate relations*. Cambridge: Polity Press.

DCFS (2007) *Statutory framework for the Early Years Foundation Stage*. Nottingham: DfES.

Dowling, E. and Osborne, E. (2003) *The family and the school: A joint systems approach to problems with children*, 2nd edn. London: Karnac.

Erera, P.I. (2002) *Family diversity: Continuity and change in the contemporary family*. London: Sage Publications.

Foucault, M. (1980) *Power/knowledge: Selected interviews and other writings 1972–1977*. Edited by Colin Gordon. New York: Pantheon Books.

Foucault, M. (1995) *Discipline and punish: The birth of the prison*. Translated by Alan Sheridan. New York: Vintage Books.

Gramsci, A. (1971) *Selections from the prison notebooks*. London: Lawrence and Wishart.

Hutchison, E.D. (2012) *Essentials of human behavior: Integrating person, environment, and the life course*. London: Sage.

Ingoldsby, B.B. and Smith, S.D. (eds) (2006) *Families in global and multicultural perspective*, 2nd edn. London: Sage.

Lacan, J. (2003) *Jacques Lacan: Family complexes in the formation of the individual*. Translated by C. Gallagher. London: Karnac.

Li, Y. and Mumford, K.A. (2009) 'Family structure and educational outcomes of British children: Some preliminary evidence', *International Journal of Learning*, 16 (7), pp.643–655.

Loveless, S. and Holman, T. (2007) *The family in the new millennium: The place of family in human society*. London: Praeger Perspectives.

McLanahan, S. and Garfinkel, I. (2012) 'Fragile families: debates, facts, and solutions', in Garrison, M. and Scott, E.S. (eds) *Marriage at the crossroads: Law, policy, and the brave new world of twenty-first-century families*. New York: Cambridge University Press, pp.142–169.

Meltzer, D. (1976) 'A psychoanalytic model of the child-in-the-family-in-the-community', in Hahn, A. (ed.) *Sincerity and other works: Collected papers of Donald Meltzer*. London: Karnac, 1994, pp.387–454.

Newman, D.M. (2009) *Families: A sociological perspective*. New York: McGraw-Hill Higher Education.

Newson, E. (1978) 'Unreasonable care: The establishment of selfhood', in Vesey, G. (ed.) *Human values: Lectures of the Royal Institute of Philosophy*. London: Harvester Press, pp.1–26.

ONS (2014) *Statistical bulletin: Live births in England and Wales by characteristics of Mother 1, 2013*. Available at: www.ons.gov.uk/ons/rel/vsob1/characteristics-of-Mother-1–england-and-wales/2013/

stb-characteristics-of-mother-1–2013.html#tab-Partnership-Status-of-Parents (accessed 26 October 2016).

ONS (2015) *Families and Households, 2015.* Available at: www.ons.gov.uk/ons/dcp171778_393133.pdf (accessed 26 October 2016).

Silva, E.B. and Bennett, T. (2004) *Contemporary culture and everyday life.* Durham: Sociologypress.

Slee, P. (2002) *Child, adolescent and family development.* Cambridge: Cambridge University Press.

Taylor, C (2012) 'Foucault and the family', *Hypatia*, 27 (1), pp.201–218.

Wharton, A.S. (2012) *The sociology of gender: An introduction to theory and research* (Key Themes in Sociology), 2nd edn. London: Wiley-Blackwell.

KEY CONCEPT: GENDER

Roger Willoughby

Concept origins

Gender, here referring predominantly to socio-cultural dimensions of females and males as opposed to their physical sex characteristics, is a relatively recent conceptual category in academic **discourse**. Originating with the introduction of the term 'gender role' by Money (1955; Money *et al.*, 1955) and 'gender **identity**' later by Stoller (1968; Green, 2010), its subsequent popularisation was due to its take up by feminism as a powerful conceptual tool (Haig, 2004; Germon, 2009). Gender stereotypes were (and continue to be) framed in terms of binaries or polar opposites, such as dominant/submissive, rational/emotional, or active/passive, one pole of which would be predominantly associated with masculinity and the other with femininity. The flexibility of such associations varies socially, culturally and historically (Mead, 1935, 1949), but worldwide such gender binaries have been repeatedly found to limit gender expression and support discriminatory norms (Naples *et al.*, 2016). As such, gender is of strong relevance in education, particularly given education's socialising function and its role as a potential agent of social change.

Current status and usage

As a concept, gender (rather than sex, here linked to **sexuality**), as Haig (2004) has pointed out, has become the predominant term in research in education and the other **social science**s, arts and **humanities**. In particular, the processes of gender socialisation in education have attracted significant feminist and wider cross-disciplinary interest (Helgeson, 2016; Naples *et al.*, 2016). In these social processes gender roles, norms and their behavioural expression are learned and perpetuated (Chodorow, 1978) in ways specific to the host **culture**, through various primary and secondary socialising agents (such as parents, **teacher**s and the media). Building particularly on Foucault's ideas, as well as on **psychoanalysis**, Judith Butler's (1990, 1993) work on gender has impacted considerably on contemporary academic debate (Brady and Schirato, 2011). Discarding the gender binary and any naturalisation of sexual identities, Butler situates gender as a cultural 'performance', which articulates contested **power** relations. The traditional performance of gender reinforces a **hegemony** of a heteronormative social order, and may be thus regarded as a disciplinary practice. Given the inherently unstable and contested nature of gender, performances that fall outside of these norms create 'gender trouble' (Butler, 1990) and can attract sanctions both from within and beyond educational circles. Prominent among the contemporary gender debates in British education is the rise in attainment rates by girls and young women in **school** and higher education. Unsurprisingly, the common response is not so much celebration of female achievement but the emergence of anxiety about failing boys (Marchbank and Letherby, 2014). In education, the task of developing Butlerian type questioning has been taken forward by a significant number of writers in rethinking a critical edge for education (e.g., Davies, 2006; Nayak and Kehily, 2006; Vlieghe, 2010; and Giuliano, 2015).

 When a child is born (and now often before this happens), one of the first questions posed is: 'Is it a girl or a boy?' This deceptively simple binary choice, which seems to offer just two fundamental categories of being, traditionally resulted in a stereotypical biologically based answer: 'He is a boy'; 'She is a girl'. Key differential markers in reaching this decision might include the possession of a vagina or penis, chromosomal differences, and other biological characteristics. The results would be generally clear and unambiguous. However, this is not always the case. Some children are born intersex or with medical conditions (e.g., Klinefelter syndrome, Turner syndrome) that can raise doubts over a simple binary attribution of sex. Estimates of the prevalence of such births vary, from 1.7% for the compound range of births being cited by Fausto-Sterling (2000), down to 0.018% for those strictly defined as intersex by Sax (2002). Irrespective of the size of these numbers, they problematise any simple binary classification according to biological sex. Gender, however, complicates the picture further. Alcoff (2006, p.146) argues that gender is 'formalizable in a nonarbitrary way through a matrix of habits, practices, and **discourses**', and goes on to note that the dynamic socio-historical context is one in which 'we are both subjects of and subjected to social construction'. Culturally and historically determined as stereotypes, femininity might typically include dependent, emotional, passive, graceful, nurturing, empathising and submissive characteristics, while independent, rational, competitive, active, systematising and confident ones would be ascribed to masculinity. These are not mere stereotypes: the language of gender is a language of hierarchy and **power**. It is a core aspect of patriarchy, a social system under which men dominate women and gender roles are reinforced (Marchbank and Letherby, 2014). Thus, those attributes more commonly associated with males and masculinity attract higher valuations than those associated with females and femininity. This all impacts on and is insidiously reproduced through the world of education (as well as in work and **society**); for example, with gendered subject choices, encouragement towards particular careers, future domestic arrangements, and so on (Dyhouse, 2006; Jackson *et al.*, 2011; Fineman, 2012).

 Masculinity and femininity, as a binary concept, are problematic. Such—substantially learned—characteristics are, of course, found in varying amounts in both males and females. Winnicott (1971) related the interrelationship of these elements in the personality to **creativity**. Yet when femininity is conspicuous in males, and masculinity in females, social censure can result, the degrees of which vary according to social, cultural and historical factors. Inevitably this increases still further the vulnerability of these groups in education and wider **society**. The term transgender (Oliven, 1965) was introduced to recognise individuals who experienced **dissonance** between their subjectively experienced gender **identity** and their assigned biological sex. More recently, an abbreviation simply to trans has gained some currency (Killermann, 2013), particularly given its greater inclusivity. The term cisgender (Sigusch, 1991) was coined to describe the non-trans population, though it is problematic for its clustering of LGB groups in with heterosexuals. Flores *et al.* (2016) estimated that 0.6% of the US population identify as transgender. Increasing social and legal recognition of trans groups in various countries, such as the hijra in India and two-spirit Native Americans, has underscored the important **human rights** issues involved, not just for these groups, but more broadly. Currently, in Europe, only Denmark, Malta and Ireland have legislation that allows individuals over the age of 18 to self-declare their preferred gender. In other countries, where gender recognition legislation exists, various restrictive forms of expert certification are required. In education, these issues are reflected at multiple levels, including in policies, in **institutional culture**s, in curricular options, in the segregation of toilets and changing facilities, and in varying degrees of violence and bullying.

Efforts to recognise the complex issues involved and develop practice guidance are slowly gathering pace, with Cornwall (Cannon and Best, 2015) and East Sussex (Allsorts Youth Project *et al.*, 2014) being among English local authorities leading the way.

Seeing the body as a cultural situation, Judith Butler (1990, 1993; Boucher, 2006; Brady and Schirato, 2011) argues that gender and **sexuality** are contingent, assumed, and the product of identifications with figures within dominant narratives. Objects of desire are offered and substantially delimited through these same narratives, which are typically heteronormative. They thus represent varieties of **ideology** (Althusser, 1971) that are essentially hegemonic (Gramsci, 1971), disciplinary (Foucault, 1977) and oppressive (Freire, 1972). One example of gender trouble important to note here are the debates accompanying the rise in female academic attainment rates in **school**s and universities, as well as the changing gender profile of academics. Aside from the continued utilisation of the gender binary and neglect of recognising female achievement, is a narrative—something of a moral panic—about 'failing boys' in a 'feminised' educational system, which lacks adequate male role models. While this may be crudely regarded as yet a further example of misogyny (and that would be too simple a story), disaggregating of **assessment** data reveals not only significant gender effects, but that these are far less significant than either social **class** or **ethnicity** (Marchbank and Letherby, 2014). It is thus important to take such research forward in a far more nuanced way, paying due attention to issues of **intersectionality** (Crenshaw, 1989; Carastathis, 2014) across the gender range. The result should offer not just greater opportunities for individual subversion (Butler, 1993), but also more transformative educational and social possibilities.

Questions to consider

1. Considering your own **identity** and **culture**, how do you express your gender and has this changed over time?
2. How has your gender affected your educational career?
3. Considering Butler's work on **performativity**, what factors contribute to (a) rigid gender performances and (b) iterations of gender with greater variability?
4. How does the design of **school**s and educational institutions impact on the gender identity and freedom of gender expression of their users?

References (with recommended readings in bold)

Alcoff, L.M. (2006) *Visible identities: Race, gender, and the self.* New York: Oxford University Press.

Allsorts Youth Project and Brighton and Hove City Council (2014) *Trans* inclusion school toolkit: Supporting transgender and gender questioning children and young people in East Sussex schools and colleges.* Brighton: East Sussex County Council.

Althusser, L. (1971) 'Ideology and ideological state apparatus', in Althusser, L. (ed.) *Lenin and philosophy and other essays.* New York: Monthly Review Press, pp.127–186.

Boucher, G. (2006) 'The politics of performativity: A critique of Judith Butler', *Parrhesia*, 1, pp.112–141.

Brady, A. and Schirato, T. (2011) *Understanding Judith Butler.* London: Sage.

Butler, J. (1990) *Gender trouble: Feminism and the subversion of identity.* New York: Routledge.

Butler, J. (1993) *Bodies that matter: On the discursive limits of sex.* New York: Routledge.

Cannon, S. and Best, T. (eds) (2015) *Schools transgender guidance.* Truro: The Intercom Trust & Devon and Cornwall Police.

Carastathis, A. (2014) 'The concept of intersectionality in feminist theory', *Philosophy Compass*, 9, pp.304–314.

Chodorow, N. (1978) *The reproduction of mothering: Psychoanalysis and the sociology of gender.* Berkeley: University of California Press.

Crenshaw, K. (1989) 'Demarginalizing the intersection of race and sex: A black feminist critique of antidiscrimination doctrine, feminist theory and antiracist politics', *The University of Chicago Legal Forum*, 140, pp.139–167.

Davies, B. (2006) 'Subjectification: the relevance of Butler's analysis for education', *British Journal of Sociology of Education*, 27, pp.425–438.

Dyhouse, C. (2006) *Students: A gendered history*. Abingdon: Routledge.

Fausto-Sterling, F. (2000) *Sexing the body: Gender politics and the construction of sexuality.* New York: Basic Books.

Fineman, S. (2012) *Work: A very short introduction.* Oxford: Oxford University Press.

Flores, A.R., Herman, J.L., Gates, G.J. and Brown, T.N.T. (2016) *How many adults identify as transgender in the United States.* Los Angeles: The Williams Institute.

Foucault, M. (1977) *Discipline and punish: The birth of the prison.* Translated by A. Sheridan. Harmondsworth: Penguin.

Freire, P. (1972) *Pedagogy of the oppressed*. Harmondsworth: Penguin.

Germon, J. (2009) *Gender: A genealogy of an idea*. New York: Palgrave Macmillan.

Giuliano, F. (2015) '(Re)thinking education with Judith Butler: A necessary meeting between philosophy and education (interview with Judith Butler)', *Encounters in Theory and History of Education*, 16, pp.183–199.

Gramsci, A. (1971) *Selections from the prison notebooks of Antonio Gramsci*. Translated and edited by Q. Hoare and G. Norwell-Smith. London: Lawrence & Wishart.

Green, R. (2010) 'Robert Stoller's *Sex and gender*: 40 years on, *Archives of Sexual Behavior*, 39(6), pp.1457–1465.

Haig, D. (2004) 'The inexorable rise of gender and the decline of sex: Social change in academic titles 1945–2001', *Archives of Sexual Behavior*, 33(2), pp.87–96.

Helgeson, V.S. (2016) *The psychology of gender*, 4th edn. Abingdon: Routledge.

Jackson, S., Malcolm, I. and Thomas, K. (eds) (2011) *Gendered choices: Learning, work, identities in lifelong learning*. Dordrecht, Netherlands: Springer.

Killermann, S. (2013) *The social justice advocate's handbook: A guide to gender*. Austin, TX: Impetus Books.

Marchbank, J. and Letherby, G. (2014) *Introduction to gender: Social science perspectives*. London: Routledge.

Mead, M. (1935) *Sex and temperament in three primitive societies*. New York: Perennial, 2003.

Mead, M. (1949) *Male and female: A study of the sexes in a changing world*. New York: William Morrow.

Money, J. (1955) 'Hermaphroditism, gender and precocity in hyper-adrenocorticism: Psychologic findings', *Bulletin of the Johns Hopkins Hospital*, 96, pp.253–264.

Money, J., Hampson, J.G. and Hampson, J.L. (1955) 'An examination of some basic sexual concepts: The evidence of human hermaphroditism', *Bulletin of the Johns Hopkins Hospital*, 97, pp.301–319.

Naples, N., Hoogland, R.C., Wickramasinghe, M. and Wong, W.C.A. (eds) (2016) *The Wiley Blackwell encyclopedia of gender and sexuality studies*. Malden, MA: John Wiley & Sons.

Nayak, A. and Kehily, M.J. (2006) 'Gender undone: subversion, regulation and embodiment in the work of Judith Butler', *British Journal of Sociology of Education*, 27, pp.459–472.

Oliven, J. F. (1965) *Sexual hygiene and pathology*. London: Pitman Medical Publishing.

Sax, L. (2002) 'How common is intersex? A response to Anne Fausto-Sterling', *Journal of Sex Research*, 39, pp.174–178.

Sigusch, V. (1991) 'Die Transsexuellen und unser nosomorpher Blick', *Zeitschrift für Sexualforschung*, 4, pp.225–256 and 309–343.

Stoller, R. J. (1968) *Sex and gender: The development of masculinity and femininity*. London: Hogarth Press.

Vlieghe, J. (2010) 'Judith Butler and the public dimension of the body: Education, critique and corporeal vulnerability', *Journal of the Philosophy of Education*, 44, pp.153–170.

Winnicott, D.W. (1971) *Playing and reality*. London: Tavistock.

KEY CONCEPT: IDENTITY

Roger Willoughby

Concept origins

Identity as a concept occurs in many **disciplines**, with its take-up within philosophy, sociology, **politics**, anthropology, theology and **psychoanalysis** being particularly prescient for the concept's utilisation within education. Unsurprisingly, usage of the term across these different fields is inconsistent and the resultant polyphony does not always lead to easy or indeed possible integration. Any discussion of identity necessitates an understanding of the closely related notion of the self. From a psychoanalytic perspective, the self has been regarded as an agent who is endowed with awareness of both their own identity and of their degrees of agency and subjective status (Rycroft, 1972). Here identity is predicated on a consciousness of one's self or self-experience across time, with this being more or less coherent and distinct from others. This understanding of the self builds on substantial philosophical work, particularly: (1) Descartes' (1641) search for epistemological certainty during the seventeenth century, which culminated in his 'cogito, ergo sum' (I think, therefore I am) dictum; and (2) Hegel's (1807) very different emphasis on recognition within **relationships** as essential to emergent self-consciousness, a thesis importantly revisited and developed by Honneth (1995).

Current status and usage

The concept has developed as its subject has become more problematic. As du Gay *et al.* (2000) emphasised, modern views of identity have increasingly depicted it as variegated, patchwork and complex. Within **politics** in general and in education in particular, current deployments of the concept of identity involve micro-identities, with **class**, **ethnic** and **gender** vertices and their **intersectionality** being particularly highlighted.

Questions of filiation and belonging, whether, for example, in terms of a notional national identity or in terms of traditional student identities, of engagement with the offered normative narratives, have become increasingly prominent (May, 2013). For education, an important part of the tension here relates to its own competing functional **discourses**: is it elucidatory, maintaining, transformative, challenging to or repressive of student, **teacher** and **institutional** identities?

 Identity is about who and what I am, and who and what I am not. This may be initially understood as an amalgam of many internal and external elements. These would include bodily experience, thoughts, fantasy and **imagination**, **gender**, **class**, **race**, **ethnicity**, multi-layered history, habitus, capital, one's jobs or roles, one's **relationships**, values, spirituality, future plans and aspirations. Central to our identity is our life experienced through our own individual consciousness, our sense of self, of 'I' and of 'me'. All this develops over time (Erikson, 1968), being a negotiated interpersonal achievement, one which remains *in-process*. Our own personal identity (how we privately perceive and construe ourselves) and our social identity (how our social worlds frame us) represent a double aspect of our identities (Stevens, 1996). How comfortably these aspects integrate or how much **dissonance** or conflict exists between them is important and can be regarded as a contributor to adjustment and well-being. With education mediating social and political processes (from the **hidden** **curriculum**, through nationalism, patriarchy, the monitoring of so-called radicalisation, to acceptance of the supremacy of democracy and market **capitalism**), **schooling** can exert a significant formative effect on identity. Processes of **labelling** are essential to consider here. Key theorists, from Durkheim (1897) through Cooley (1902) to Goffman (1963), have emphasised how deviating from cultural norms can attract negative labels, which stigmatise and devalue their recipients, processes exacerbated through sometimes resulting phenomena, such as the **self-fulfilling prophecy** (Merton, 1948). Almost inevitably, processes of educational **assessment**, within which there are winners and losers, cultivate and jeopardise students' identities as learners (Reay and Wiliam, 1999). Relatedly, **ideology** exerts similar influence on students, albeit more insidiously (Illich, 1973).

✿ While **labelling**, the **self-fulfilling prophecy** and **ideology** negatively impact on personal identity (both in and outside education), in an effort to regulate **society** (a functionalist view), correlates such as the Pygmalion effect (Rosenthal and Jacobson, 1992) highlight the potentially positive effect on performance of high expectations. Positive outcomes, of course, impact not only on student identity, but also on **teacher** identity (Zembylas, 2003; Beauchamp and Thomas, 2009) and that of the institution (Avest and Bakker, 2007). Considering identities beyond those of students further highlights variation. How *difference* is responded to is here significant, particularly as identity can be constructed in terms of that which one is not (e.g., not black, not female, not Christian, not heterosexual, etc.). Often such clustering thinking is predicated on binary oppositions and a magnification of the significance of minor differences (Freud, 1930; Blok, 1998). Identities thus formed can be precarious and can promote thinking that dehumanises the other; they are not me, not as good, less civilised, and so on as the self (or one's group) is promoted and the other is devalued. The result can be sexist, racialised, denigratory, and other forms of frankly aggressive thinking and **behaviour**. The degree to which there is an active sponsorship or passive complicity in such **culture**s by individuals, institutions and/or the state, as opposed to challenging such thinking and offering an alternative, more nuanced empathic reading of identity of self and other, may be seen not just as a measure of moral standing (see **ethics**) but also of risk.

☺ As suggested previously, just as identity as a concept is disputed territory, so too are identities. In the face of the State's encouragement of normalcy and pressure to adhere to dominant, **hegemonic** identity narratives, these same sets of signification are often met with scepticism and actually command decreasing allegiance. Theoretical responses, such as the psychosocial fragmentation or individualisation theses (May, 2013), tend to emphasise (1) the erosion of so-called traditional certainties on the one hand and (2) new freedom and agency for individual identity creation on the other. The work of Willis (1977; Dolby *et al.*, 2004) offers a classic example of a sub-group critique of education as a middle-**class** project; the 'lads' resistance to subordination and concomitant creation of a counter **school** culture, disqualifies them from **transformation** possibilities, leaving them, instead, apparently choosing traditional low-skilled manual factory work. Such identity construction, Willis argues, rests not so much on a rejection of educational aspiration, but on binaries involving mental/manual labour, **gender** and **race**, alongside a perception of the structural and value barriers they face in the labour market. While questions of class and agency pervade Willis's argument, race and gender identity (and the **intersectionality** of such dimensions) have increasingly focused critical debates. With a history of **racism** (Mac an Ghaill, 1988) and postcolonial problems, particularly around alienation (Fanon, 1952), negatively impacting on educational attainment, and contemporary anxieties around the Muslim other, traditional education itself has come to be questioned as a colonising **discourse** that distorts identity (Dei and Simmons, 2010; Hoerder, 2014). Similar questions arise in relation to gender identity, with the work of Butler (1990, 1993; Brady and Schirato, 2011), for example, situating gender identity as a cultural performance that is contingent, assumed and the product of identifications. In both arenas, choice can be limited essentially through dominant narratives, resulting in a partial or premature identity, with other possibilities foreclosed.

Questions to consider

1. Thinking about your own life, what are central pillars of your identity? Will these change?
2. How does having a minority status (such as BAME) impact on social identity and the potential constructions of self within **school**s?
3. How does the **gender** identity of a **teacher** figure impact on students?
4. Which theorists and research would you cite in support of your ideas about identity?

References (with recommended readings in bold)

Avest, K.H.T. and Bakker, C. (2007) 'School identity: A living document on the relationship between the biography of the principal relating to school identity', *Interacções*, 7, pp.116–140.

Beauchamp, C. and Thomas, L. (2009) 'Understanding teacher identity: Overview of issues in the literature and implications for teacher education', *Cambridge Journal of Education*, 39, pp.175–189.

Blok, A. (1998) 'The narcissism of minor differences', *European Journal of Social Theory*, 1, pp.33–56.

Brady, A. and Schirato, T. (2011) *Understanding Judith Butler*. London: Sage.

Butler, J. (1990) *Gender trouble*. London: Routledge.

Butler, J. (1993) *Bodies that matter*. London: Routledge.

Cooley, C.H. (1902) *Human nature and the social order*. New York: Charles Scribner's Sons.

Dei, G.J.S. and Simmons, M. (eds) (2010) *Fanon & education: Thinking through pedagogical possibilities*. New York: Peter Lang.

Descartes, R. (1641) *Meditations of first philosophy*. Translated by J. Cottingham. Cambridge: Cambridge University Press, 1996.

Dolby, N., Dimitriadis, G. and Willis, P. (2004) *Learning to labor in new times*. London: RoutledgeFalmer.

du Gay, P., Evans, J. and Redman, P. (eds) (2000) *Identity: A reader*. London: Sage.

Durkheim, E. (1897) *Suicide: A study in sociology*. Abingdon: Routledge Classics, 2002.

Fanon, F. (1952) *Black skin white masks*. Translated by Charles Lam Markmann. London: Pluto Press, 1986.

Erikson, E.H. (1968) *Identity, youth and crisis*. New York: Norton.

Freud, S. (1930) *Civilization and its discontents*, in Strachey, J. (ed.) *The standard edition of the complete psychological works of Sigmund Freud*, vol. 18, London: Hogarth Press, 1961, pp.57–146.

Goffman, E. (1963) *Stigma: Notes on the management of spoiled identity*. Englewood Cliffs, NJ: Prentice-Hall.

Hegel, G.W.F. (1807) *The phenomenology of spirit*. Translated by A.V. Miller. Oxford: Clarendon Press, 1977.

Hoerder, D. (2014) 'Education for a transcultural life-world or for a hegemonic nation? Schooling in the British empire, in France, and in Canada, 1830s–2000s', *Studia Migracyjne—Przeglad Polonijny*, 40 (3), pp.17–32.

Honneth, A. (1995) *The struggle for recognition: The moral grammar of social conflicts*. Cambridge: Polity Press.

Illich, I. (1973) *Deschooling society*. Harmondsworth: Penguin.

Mac an Ghaill, M. (1988) *Young, gifted and black: Student–teacher relations in the schooling of black youth*. Milton Keynes: Open University Press.

May, V. (2013) *Connecting self to society: Belonging in a changing world*. Basingstoke: Palgrave Macmillan.

Merton, R.K. (1948) 'The self-fulfilling prophecy', *Antioch Review*, 8, pp.193–210.

Reay, D. and Wiliam, D. (1999) '"I'll be a nothing": Structure, agency and the construction of identity through assessment', *British Educational Research Journal*, 25 (3), pp.343–354.

Rosenthal, R. and Jacobson, L. (1992) *Pygmalion in the classroom*, expanded edition. New York: Irvington.

Rycroft, C. (1972) *A critical dictionary of psychoanalysis*. Harmondsworth: Penguin.

Stevens, R. (ed.) (1996) *Understanding the self*. Milton Keynes: Open University Press.

Willis, P. (1977) *Learning to labor: How working class kids get working class jobs*. New York: Columbia University Press.

Zembylas, M. (2003) 'Interrogating "teacher identity": Emotion, resistance, and self-formation', *Educational Theory*, 53, pp.107–127.

KEY CONCEPT: IMAGINATION

Dave Trotman

Concept origins

In its English usage imagination is commonly associated with mental conceptions of 'seeing' things that do not exist and that are not visible (Williams, 1988, p.158). For White (1990, p.184) to imagine is 'to think of it as possibly being so'. In ancient Greek and Hebrew traditions, imagination was regarded not as a benign or positive aspect of human **behaviour**, but as troublesome and problematic, generating disruption to the harmonious state that exists between the human and divine world—a rebellion against divine order (Egan, 1992). The idea, then, of the imagination being something to be distrusted—a hindrance and distraction to philosophical reason and the spiritual life—persisted largely until the eighteenth century, with the emergence of a positive romantic conception of imagination. In this romantic development of the concept, the poet Samuel Taylor Coleridge cast the 'primary imagination' as: 'the living **power** and prime agent of all human perception, and as a repetition in the finite mind of the eternal act of creation in the infinite I AM' (Coleridge, 1817, p.313).

Current status and usage

In contrast to the early origins of the term, imagination is now widely regarded as an important and powerful attribute of human endeavour. Often closely associated with **creativity, play** and thinking skills, imagination involves the freedom to think up and experiment with a range of possibilities, ideas, images and experiences. Hence, imagination is frequently linked to invention, originality and discovery, principally because it is 'thought of the possible rather than the actual' (White, 1990, p.186).

In order to begin to better understand the role of imagination and its educational possibilities, it is useful to first deconstruct some of the components of the concept. Passmore (1980) offers a distinction between imaging, imagery and imagination. He considers imaging as something that takes place through various forms of mental representation; involving visual, auditory, olfactory, kinaesthetic, gustatory and other forms of sense data. Imagining, he contends, involves such things as pretence, supposition, hypothesising and empathy, while being imaginative implies the generation of a novel outcome. According to Eisner (2005) our ability to conceive of things that never were, but which might become, provides the engine of social and cultural progress:

> To imagine is to create new images, images that function in the development of a new science, the creation of a new symphony, and the invention of a new bridge. It is a process critical for the creation of poetry and for innovation in our practical lives.
>
> (Eisner, 2005, pp.107–108)

In similar vein, Fisher and Williams (2004, p.9) contend that to imagine is to conceive possible or impossible worlds that lie beyond a given time and place.

In her seminal text on the subject, Mary Warnock (1976) examines imagination from the perspective of the European philosophical traditions of Hume, Kant, Schelling, Sartre and Wittgenstein to reveal how features of imagination emerge as both essential and universal. From these different perspectives Warnock's contention is that meanings arise in parallel with the immediacy of our consciousness and that it is the imagination which ascribes these meanings. In our day-to-day lived experience, we then use imagination to apply concepts to things. This, she argues, is the way in which the world is made familiar and subsequently manageable (Warnock, 1976, p.207). She suggests that we may also 'render our experience unfamiliar and mysterious', speculating that below the level of consciousness our imagination is at work 'tidying up the chaos of sense experience', yet, at a different level, it may also 'untidy it again'. This leads her to consider the existence of 'unexplored areas, huge spaces of which we may only get an occasional awe-inspiring glimpse, questions raised by experience about whose answers we can only with hesitation speculate' (Warnock, 1976, p.208; see **psychoanalysis**).

Turning to the idea of imaginative growth, Gajdamaschko (2005) draws on Vygotsky's psychology to describe how imagination develops from its most basic forms to the more complex, in which imaginative growth is contingent upon other forms of human activity and the accrual of experience. In this regard, emotional development and imagination are closely related to children's **play** and the ability to create and sustain imaginary situations that eventually lead to the development of abstract thought (Gajdamaschko, 2005, p.19). This approach to imagination in education has been subject to extensive treatment by Egan (1997, 2005). In advancing a theory and **curriculum** of imaginative education that is primarily culturally situated, Egan turns to the possibilities offered by Vygotsky's concept of cultural/psychological tools. Beginning with psychological tools, imaginative activities are developed through an interiorisation of correspondent cultural forms. In early **childhood**, imagination emerges as a characteristic of play and through gradual development appropriates new cultural tools in **learning** activities. As these change it 'gradually turns into the imagination of adolescence and then into the productive imagination of the adult' (Gajdamaschko, 2005, p.20). Examples of psychological tools would then include such things as language, writing, forms of numeration, symbols and signs, works of art, diagrammatic representations, maps and so on. It is these tools, Egan argues, that assist us in making sense of the world of experience in relation to particular kinds of understanding (Egan, 2010, p.38).

Questions to consider

1. What makes someone imaginative?
2. What sort of things might help shape our imaginative development?
3. How can we best avoid stifling the imagination?
4. What are the main differences between imagination in **childhood** and imagination in adulthood?
5. How can we make the imagination more central to the **curriculum**?

References (with recommended readings in bold)

Coleridge, S.T. (1817) *Biographia literaria*, in Jackson, H.J. (ed.) *Samuel Taylor Coleridge: The major works*. Oxford: Oxford University Press, 2000, pp.155–482.

Egan, K. (1992) *Imagination in teaching and learning: Ages 8–15.* **London: Routledge.**

Egan, K. (1997) *The educated mind: How cognitive tools shape our understanding.* Chicago: University of Chicago Press.

Egan, K. (2005) *An imaginative approach to teaching.* San Francisco: Jossey-Bass.

Egan, K. (2010) 'Culture, imagination and the development of the mind' in Nielsen, T.W., Fitzgerald, R. and Fettes, M. *Imagination in educational theory and practice: A many-sided vision.* Newcastle: Cambridge Scholars, pp.21–41.

Eisner, E. (2005) *Reimagining schools: The selected works of Elliot W. Eisner.* London: Routledge.

Fisher, R. and Williams, M. (2004) *Unlocking creativity: Teaching across the curriculum.* London: David Fulton.

Gajdamaschko, N. (2005) 'Vygotsky on imagination: Why an understanding of the imagination is an important issue for school teachers', *Teaching Education,* **16 (1), pp.13–22.**

Passmore, J. (1980) *The philosophy of teaching.* London: Duckworth.

Warnock, M. (1976) *Imagination.* **London: Faber and Faber.**

White, A. (1990) *The language of imagination.* Oxford: Blackwell.

Williams, R. (1988) *Key words.* London: Fontana Press.

KEY CONCEPT: MOTIVATION

Parminder Assi

Concept origins

The word motivation derives from the Latin verb *movere* meaning 'to move', and in educational terms focuses on the understanding of factors which influence individuals in their engagement, effort and persistence in activities. There are numerous differing perspectives on motivation; however, historically, the study of motivation has been dominated by **behaviourist** perspectives. For example, Watson (1913) argued that inner experiences of individual motivation cannot be properly studied as these are not observable but **behaviour** can be studied. This perspective led to focus on extrinsic motivational strategies and manipulation of the environment to motivate individuals to achieve results.

Current status and usage

The current interest in motivation within **learning** and **teaching** is dominated by goal-directed performative **discourses** of standards and compliance (Carr, 2016). Increasingly **neuroscience** is being brought into the picture (Dommett *et al.*, 2013), as are humanist desires to focus on the value of **relationships** (Rogers, 2015). Nevertheless, approaches involving **behaviourism** still hold the day. This is being challenged by a realisation that behaviourism may not suit all learners, particularly those whose early years were disrupted or neglectful and who may also be from, or in, state provided **care** settings (Parker *et al.*, 2016). In a **neoliberal** climate, the lack of motivation is increasingly conceptualised as a problem, where those who fail to achieve are personally penalised for their 'failure' to attain goals. This view ignores contextual factors of environment and relationships, as well as home life, well-being, mental life and relevance to the individual and so is open to challenge.

Psychologically based perspectives on motivation tend to explore the effects of external, extrinsic factors including rewards, certificates and privileges. Sociologically based perspectives focus on the interactions between internal thinking and social experiences. Extrinsic motivation comes from an outside source such as money, grades, praise or the status that achievements bring (Skinner, 1973). Intrinsic motivation can be influenced by the activity itself because it gives an individual pleasure, helps develop a skill they value, or they consider it ethically and morally right (Weiner, 1974). While there are arguments across and within perspectives stemming from **behaviourist, cognitivist, social-constructivist** and humanist models on motivation (e.g., that extrinsic motivation more efficiently leads to good grades or compliance, or that intrinsic motivation can be effective, kinder and closer to a **holistic** approach), all theories concern themselves with outcomes. As a response to **behaviourism, cognitive** approaches to motivation focus on how information is processed and interpreted by individuals to inform and motivate actions when rewards are withdrawn, (Deci and Flaste, 1995; Kohn, 1996). Internal, intrinsic motives and the contribution of cognitive feedback about 'success' or 'failure' (Weiner, 1974) has been developed by Bandura (1986, 1997) to address aspects such as self-belief and self-efficacy (how individuals expect success and how they evaluate the goal and any potential cost involved). The influence of a social context sees increased motivation linked to competition with others who are observed and seen to be 'successful' (Ames, 1992). Humanistic approaches such as in the work of Maslow (1943) and Rogers (2015), look at social environments and the individual's experience of competence, personal freedom and **autonomy** as an intrinsic motivation for **learning**. These perspectives are utilised widely in education, business and management.

Individual motivation reflects, and is influenced by, wider socio-political contexts and **discourses** on prescribed goals, normative standards, performance and accountability (Carr, 2016). How one perceives the 'self' in this wider context of education influences motivation, self-regulation, interpersonal processes and achievement. Dweck's mind-set theory (2013) shows how individuals develop beliefs about themselves (self-theories), which direct their unique understanding of environments. Individuals may regard **intelligence** and other abilities not as fixed traits (that they either have or lack), but as attributes to be improved through effort. Dweck argues for the growth of 'mind-set' attitudes or beliefs through targeted praise for *effort* to motivate learners towards goals. She identifies three different goals: mastery goals (**learning** goals), which focus on gaining competence or mastering a new area of knowledge or skills; performance goals (ego-involvement goals), which focus on achieving normative-based standards, doing better than others, or doing well without a lot of effort; and social goals, which focus on **relationships** among people. Dweck indicates that in the relatively structured context of the **school** learning environment, students with mastery goals are shown to outperform students with either performance or social goals.

Definitions of motivation can operate in specific social, cultural and political contexts to reproduce existing educational inequalities, rather than support everyone by addressing their unique **learning** needs. Motivation is influenced by the social construction of terms such as 'achievement', 'ability' and '**performativity**' (McClelland, 1985). Socio-cultural views of motivation—including those by Vygotsky (1978), Nolen (2007), Turner and Meyer (2000) and Hickey and Granade (2004)—argue that motivation needs to be understood in the context of the 'quality' of the **curriculum**, **pedagogy** and **assessment**. This social process of engagement has been explored by Lave and Wenger (1991), who stress that identities are established through the acquisition of new strategies, which bring knowledge and **culture** through interaction ('legitimate peripheral participation'). Criticisms of this view, such as that by Amin and Roberts (2008), explore how stereotypes, prejudice and **discrimination** may affect the motivation of disadvantaged groups. Asymmetrical social relations in **society** may thus result in some remaining 'peripheral' rather than 'participative' in events, thereby limiting their motivation. Any consideration of motivation must consider the unique learner and learning and **teaching** processes, which encourage self-determination and independence (rather than desired responses and compliance), if students are to be prepared for **life-long learning** and **adult education**.

Questions to consider

1. Does being motivated to learn matter?
2. Why should we see motivation from a variety of perspectives?
3. How might factors such as of the quality of the **curriculum** or the nature of **pedagogy**, feedback, guidance and **assessment** affect learner motivation?
4. How does **power** (one's own and that of others) affect motivation?

References (with recommended readings in bold)

Ames, C. (1992) 'Classroom goals, structures, and student motivation', *Journal of Educational Psychology*, 84 (3), pp.261–271.

Amin, A. and Roberts, J. (2008) 'Knowing in action: Beyond communities of practice', *Research Policy*, 37, pp.353–369.

Bandura, A. (1986) *Social foundations of thought and action: A social cognitive theory*. Englewood Cliffs, NJ: Prentice-Hall.

Bandura, A. (1997) *Self-efficacy: The exercise of control*. New York: Freeman.

Carr, S. (2016) *Motivation: Educational policy and achievement, a critical perspective*. Abingdon: Routledge.

Deci, E.L. and Flaste, R. (1995) *Why we do what we do: Understanding motivation*. London: Penguin Books.

Dommett, E., Devonshire, I., Sewter, E. and Greenfield, S. (2013) 'The impact of participation in a neuroscience course on motivational measures and academic performance', *Trends in Neuroscience and Education*, 2 (3–4), pp.122–138.

Dweck, C. (2013) *Self theories: Their role in motivation, personality, and development*. Hove: Psychology Press.

Hickey, D.T. and Granade, J. (2004) 'The influence of sociocultural theory on our theories of engagement and motivation', in McInerney, D.M. and Van Etten, S. (eds) *Big theories revisited: Research on socio-cultural influences on motivation and learning*, vol. 4. Greenwich, CO: Information Age, pp.223–247.

Kohn, A. (1996) 'By all available means: Cameron and Pierce's defence of extrinsic motivators', *Review of Educational Research*, 66, pp.1–4.

Lave, J. and Wenger, E. (1991) *Situated learning: Legitimate peripheral participation*. Cambridge: Cambridge University Press.

McClelland, D. (1985) *Human motivation*. Glenview, IL: Scott, Foresman.

Maslow, A.H. (1943) 'A theory of human motivation', *Psychological Review*, 50, pp.370–396.

Nolen, S.B. (2007) 'Young children's motivation to read and write: Development in social contexts', *Cognition and Instruction*, 25, pp.219–270.

Parker, R., Rose, J. and Gilbert, L. (2016) 'Attachment aware schools: An alternative to behaviourism in supporting children's behaviour?', in Lees, H.E. and Noddings, N. (eds) *The Palgrave international handbook of alternative education*. London: Palgrave Macmillan, pp.463–483.

Rogers, B. (2015) *Classroom behaviour: A practical guide to effective teaching, behaviour management and colleague support*, 4th edn. London: Sage.

Skinner, B.F. (1973) *Beyond freedom and dignity*. London: Penguin.

Turner, J.C. and Meyer, D.K. (2000) 'Studying and understanding the instructional contexts of classrooms: Using our past to forge our future', *Educational Psychologist*, 35 (2), pp.69–85.

Vygotsky, L.S. (1978) *Mind and society: The development of higher psychological processes.* Cambridge, MA: Harvard University Press.

Watson, J.B. (1913) 'Psychology as the behaviorist views it', *Psychological Review*, 20, pp.158–177.

Weiner, B. (1974) *Achievement, motivation and attribution theory.* Morristown, NJ: General Learning Press.

KEY CONCEPT: NEUROSCIENCE

Steve Griffin

Concept origins

Neuroscience is described by the *Oxford English Dictionary* as the **interdisciplinary** field of science that concerns itself with 'the structure or function of the nervous system' (OED, 2017). As the Centre for Science and **Policy** at Cambridge University suggests, 'Neuroscience now transcends biology and, increasingly, involves novel intellectual alliances such as computational neuroscience, social neuroscience, educational neuroscience, neuroeconomics, neurophilosophy and neuroethics' (2016). Configured with education, educational neuroscience seeks to draw on neuroscientific research to explore the neural apparatus and mechanisms that underpin **learning** processes, learning deficits and behaviourial concerns in order to improve educational practice. There are other uses of neuroscience in **educational research** which could be said to be inflected more towards a **social science** commentary perspective, such as research by De Meyer (2016) on controversies and the erroneous maintenance of conservative thinking in education, but these are still the exception to a current learning/**behaviour**-focused approach.

Current status and usage

Drawing on educational psychology, **cognitive** neuroscience and developmental cognitive neuroscience, educational neuroscience 'investigates educationally inspired research questions' that 'might lead to applications in educational practice and **policy**, **pedagogy** and **curriculum**' (Geake, 2008, p.12). In recent years, the idea of 'brain based education' has gathered significant interest from educators, parents and the media. Despite the populist appeal of many of these approaches, Goswami has cautioned that 'Neuroscience does not at yet study **teaching**' (2008, p.34), while Illeris states that 'even though brain research has made colossal progress, it is as yet far from being able to give exhaustive answers to the more advanced brain functions, including **learning**' (2007, p.12). In terms of neuroscience's reach, **educational theory** and pedagogy are largely uninfluenced, but some work begins to question and investigate the remit of neuroscience as having potential to inform us more about purpose-led reflections on how, why and what educators and families do when it comes to any kind of education (Joldersma, 2016).

In order to understand the potential of neuroscience for education, we must first consider the scientific concept of *levels of analysis*. As an emerging field of scientific exploration, neuroscience currently studies activity at the level of anatomic structures of the brain. This is a low level of analysis, involving the 'mapping of brain structure and activity to **cognitive** functions (e.g., memory, attention) or function interactions (e.g., the impact of emotion on **learning**)' (Willingham, 2009, p.545). Neuroscientists do not study the whole nervous system, whereas **teacher**s focus their attention on individual children, groups of children or indeed whole classes; these are very different, and indeed more complicated, levels of analysis. As Willingham further explains, working in isolation neuroscientists might identify that repetition helps with memory, but in a classroom environment, children's **motivation** may suffer if they are asked to regularly repeat work. Thus, neuroscientific findings made at an anatomical level do not necessarily translate well to the more complex, socially interactive level of analysis of the whole child or classroom.

Despite some of the reservations about the value of neuroscience in education (see Hirsch-Pasek and Bruer, 2007), Geake and Cooper (2003) suggest that, if applied thoughtfully, neuroscientific findings offer significant pedagogical enhancements in the classroom to support 'intuitive high-quality **teaching** practices' (p.16). As hinted at above, however, questioning those practices as choices of **pedagogy**, underpinned by reflection, is still to be an embedded offer. Geake (2008) makes the case for educational neuroscience by suggesting that 'human beings are biological entities' and brain **behaviour** is neurobiological and that consequently education is neurobiological (p.5). He also explains that **cognitive** neuroscience could potentially answer key educational questions such as when children should start **school**. Geake asserts the need for **teachers** to be able to access and critically interpret the many research papers that neuroscientists produce each year. However, Weisberg *et al.* (2008) have demonstrated in their research that there is a 'seductive allure' concerning neuroscientific explanations (p.470), causing non-experts and even students studying neuroscience to believe scientific explanations when they are presented alongside irrelevant neuroscientific information. Lindell and Kidd (2013) and McCabe and Castel (2008) demonstrate that including the word 'brain' or images of the brain in educational materials causes teachers to believe they are more scientifically valid. The issue, then, for education is to question the neuroscientific 'movement' into education: to test it in the context of the multiple **disciplines** of education as a complex **social science** of the interpersonal.

Much of the challenge for the educational community is then how best to access, understand and ultimately utilise findings from neuroscience in purposeful and advantageous ways, which serve them *on their own terms* rather than blind them with 'science'. Among these challenges is that **education research** typically concerns itself with the social context of **school** and classroom processes, and the impact this has on pupil **learning** and not on brain anatomy, which is seen as someone else's job: someone in a neuroscience laboratory rather than with an educational background. Added to this **dissonance** is the proliferation of educational products and consultancy, creating what Geake (2008) refers to as 'neuromythologies' of efficiency for educational practice, which are seen as different in quality and value from actual facts. Howard-Jones (2014) suggests that significant work is needed to bridge the gap between myths and utility of neuroscience. Bruer and Hirsh-Pasek (2007) question what they see as the brain/education barrier that separates the neuroscientific and educational communities, suggesting developmental evidence, drawn from **teacher** observation and experience, is the ultimate signifier of worth. In other words, for some, it is not the impersonal natural sciences that can help the child, but the **care** and attention of a teacher following their **profession** as an educationist. In the face of such a claim is the rise of the 'gold standard' **randomised controlled trial** to test neuro 'facts'—which *may* one day offer acceptable *educationally* sound suggestions for practice—as though they had better answers than teachers. The debate continues.

Questions to consider

1. What are neuromythologies?
2. Is it useful for **teachers** to develop a clearer understanding of how children's brains work? Why and how might they do this?
3. How can teachers guard against the claims made by commercial providers of 'brain-based' **learning** materials?
4. Can neuroscience **teach** us about **pedagogy**?
5. Who does neuroscience in education serve?

References (with recommended readings in bold)

Centre for Science and Policy (2016) Cambridge University. Available at: www.csap.cam.ac.uk/organisations/cambridge-neuroscience (accessed 12 November 2016).

De Meyer, K. (2016) 'The mind of the educator', in Lees, H.E. and Noddings, N. (eds) *The Palgrave international handbook of alternative education*. London: Palgrave Macmillan, pp.17–30.

Geake, J. (2008) 'Neuromythologies in education', *Educational Research,* **50 (2), pp.123–133.**

Geake, J.G. and Cooper, P.W. (2003) 'Implications of cognitive neuroscience for education', *Westminster Studies in Education*, 26 (10), pp.7–20.

Goswami, U. (2008) 'Neuroscience and education', in *The Jossey Bass reader on the brain and learning.* **San Francisco: Wiley, pp.33–50.**

Hirsh-Pasek, K. and Bruer, J.T. (2007) 'The brain/education barrier', *Science*, 317 (5843), p.1293.

Howard-Jones, P.A. (2014) 'Neuroscience and education: Myths and messages', *Nature Reviews Neuroscience*, 15, pp.817–824.

Illeris, K. (2007) *How we learn: Learning and non-learning in school and beyond*. London: Routledge.

Joldersma, C.W. (2016) 'Promise and peril of neuroscience for alternative education', in Lees, H.E. and Noddings, N. (eds) *The Palgrave international handbook of alternative education*. London: Palgrave Macmillan, pp.79–95.

Lindell, A. and Kidd, E. (2013) 'Consumers favour "right brain" training: The dangerous lure of neuromarketing', *Mind, Brain and Education,* **7 (1), pp.35–39.**

McCabe, D.P. and Castel, A.D. (2008) 'Seeing is believing: The effect of brain images on judgments of scientific reasoning', *Cognition,* 107 (1), pp.343–352.

OED (2017) *Oxford English Dictionary*. Available at: www.oed.com.

Weisberg, D.S., Keil, F.C., Goodstein, J., Rawson, E. and Gray, J. (2008) 'The seductive lure of neuroscience explanations', *Journal of Cognitive Neuroscience*, 20 (3), pp.470–477.

Willingham, D. (2009) 'Three problems in the marriage of neuroscience and education', *Cortex*, 45, pp.544–545.

KEY CONCEPT: PERFORMATIVITY

Dave Trotman

Concept origins

Performativity, in this account of the concept, is drawn from Lyotard's 1984 work *The postmodern condition: A report on knowledge.* For Lyotard, performativity is both a **culture** and **technology**, in which regulation serves to drive performance against generalised standards. Performativity, in the Lyotardian sense, involves the macro-societal pursuit of efficiency and outcomes. This, he argues, is governed by narrow bureaucratic forms of output and accountability to serve capitalist interests. A corollary of the performative drive for efficiency is the assumption that it is possible to precisely gauge and make transparent the performance of so-called core activities of organisations through the use of audit technologies.

Current status and usage

Lyotard's performativity has been hugely popularised in the literature of educational sociology, most notably in the UK in the work of Stephen Ball (2003, 2012a, 2012b). In particular, the concept of performativity has been used to explain and critique **policy** imperatives that promote particular forms of educational standardisation, measurement, comparison and ranking and their subsequent effects (see, for example, Lingard and Blackmore, 1997; Jeffrey and Troman, 2012). While the presence of performativity in **school** systems has been made manifest in the form of standardised testing, league tables and school inspections in England, the use of audit **technology** described by Lyotard is increasingly visible across other public sector areas of work, including healthcare, policing and social services.

'Performativity', as the term implies, concerns the continuous pursuit of improvement in performance outputs that can be applied to a range of activities. While approaches to business, economics and sport science are among those areas that typically have performativity at their heart, performative **cultures** can now be found in education, health, policing and social **care**, where 'outputs' are specifically defined by the means of measurement. In statutory-age education in England, performativity is visible in the reliance on routine testing in **literacy** and numeracy in primary **school**s and the use of A–C grading in designated exam subjects in secondary schools. The use of these measures by the Office for Standards in Education (Ofsted) as an over-riding indicator of school effectiveness in England has served to amplify the role of 'high stakes' testing as a key feature of performativity in education. Performativity, then, works best when organisations are made accountable for their outputs. Often involving a reliance on paper and pencil tests, performativity, in turn, privileges those aspects of the **curriculum** that are easy to test while also serving to promote this as a preferred method of **assessment**. As a consequence, performative cultures, by intention, exclude those aspects of education that are difficult to standardise, regulate or measure, such as **creativity**, **imagination**, socialisation and character. In turn, this aspect of performativity communicates via the **hidden curriculum** the particular forms of knowledge, skills and abilities regarded as more important than others.

Placed in a national context, performativity in the UK has extended to a range of public services where audit technologies are now commonly used to regulate and, in turn, valorise forms of **institutional** processes and outcomes. In medicine, waiting times and recovery rates now dominate organisational imperatives, as do conviction rates for particular forms of crime with regard to policing (specifically those deemed more serious than others), while surveillance and control are now common to the field of social work. In an international educational context, performativity finds global form in programmes of international educational comparison, most notably the Organisation for Economic Co-operation and Development's (OECD) triennial Programme of International Student **Assessment** (PISA). With its reliance on rudimentary tests in reading, mathematics and science as a means of ascertaining the skills of 15-year-olds, PISA has for many critics become nothing less than 'global educational governance' (Meyer and Benavot, 2013) with education **policy** reforms initiated among OECD countries in direct response to international test results of young people.

In the Lyotardian meaning of the concept, the 'reach' of performativity is not simply restricted to the technologies of **schooling** (regulation, standardisation and outcomes) but, as Lyotard argues, it is a **culture**. In this regard, the **power** of performativity lies in its ability to both affect and shape personal and collective **behaviour**. Priestly *et al.* (2012) note that with its emphasis on short-term goals, performativity encourages 'detachment from big-picture ideas' and the distancing of personal values, as professional educators are increasingly pressurised into 'playing the game'. This game-playing, they conclude, involves anything from the impression management and fabrication of **school** image to more serious matters of corruption and cheating (Ball, 2003; Sahlberg, 2010). In other provinces of public-sector work, performativity has had similar negative effects, involving such things as the falsification of hospital records in order to meet national targets, and the manipulation of crime statistics among regional police forces. In its more subtle but equally corrosive form, performativity permeates the **institutional** and professional language of educational cultures to the extent that this is colonised and subsequently supplanted by what Kenway (1987) has called a '**discourse of derision**'. For observers of performativity in education, the technologies of educational reform dramatically affect the construction of individual identities, to the extent that it is nothing less, according to Ball, than a struggle over the very soul of the **teacher** (Ball, 2003).

Questions to consider

1. In what ways and in what areas might performativity be considered a good thing?
2. What aspects of performativity should we be most concerned about?
3. What makes performativity so powerful as an agent of accountability?
4. In what ways might performativity be positively addressed?

References (with recommended readings in bold)

Ball, S. (2003) 'The teacher's soul and the terrors of performativity', *Journal of Education Policy*, 18 (2), pp.215–228.
Ball, S. (2012a) 'Performativity, commodification and commitment: An I-spy guide to the neoliberal university', *British Journal of Educational Studies*, 60 (1), pp.17–28.

Ball, S. (2012b) 'Performativities and fabrications in the education economy: Towards the performative society?, *Australian Educational Researcher,* 27 (2), pp.1–23.

Jeffrey, B and Troman, G. (eds) (2012) *Performativity in UK education: Ethnographic cases of its effects, agency and reconstructions.* Painswick: EandE Publishing.

Kenway, J. (1987) 'Left right out: Australian education and politics of signification', *Journal of Education Policy,* 2 (3), pp.189–203.

Lingard, B. and Blackmore, J. (1997) 'The "performative" state and the state of educational research', *Australian Educational Researcher,* 24 (3), pp.1–22.

Lyotard, J.-F. (1984) *The postmodern condition: A report on knowledge.* Translated by G. Bennington and B. Massumi. Manchester: Manchester University Press.

Meyer, H.-D. and Benavot, A. (2013) (eds) *PISA, power, and policy.* Oxford: Symposium Books.

Priestley, M., Robinson, S., and Biesta, G. (2012) 'Teacher agency, performativity and curriculum change: Reinventing the teacher in the Scottish curriculum for excellence?' in Jeffrey, B. and Troman, G. (eds) *Performativity in UK education: Ethnographic cases of its effects, agency and reconstructions.* Painswick: EandE Publishing, pp.87–108.

Sahlberg, P. (2010) 'Rethinking accountability in a knowledge society', *Journal of Educational Change,* 11 (1), pp.45–61.

KEY CONCEPT: PSYCHOANALYSIS

Roger Willoughby

Concept origins

Developed by Sigmund Freud (1856–1939), the founding moment of psychoanalysis is typically associated with Freud's self-analysis, commenced in 1897 following the death of his father. A series of key texts from this period, beginning with *Studies on Hysteria* (Breuer and Freud, 1893–1895), the seminal *Interpretation of Dreams* (Freud, 1900), and then works on **sexuality**, jokes, parapraxes ('Freudian slips'), and other topics, ensued, in which basic tenets were outlined. These depicted psychoanalysis as a way of investigating and understanding the mind (the Greek *psyche* referring to soul), much of which it depicted as unconscious to both the individual and the wider world, with mental conflict being ubiquitous, and its life driven by sexual and aggressive instincts, which were often expressed as wishes, dreams and fantasies. The early psychoanalytic emphasis on sexuality and repressed mental contents gave rise to much popular opposition, conflicting as it did with nineteenth- and early-twentieth-century values, while others criticised its subjectivity and methodology. Nevertheless, psychoanalysis influenced, not only much of the rise of psychological therapies and counselling, but would also become an important tool for understanding **culture**, arts and **humanities**, while offering a liberating model for many involved in **alternative education.**

Current status and usage

Like other **disciplines**, psychoanalysis has considerably changed and developed over its history. An important turning point towards contemporary psychoanalytic thinking began with the introduction of the structural model (Id, Ego and Super-Ego) of the mind by Freud (1923). This subsequently developed into a profound focus on **relationships**, both in the social world and as internalised object-representations, as key drivers of human action. While psychoanalysis is now an umbrella concept, incorporating many divergent models (Frosh, 2012), this emphasis on relationships, the subjective meanings constructed within them, and struggles for freedom and expression are part of their common focus. While its strict use—of long duration and commitment on an analysand's part—is in decline as a therapeutic option, in the face of psychopharmacology and very brief forms of therapy, psychoanalysis continues to exercise a significant influence within intellectual and academic circles (Bell, 1999). Within education, psychoanalytic ideas offer profound ways of approaching its relational and affective dimensions, while challenging repressive and alienating practices (Salzberger-Wittenberg et al., 1999; Youell, 2006; Willoughby and Demir Atay, 2016).

Popular depictions of psychoanalysis concentrate on it as a form of psychological treatment, but it can be additionally positioned as a body of knowledge of the mind and human **culture** and as a research activity (Bell, 1999). Typically, it concentrates on aspects of experience that are consciously unknown, through repression or various forms of denial, for example, and seeks to make these conscious. Our subjectivity and everyday human experience can thus be expanded, allowing greater freedom of action and life satisfaction. Psychoanalysis can allow educationalists one way of beginning to enquire into hidden aspects of human experience, whether those relate to an individual, a **class**, a total institution or wider **society**. The results of such enquiries can be unsettling. Freud (1907) saw traditional education as part of a 'civilizing' process that often entails the repression of spontaneity and the creation of emotional inhibitions. Within the **curriculum**, Freud regarded religious instruction as particularly problematic, while inadequate sex and relationship education compounded problems. Simply put, education can be dangerous to your emotional health. In such cases, psychoanalysis could offer a limited 'after-education' (Freud, 1913; Britzman, 2003), seeking to undo the excesses of an individual's earlier experiences, here including their toxic education. The challenge, of course, and Freud saw this clearly, was how to bring about systemic change in the education system.

Within **alternative education**, psychoanalysis has had a wider impact, its influence on the thinking of A.S. Neill at Summerhill School being perhaps one of the best-known examples (Bailey, 2013). However, Neill's model included ideas from non-psychoanalytic sources and few would thus regard Summerhill as a test case for psychoanalytic educational ideas. More generally, psychoanalysis has been used within **critical theory** and critical **education studies** (Appel, 1996), not so much as a utopian model for **schooling**, but as a means for inter-rogating **ideology** and opening up a reflective space on existing edu-cational **praxis**. Such usage may be indirect or inexplicit. For example, when Althusser (1971, p.161) hypothesises that 'ideology interpellates individuals as subjects', he is implicitly drawing on ideas from his own psychoanalytic formation with Rene Diatkine and Lacan. Similarly, Gramsci's important ideas on ideology may be elucidated using psy-choanalytic insights into the ways in which we sustain incompatible and conflictual thoughts in our minds, using dissociation, negation and other coping or defence mechanisms.

Psychoanalysis is a site of contest. It is disputed both from within (and thus has multiple divergent sub-types, e.g., Freudian, Kleinian, Lacanian, Object Relations Theory, Self-Psychology, Ego-Psychology, **Attachment** Theory, etc.) and without, having numerous philosophi-cal and scientific critics. Robinson (1993), however, argues that these latter critiques tend to be poorly founded. Nevertheless, it is incum-bent on students to question and evaluate this as much as any other tool they may use in educational **praxis**. This imperative comes from academic formation, **identity**, and reflective practice: processes that indelibly carry the imprint of psychoanalysis. Taking these issues up from the point of view of the **learning** and **teaching** relationship, we may here use Bion's (1962) psychoanalytic model of mental develop-ment to highlight one such understanding of their affective founda-tions. Bion argues that these essentially interpersonal processes entail repeated meaning-conferring cycles of projection, containment and **transformation** of psychic elements into higher-order thoughts. In a way reminiscent of Vygotsky's more **social constructivist** model, Bion proposes that it is the significant other's developed capacities for thought that allows them (traditionally the infant's mother, but in this case, the person in the position of the **teacher**) to both wit-ness and assist the child in the painful and uncertain process of learn-ing from emotional experience. Transposing Bion's ideas to education contexts, Alcorn (2010, 2013), and others (e.g., Britzman, 2003; Youell,

2006; Archangelo, 2007, 2010; Mintz, 2014) have increasingly explored defences against thinking, learning and academic engagement. While such work is very promising, its extension within the standards-driven climate will be challenging.

Questions to consider

1. Is it important to know about psychoanalysis to be a good **teacher**?
2. Can we compare psychoanalysis with other models of the mind?
3. Considering Freud's ideas on education and the '**hidden curriculum**', is education consciousness raising or a form of repression?
4. What might a truly psychoanalytically informed **school** look like?
5. How might psychoanalysis help us understand and address barriers in **learning** and widespread student disaffection?

References (with recommended readings in bold)

Alcorn, M.W. (2010) 'The desire not to know as a challenge to teaching', *Psychoanalysis, Culture & Society*, 15, pp.1–15.

Alcorn, M.W. (2013) *Resistance to learning: Overcoming the desire-not-to-know in classroom teaching*. New York: Palgrave Macmillan.

Althusser, L. (1971) *Lenin and philosophy and other essays*. London: New Left Books.

Appel, S. (1996) *Positioning subjects: Psychoanalysis and critical educational studies*. Westport, CT: Bergin and Garvey.

Archangelo, A. (2007) 'A psychoanalytic approach to education: "Problem" children and Bick's idea of skin formation', *Psychoanalysis, Culture & Society*, 12, pp.332–348.

Archangelo, A. (2010) 'Social exclusion, difficulties with learning and symbol formation: A Bionian approach', *Psychoanalysis, Culture & Society*, 15, pp.315–327.

Bailey, R. (2013) *A. S. Neill*. London: Bloomsbury.

Bell, D. (ed.) (1999) *Psychoanalysis and culture: A Kleinian perspective*. London: Duckworth.

Bion, W.R. (1962) 'A theory of thinking', *International Journal of Psycho-Analysis*, 43, pp.306–310.

Breuer, J. and Freud, S. (1893–1895) *Studies on Hysteria*, in Strachey, J. (ed.) *The standard edition of the complete psychological works of Sigmund Freud*, vol. 2. London: Hogarth Press, 1955.

Britzman, D. P. (2003) *After-education: Anna Freud, Melanie Klein, and psychoanalytic histories of learning.* **Albany, NY: SUNY Press.**

Freud, S. (1900) *The interpretation of dreams*, in Strachey, J. (ed.) *The standard edition of the complete psychological works of Sigmund Freud*, vols 4–5. London: Hogarth Press, 1958.

Freud, S. (1907) 'The sexual enlightenment of children (an open letter to Dr M Furst)', in Strachey, J. (ed.) *The standard edition of the complete psychological works of Sigmund Freud*, vol. 9. London: Hogarth Press, 1959, pp.131–139.

Freud, S. (1913) 'Introduction to Pfister's *The psycho-analytic method*', in Strachey, J. (ed.) *The standard edition of the complete psychological works of Sigmund Freud*, vol. 12. London: Hogarth Press, 1958, pp.327–332.

Freud, S. (1923) *The ego and the id*, in Strachey, J. (ed.) *The standard edition of the complete psychological works of Sigmund Freud*, vol. 19. London: Hogarth Press, 1961, pp.3–59.

Frosh, S. (2012) *A brief introduction to psychoanalytic theory*. Basingstoke: Palgrave Macmillan.

Mintz, J. (2014) *Professional uncertainty, knowledge, and relationship in the classroom: A psycho-social perspective.* Abingdon: Routledge.

Robinson, P. (1993) *Freud and his critics*. Berkeley: University of California Press.

Salzberger-Wittenberg, I., Henry, G. and Osbourne, E. (1999) *The emotional experience of learning and teaching*. London: Karnac.

Willoughby, R. and Demir Atay, H. (2016) 'Psychoanalysis and the challenge of educational fantasies', in Lees, H.E. and Noddings, N. (eds) *The Palgrave international handbook of alternative education*. London: Palgrave Macmillan, pp.113–128.

Youell, B. (2006) *The learning relationship: Psychoanalytic thinking in education*. **London: Karnac.**

KEY CONCEPT: RELATIONSHIPS

Clare Bright

Concept origins

A relationship can be most simply defined as the way in which two things are connected. Within the context of human **behaviour**, a relationship is an interaction with another person. According to Moxon (2001, p.1) it is helpful to consider these on a continuum of closeness or 'emotional **attachment**', which can include friendship, love, platonic, **family** and professional relationships. Moxon argues that forming relationships is a 'natural human tendency'. This is affirmed by Maslow, who, in his theory of a 'hierarchy of needs', identifies seeking the company of others and engagement in relationships with them as a basic human need. American **care** theorist Nel Noddings suggests 'Every human life starts in relation, and it is through relations that a human individual emerges' (Noddings, 2013, p.771).

Current status and usage

Successful relationships are based on trust, respect and communication (see, e.g., Rogers, 1961, 1983). The importance of interpersonal skills (such as working with others, expressing personal feelings and understanding the emotions of others) were highlighted in 1996 by Daniel Goleman, who popularised the term 'emotional **intelligence**'. Much of the work on emotional intelligence has been conducted in the US in the context of business and management, and so there is concern that this does not apply directly to the educational context. However, Weare (2004) suggests interest in 'affective education' is developing at an extraordinary pace in the **teaching profession**. Some of the earliest significant relationships are formed with **teacher**s who are in a very strong position to be able to influence a child or young person's emotional well-being (Pollard, 2014, p.149). Recent advances in the neurobiology of emotions reveal connections between emotional state and capacity for **learning** (Immordino-Yang and Damasio, cited in Pollard, 2014, p.144). Work on love in infancy suggests that babies without it suffer life-long detrimental effects to their brains and social relational capacities (Gerhardt, 2004). New work on **attachment** has begun to frame attitudes to emotionally driven mis-**behaviour** as *necessarily* requiring more **child-centred**, *relational* understanding of a need for empathy and listening, rather than sanctions or punishments within a set of school rules (Parker *et al.*, 2016).

The development of meaningful relationships with others begins with interactive **behaviour**s between babies and adults. In their landmark studies of the 1960s, John Bowlby and Mary Ainsworth introduced **attachment** theory, which has since been used to help explain early **childhood** relationships. According to Bowlby (1969), secure attachments are achieved when the child is cared for by sensitive and responsive caregivers. Securely attached children have 'internal working models', which guide their feelings and enable them to regulate any distress. Attachment disorders, they argue, where internal working models are dis-regulated, can lead to **behaviour**s, such as aggression, withdrawal or indifference, and will reduce a child's chances of developing healthy, trusting relationships with others. This work brings into stark relief the need for relational connections and problematises technological advances involving social media, for example: in a world of Facebook and Skype, do we need others in person? For many the increased use of **technology** for communication has changed the way relationships are established and maintained. Some suggest 'digital communications technology is not isolating people but rather augmenting existing social relationships' (Baym, 2011). However, in online and telephone contacts, contextual, auditory and visual cues through which humans convey meaning are reduced. This brings into question whether such means of communication successfully serve the *same* social functions as direct human contact. Baym argues that this does not follow and recognises that (rather than submitting ourselves to an impoverished, emotion-free communication experience) we come up with creative ways to work around these barriers (2011). The use of social cues, such as emoticons, or the addition of photos and other representations of ourselves, for example, can convey a range of emotions. It may be that we are at the start of realising new forms of emotional and relational connecting, or that we need to value each other face-to-face still more in a world full of dis-connectedness.

 Growing a relationship is for some a fine art and not all people are good at forming, keeping, maintaining and growing relations with others. Some people have a sensitivity to others, which enables relationships to flourish. As noted above, we do seem to need others in order to be 'well', so the primacy of relationships is not just about relating but also about **ontology** and being. Noddings describes a relationship as involving **care** if there is attention or 'engrossment' which is receptive; thus, to care, we have to consider the other's point of view and focus our attention on the cared-for and not so much on ourselves (Noddings, 2013, p.24). According to American psychologist Carl Rogers, known for his work on understanding personality and human relationships, to be effective, three significant conditions are required to create a 'growth promoting climate' of personhood. These are: (1) 'genuineness or congruence'; (2) 'unconditional positive regard', the ability to accept a person for what they are; and (3) 'empathic understanding', when the relationship is founded on a sensitive awareness of how someone is feeling without judgement (Rogers, 1961). Colverd and Hodgkin (2011, p.24) suggest that empathy 'requires the ability to understand and imaginatively enter the feelings of another person' and is a '**cognitive** skill that we learn through **attachment** and social referencing.' According to Jackson-Dwyer (2014, p.102), there are some recognised cultural differences in relationships and frequently a distinction is made between Western and non-Western relationships. The former are seen as individualistic, where the emphasis is on independence of the individual, choice and their tendency to focus on personal goals. The latter can be described as collectivist, where there is emphasis on kinship, interdependence and achieving collective aims. Jackson-Dwyer points out the dangers involved in such oversimplification as research on relationships is still limited to very few **culture**s. Bullough (1980) considers variance across cultures and history in terms of **sexuality** and finds there are huge differences of mores, traditions, patterns of interrelating and attitudes. In essence, there is perhaps no 'right' way to relate, only the way that works for self and other. Such an approach affects **ethics**, **society**, **pedagogy** and most of the contents of this book, as it challenges any given status quo for a more local set of solutions.

One of the common myths that surround professional **behaviour** and the emotional world of young people is that a **teacher** is placed in a position of trust as a professional but, as Lever (2011, p.84) suggests, 'it is a myth that to be "professional" a teacher must not engage at an emotional level with a child'. To maintain secure, healthy relationships certain 'professional boundaries' need to be clarified (Johnson, 2010, p.6), but this does not mean losing trust and emotional relation. Johnson suggests that this can be achieved within an 'ethic of **care**', which requires adults to take their cue from children so they respond appropriately to their needs (2010, p.61). However, increased awareness of child protection has forced practitioners to reflect on what Elfer *et al.* refer to as, 'appropriate professional intimacy which is an intimacy every child needs in order to feel special' but which 'requires emotional work of the highest calibre' (Elfer *et al.*, cited in Johnson, 2010, p.61). As one example, touch can be important for healthy psychological and physiological development, but in certain environments, situations and contexts, touching children can be misconstrued and interpreted as a sexual advance or a way of establishing dominance (Hall and Hall, 1988, p.196). While it does depend on how touch is understood (Stronach and Piper, 2008), adults in education settings are usually advised *not* to touch their pupils. Provided that personal and cultural differences are respected, spontaneous touching can, however, contribute to genuine communication and *healthy* interpersonal relations. Such relations are important educationally for, as Pollard suggests, 'Positive classroom relationships are a considerable source of **teacher** and pupil fulfilment' (Pollard, 2014, p.170).

Questions to consider

1. Why do relationships with **teacher**s matter?
2. How do teachers foster good relationships with their pupils?
3. How do professionals maintain appropriate professional intimacy?
4. What strategies can help develop children's emotional **intelligence**?
5. To what extent has the use of **technology** impacted on our interpersonal skills?

References (with recommended readings in bold)

Baym, N. (2011) *Personal connections in the digital age.* Cambridge: Polity Press.

Bowlby, J. (1969) *Attachment.* New York: Basic Books.

Bullough, V.L. (1980) *Sexual variance in history.* Chicago: University of Chicago Press.

Colverd, S. and Hodgkin, B. (2011) *Developing emotional intelligence in the primary school.* Abingdon: Routledge.

Gerhardt, S. (2004) *Why love matters: How affection shapes a baby's brain.* Hove: Brunner-Routledge.

Goleman, D. (1996) *Emotional intelligence.* New York: Bantam Books.

Hall, E. and Hall, C. (1988) *Human relations in education.* London: Routledge.

Jackson-Dwyer, D. (2014) *Interpersonal relationships.* Hove: Routledge.

Johnson, J. (2010) *Positive and trusting relationships with children in early years settings.* Exeter: Learning Matters.

Lever, C. (2011) *Understanding challenging behaviour in inclusive classrooms.* Abingdon: Routledge.

Moxon, D. (2001) *Human relationships.* Oxford: Heinneman Educational Publishers.

Noddings, N. (2013) *Caring: A relational approach to ethics and moral education.* London: University of California Press.

Parker, R., Rose, J. and Gilbert, L. (2016) 'Attachment aware schools: An alternative to behaviourism in supporting children's behaviour?', in Lees, H.E. and Noddings, N. (eds) *The Palgrave international handbook of alternative education.* London: Palgrave Macmillan, pp.463–483.

Pollard, A. (2014) *Reflective teaching in schools.* London: Bloomsbury Publishing.

Rogers, C. (1961) *On becoming a person.* New York: Houghton Mifflin Company.

Rogers, C. (1983) *Freedom to learn for the 80's.* London: Merrill.

Stronach, I. and Piper, H. (2008). 'The case of "relational touch" at Summerhill School: Can liberal education make a comeback?', *American Educational Research Journal*, 45 (1), pp.6–37.

Weare, K. (2004) *Developing the emotionally literate school.* London: Paul Chapman Publishing.

KEY CONCEPT: SEXUALITY

Roger Willoughby

Concept origins

Referring to a person's tendencies, preferences, habits and interests with respect to sexual activity, typically—though by no means exclusively—in an interpersonal context, sexuality is often closely associated with one's sexual orientation. As Meyer (2010, p.48) points out, however, it can 'refer to a wide variety of identities and behaviours as well' and she goes on to emphasise the inter-**relationships** between sexuality, sexual orientation (who/what one is sexually attracted to), sexual **behaviour** (the types of sexual activity one actually engages in), and sexual **identity** (how one chooses to describe one's self). As such, sexuality permeates, influences, and is inseparable from our gendered, religious, **class**, **ethnic** and other identities. Emerging as a term in the late eighteenth century, sexuality increasingly became an object of study through the following two centuries, with the work of Krafft-Ebing (1886; Oosterhuis, 2012), Hirschfeld (1910, 1935) and Havelock Ellis (1900–1928) being among the landmarks in the development of sexology (the scientific study of human sexuality). Subsequent work by Kinsey, and later, Masters and Johnson, built on these foundations, while **psychoanalysis** was more broadly influential. From an emphasis on practices, attention shifted during this period to sexuality as intertwined with identity. Such ideas influenced wider socio-political efforts towards sexual reform, the development of feminism, and a relative **liberal** change process in western **society** (Mottier, 2008).

Current status and usage

Sexuality is both powerful and potentially disruptive, especially given its private and public nature. While **liberal** political **discourses** can marginalise sexuality as something essentially private, Foucault's (1978–1986; *cf.* Fischer and Seidman, 2016;

Weeks, 2016) ideas suggest otherwise. As with the closely related concept of **gender**, Butler (1990, 1993) builds on his work and further destabilises any naïve naturalisation of sexual identities. These, in her view, are substantially fictive social constructions and performative. In tandem with such hegemonic views that Butler critiques has been the mythologising of sexuality, artificially separating it from the lived lives of children and young people. Children continue to be ill-informed and mis-informed about sex and sexuality, both by parents, educators and wider **society** (UNESCO, 2009). Part of this has been rationalised with reference to a presumed sexual innocence of **childhood** (Renold, 2005), a romanticised idea that often perpetuates myths and religious **ideology**. Unsurprisingly, with **school**s as sites of struggle and cultural negotiation, their capacity to disseminate knowledge about sex and sexuality often continues to be very variable. In Britain, legislation on the topic has been late in coming (Blair and Monk, 2009) and pedagogic efforts have been often poor (Nelson and Martin, 2004; Hall, 2009). The establishment of specialist journals, such as *Sex Education*, which began in 2001, has opened an important on-going space to further academic discussion on the topic, and World Health Organization guidance (WHO, 2010; Frans, 2016) is beginning to influence educational practice. Nevertheless, education on sexuality, as Hall (2009) notes, continues to be predominantly situated within a damage limitation framework (concentrating on the dangers of sexually transmitted infections [STIs], teenage pregnancy, reputational and moral issues), rather than on a sex-positive discourse of potential pleasure and empowerment (Vernacchio, 2014; Ponzetti, 2016).

⏻ Children and (not-so-) young people's knowledge of sex and sexuality is predominantly self-taught (Reiss, 2016), through efforts to relate to others and through exploring texts, media and the internet. This quest for knowledge, driven by biological instinct, pleasure and **culture**, is, however, troubled, being beset with reticence, censorship and/or repression, and hypocrisy. Such issues make sexuality an interesting and important exemplar of sites of contest within **education studies**, as well as within wider culture. Sex and sexuality are a central part of most people's lives, an important source of pleasure, motivating action, and supporting **relationships**, particularly when integrated into a person's psychological and emotional life (Russell, 1957; Scruton, 1986). Yet it is also often a significant source of anxiety, of awkwardness, embarrassment, pain and interpersonal conflict. Contemporary approaches to this often build on Foucault's (1978–1986) critique of so-called 'natural' sexuality, following which sexuality has been 'increasingly interpreted as a historically contingent practice closely connected to **power** relations and values' (Sauerteig and Davidson, 2009, p.1). In this context, Foucault highlights the close social and educational surveillance of children, particularly for manifestations of sex and sexuality; forms of biopower aimed at the subjugation of bodies and of sexual **diversity** (Renold, 2005). So far, education worldwide has failed to adequately disseminate clear, accurate and useful knowledge of human sexuality (UNESCO, 2009). Such failures are often ascribed to poor **teacher** training on the subject (Hall, 2009; Meyer, 2010; Allen and Rasmussen, 2016). However, clearly the discussion of stereotypically private matters in the more public space of education by teachers—who are not themselves exempt from anxieties in relation to sexuality—makes the pedagogic and human encounter a particularly problematic part of the **curriculum**, complicated as it is by socio-cultural and religious dimensions.

Religious **culture**s, while attempting to offer a level of explanation for many existential issues, have often obscured understanding of sexuality. The myth of the Garden of Eden is useful to consider in this context, given both its foundational significance and its occurrence in several of the great monotheistic religions. The myth depicts an omniscient and omnipotent god (a moral system), which appears hostile to the human search for knowledge. Reading the myth psychologically, the eating of the fruit of the tree of the knowledge of good and evil represents human curiosity and transgression: it is an important developmental step, **learning** to distinguish between good and evil. Yet the consequences of curiosity and its realisation in knowledge highlight how painful learning and development can be (Bion, 1963; Bodin, 2010; George and George, 2014). In this way Bion (1963; Bléandonu, 1994) uses such myths to offer a psychoanalytic insight into the problem of learning, especially when it is associated with a primary emotional experience such as sexuality. Knowledge of sexuality is particularly troubling in the Eden myth, leading as it does to embarrassment and punishment, but so too is concomitant curiosity. With education enmeshed with such culturally ingrained attitudes, which are repressive of sexuality (as well as antipathetic to curiosity), it is unsurprising that figures as diverse as Freud (1907) and Foucault were deeply critical of traditional education. **Psychoanalysis** thus radically challenged popular views about the supposed sexual innocence of **childhood**, for example, with Freud (1905; *cf.* Sandfort and Rademakers, 2000) emphasising and normalising its sexual **diversity**, and Ferenczi (1933) pointing to qualitative differences between its childhood and adult expressions and the damage of childhood sexual abuse. The cultural challenge in the **social science**s was extended by Foucault (1978– 1986), critiquing **essentialist** views of sexuality, which he argued were part of hegemonic regulatory **discourses**.

Butler's (1990, 1993) work offers a degree of (albeit unstable) integration of psychoanalytic and Foucauldian ideas. Her emphasis on sexuality and **gender** as socially constructed fictions, their multiplicity (as opposed to any simple binary classification), their disruptive potential (as distinct from their traditional incorporation into hegemonic heteronormative narratives), and the ways in which sexuality is also restricted through iterative doing (thus making it performative) are particularly useful ideas in critical educational contexts. Despite increasing efforts to acknowledge the sexual **diversity** in **school**s, with the variegated sexualities and identities of students and staff (Meyer, 2010), cultural narratives continue to impact on both **curriculum** and practice. UNFPA and UNESCO (2009) initiatives to promote sexuality education are substantially intertwined with HIV and AIDS strategies. In developing nations, particularly with colonial histories (themselves often sexualised through the subjugation and othering of bodies), the intersectional issues form vital sites for debate. By contrast, the WHO (2010) guidance on sexuality education for Europe offers a far more **holistic** conception, emphasising positive human potential, views which are gaining increasing acceptance in the Netherlands, Austria, Belgium and other countries (see Frans, 2016 for a review). In the British context, past efforts at sex education have typically been couched in unhelpful euphemisms (Hall, 2009; Jones and Astley, 2009), oscillating between the imperative to promote knowledge and counter misinformation on the one hand, and protect a supposed **childhood** innocence on the other (Renold, 2005). Despite improvements (Allen, 2005; Hall, 2009; Allen and Rasmussen, 2016), the content and implicit values too often tends towards deficit models, continuing expressions of biopower that seek to inhibit sexuality, particularly through prioritising risks over pleasure and a sex-positive stance.

Questions to consider

1. Considering the sources of your own knowledge of sex and sexuality, which have been the most helpful?
2. To what extent should **school**s be involved in offering **teaching** on sex and sexuality?
3. How are sexuality and **colonialism** related to each other?
4. Should sexuality education challenge cultural practices such as female genital mutilation (FGM)?

References (with recommended readings in bold)

Allen, L. (2005) *Sexual subjects: Young people, sexuality and education.* Basingstoke: Palgrave Macmillan.

Allen, L. and Rasmussen, M.L. (eds) (2016) *The Palgrave handbook of sexuality education*. London: Palgrave Macmillan.

Bion, W.R. (1963) *Elements of psycho-analysis.* London: William Heinemann.

Blair, A. and Monk, D. (2009) 'Sex education and the law in England and Wales: The importance of legal narratives', in Sauerteig, L.D.H. and Davidson, R. (eds) *Shaping sexual knowledge: A cultural history of sex education in twentieth century Europe.* Abingdon: Routledge, 2009, pp.37–51.

Bléandonu, G. (1994) *Wilfred Bion: His life and works 1897–1979.* London: Free Association Books.

Bodin, G. (2010) 'Expulsion from the Garden of Eden: The pain of growing wiser', *The Scandinavian Psychoanalytic Review,* 33, pp.96–105.

Butler, J. (1990) *Gender trouble.* London: Routledge.

Butler, J. (1993) *Bodies that matter.* London: Routledge.

Ellis, H. (1900–1928) *Studies in the psychology of sex,* 6 vols. Philadelphia: F.A. Davis.

Ferenczi, S. (1933) 'The confusion of tongues between adults and the child: The language of tenderness and passion', in Balint, M. (ed.) *Final contributions to the problems and methods of psycho-analysis.* London: Hogarth Press, 1955, pp.156–167.

Fischer, N.L. and Seidman, S. (eds) (2016) *Introducing the new sexuality studies,* 3rd edn. Abingdon: Routledge.

Foucault, M. (1978–1986) *The history of sexuality*, 3 vols. Translated by R. Hurley. New York: Pantheon.

Frans, E. (2016) 'A practical guide to holistic sexuality education', in Ponzetti, J.J. (ed.) (2016) *Evidence-based approaches to sexuality education: A global perspective*. Abingdon: Routledge, pp.52–75.

Freud, S. (1905) *Three essays on the theory of sexuality*, in Strachey, J. (ed.) *The standard edition of the complete psychological works of Sigmund Freud*, vol. 7. London: Hogarth Press, 1953, pp.123–246.

Freud, S. (1907) 'The sexual enlightenment of children (an open letter to Dr M Furst)', in Strachey, J. (ed.) *The standard edition of the complete psychological works of Sigmund Freud*, vol. 9. London: Hogarth Press, 1959, pp.131–139.

George, A. and George, E. (2014) *The mythology of Eden*. Lanham, MD: Hamilton Books.

Hall, L.A. (2009) 'In ignorance and in knowledge: Reflections on the history of sex education in Britain', in Sauerteig, L.D.H. and Davidson, R. (eds) *Shaping sexual knowledge: A cultural history of sex education in twentieth century Europe*. Abingdon: Routledge, 2009, pp.19–36.

Hirschfeld, M. (1910) *The transvestites: The erotic drive to cross-dress*. Buffalo, NY: Prometheus Books, 2003.

Hirschfeld, M. (1935) *Sex in human relationships*. London: The Bodley Head.

Jones, G. and Astley, J. (2009) *The joy of sex education*, DVD. London: British Film Institute.

Krafft-Ebing, R.F. von (1886) *Psychopathia sexualis: With especial reference to the antipathic sexual instinct, a medico-forensic study*. New York: Physicians and Surgeons Book Company, 1933.

Meyer, E.J. (2010) *Gender and sexual diversity in schools*. Dordrecht: Springer.

Mottier, V. (2008) *Sexuality: A very short introduction*. Oxford: Oxford University Press.

Nelson, C. and Martin, M.H. (eds) (2004) *Sexual pedagogies: Sex education in Britain, Australia, and America 1879–2000*. Basingstoke: Palgrave Macmillan.

Oosterhuis, H. (2012) 'Sexual modernity in the works of Richard von Krafft-Ebing and Albert Moll', *Medical History*, 56, pp.133–155.

Ponzetti, J.J. (ed.) (2016) *Evidence-Based Approaches to Sexuality Education: A Global Perspective*. Abingdon: Routledge.

Reiss, M.J. (2016) 'Alternatives to school sex education', in Lees, H.E. and Noddings, N. (eds) *The Palgrave international handbook of alternative education*. London: Palgrave Macmillan, pp.401–413.

Renold, E. (2005) *Girls, boys and junior sexualities: Exploring children's gender and sexual relations in the primary school.* Abingdon: RoutledgeFalmer.

Russell, B. (1957) *Marriage and morals.* New York: H. Liveright.

Sandfort, T.G.M. and Rademakers, J. (eds) (2000) *Childhood sexuality: Normal sexual behavior and development.* New York: Haworth Press.

Sauerteig, L.D.H. and Davidson, R. (eds) (2009) *Shaping sexual knowledge: A cultural history of sex education in twentieth century Europe.* Abingdon: Routledge.

Scruton, R. (1986) *Sexual desire: A philosophical investigation.* London: Weidenfeld and Nicolson.

UNESCO (2009) *International technical guidance on sexuality education: An evidence-informed approach for schools, teachers and health educators.* Paris: UNESCO. Available at: http://unesdoc.unesco.org/images/0018/001832/183281e.pdf.

Vernacchio, A. (2014) *For goodness sake: Changing the way we talk to teens about sexuality, values, and health.* New York: HarperCollins.

Weeks, J. (2016) *Sexuality*, 4th edn. Abingdon: Routledge.

WHO (2010) *Standards for sexuality education in Europe: A framework for policy makers, educational and health authorities and specialists.* Cologne: Federal Centre for Health Education, BZgA. Available at: www.bzga-whocc.de/?uid=20c71afcb419f260c6afd10b684768f5&id=home.

KEY CONCEPT: TRANSFORMATION

Helen E. Lees

Concept origins

Transformation is a key concept in a variety of **disciplines**, from science to religion. In education, it can be regarded as a key concept in that any claim to a meaningful education will almost certainly involve personal transformation—in terms of any aspect of the **cognitive**, affective, social or spiritual. This is based on the idea of **learning** as *adding* something to the learner, often added by a teacher. Thus, transformation generates. Transformative **learning** is a concept originating in **adult education**, but it is not its exclusive domain. We could argue that there has never been education without transformation of some kind, such that the origins of this concept lie with the origins of the idea of education. In modern academic terms, the notion of educational transformation can be traced back to Carl Rogers' work on freedoms of the self to learn (1969), Jack Mezirow's work, begun in the 1970s using the women's liberation movement as inspiration to discuss changes of perspectives, frames of reference, and habits of mind in adults (1978), and Paulo Friere, a Brazilian political activist, whose work offered education to workers for social and personal 'conscientisation' (1972), with a view to transformation of their social conditions.

Current status and usage

Transformation in and through education has developed since Mezirow and Friere from the **cognitive**-rational and political to now again re-emphasise the kind of **holistic** vision of Rogers (Lauricella and MacAskill, 2015). It is unclear, however, whether this trend is in any large degree to be found within the **mainstream** of education in the UK and other international contexts, or instead expresses itself merely in isolated examples of practice where transformation is actively sought and valued as a discrete aim. A more **instrumental** approach in **neoliberal** times can be found in the plethora of **qualifications** and forms of **assessment** and examination that claim to transform life chances. **Education research** continues to support the **inclusion** of emotional, affective and self **identity** transformation approaches (Illeris, 2014) in education, but their realisation is often impeded by the **politics** and **policy** agendas of education, that both constrain educational innovation and limit available resource. Pedagogically, such things as 'threshold concepts', as gateways into new kinds of thinking (e.g., Meyer and Land, 2003) or social **equality**, where pedagogic forms and practice affect justice (Reay, 2012) can be regarded as forms of transformative educational activity. The key currency of transformation can then be understood in light of the problematic nature of education, with regard to the **mainstream** and hegemonic, **authoritarian** global model of the **schooling** system (Harber, 2009) and for which a transformation of education *as system* is being sought (Lees and Noddings, 2016).

Transformation can be regarded as an expansion of, or, at least, change in consciousness. This can occur in different ways in and through education, although different disciplinary lenses can help identification of what occurs and why. Thomas Kuhn suggests that transformation always occurs via a sudden breakthrough of perception (Kuhn, 1962). Gladwell (2002) focuses on minor things, happening incrementally day after day through small shifts which then cause a transformational 'tipping point'. Mezirow (1978) and Hase and Kenyon (2007) both consider shifts in perspective—such as Kuhn's focus on anomalies in scientific knowledge causing crisis (1966). Following crisis moments involving suffering, Mezirow speaks of a 'disorienting dilemma', while Hase and Kenyon state 'people only change in response to a very clear need. This usually involves distress such as confusion, **dissonance**, and fear or a more positive motive such as intense desire' (2007, p.112). Similarly, O'Sullivan, Morrell and O'Connor speak of a 'deep, structural shift in the basic premises of thought, feelings, and actions' (2002, p.xvii). Whatever the change, change it is: the previous state of self and mind is altered.

Education of any kind has the **power** to be both transformative of the self—as with **learning** a musical instrument, becoming good at a sport, discovering the joy of mathematics, or **adult education**—or it is able to be transformative of societies. We see this latter impact reflected in political policies, where the **ideology** linked to the party in power uses the transformative nature of education to mould **society** after its own image. Increasingly this appropriation of education for transformation of the social (and therefore the personal) is treated as a given good, without question. In the wrong hands, of course, education has been used for nefarious, evil transformative ends such as genocide—as we see in the use of education by the Nazis during the 1930s and Pol Pot's regime in Cambodia. In the right hands, the transformative potential of education can allow disenfranchised people to transform society themselves, as with the use of **literacy** education by Friere (1972) to empower the poor. Transformation of and in education can also be utilised both to unite or maintain differences by disparate factions. On the one hand are the **alternative education** 'progressives', seeking more **child-centred** approaches and less coercive academic pressure; on the other are the traditionalists demanding more rigour (testing) and back to basics (e.g., the 3 Rs—reading, writing and arithmetic) and 'classic' values of obedience to a politically desirable norm (e.g., 'British values' education). The political appropriation of transformation of self through education is at odds then with 'journeys' as 'careership' (Hodkinson and Sparkes, 1997), where happenstance force pragmatically rational decisions creating transformations which 'can be comfortable or traumatic' (p.39).

Transformation, then, needs conditions of **social justice** and fairness to be in place for the impact of 'mere' education to effect change in conscious awareness of self and others (Formosa, 2010). If the social setting fails to provide such an environment, people can and do undergo freely arranged and relative 'free cost' educational transformations in their private spaces and spare time, where conditions of fairness are more controllable and affordable, e.g., rather than pay expensive fees, the cost is of a book, a broadband connection or a bus fare to the library. It is not the case that transformation needs to come about through interaction in or with education of any formal and **teacher**-led kind. As Ang (1996) shows with her analysis of the impact of the 1980s TV programme *Dallas* on avid viewers, and Jarvis and Burr (2011) with their discussion of the TV series *Buffy the Vampire Slayer*, transformation comes through a wide range of media and occurs thus in intimate ways, where informal engagements with such drama allows for self reflection and enactments of possibilities for change via imaginary mirroring of the storyline. Education in the formal, schooled sense is then not necessary for the transformative potential of **learning** to occur: it can happen 'just' through conversations within the home and be as effective through this means as via formalised **school** attendance (Thomas and Pattison, 2007). To think of transforming oneself thus through an education one does to oneself is along the lines of Foucauldian 'care of the self' (Foucault, 1988); this might involve the use of techniques or 'technologies of the self' such as speaking fearlessly, engaging with the reality of emotions or writing in a journal to transform via reflection and deep engagement with the self and other (Besley, 2007; Zembylas and Fendler, 2007).

Questions to consider

1. What is transformation through education?
2. Is transformation necessary for education to be good?
3. How do we best achieve transformation in education?
4. Who transforms?
5. Why transform oneself or others?

References (with recommended readings in bold)

Ang, I. (1996) *Watching Dallas: Soap opera and the melodramatic imagination*. London: Routledge.

Besley, T.A.C. (2007) 'Foucault, truth-telling and technologies of the self: Confessional practices of the self and schools', in Peters, M.A. and Besley, T.A.C. (eds) *Why Foucault? New directions in educational research*. New York: Peter Lang.

Formosa, M. (2010) 'Universities of the Third Age: A rationale for transformative education in later life', *Journal of Transformative Education*, 8 (3), pp.197–219.

Foucault, M. (1988) 'Technologies of the self', in Martin, L.H., Gutman, H. and Hutton, P.H. (eds) *Technologies of the self: A seminar with Michel Foucault*. London: Tavistock Publications, pp.16–49.

Freire, P. (1972) *Pedagogy of the oppressed*. New York: Seabury.

Gladwell, M. (2002) *The tipping point: How little things can make a big difference*. London: Abacus.

Harber, C. (2009) *Toxic schooling: How schools became worse*. Nottingham: Educational Heretics Press.

Hase, S. and Kenyon, C. (2007) 'Heutagogy: a child of complexity theory', *Complicity: An International Journal of Complexity and Education*, 4 (1), pp.111–118.

Hodkinson, P. and Sparkes, A. (1997) 'Careership: A sociological theory of career decision making', *British Journal of Sociology of Education*, 18 (1), pp.29–44.

Illeris, K. (2014) 'Transformative learning and identity', *Journal of Transformative Education*, 12 (2), pp.148–163.

Jarvis, C. and Burr, V. (2011) 'The transformative potential of popular television: The case of *Buffy, the Vampire Slayer*', *Journal of Transformative Education*, 9 (3), pp.165–182.

Kuhn, T.S. (1962) *The structure of scientific revolutions*. Chicago: Chicago University Press.

Lauricella, S. and MacAskill, S. (2015) 'Exploring the potential benefits of holistic education: A formative analysis', *Other Education*, 4 (2), pp.54–78.

Lees, H.E. and Noddings, N. (eds) (2016) *The Palgrave international handbook of alternative education*. London: Palgrave.

Meyer, J. and Land, R. (2003) *Threshold concepts and troublesome knowledge: Linkages to ways of thinking and practising within the disciplines*. Edinburgh: University of Edinburgh in association with the TLRP and ESRC. Available at: www.etl.tla.ed.ac.uk//docs/ETLreport4.pdf (accessed 26 October 2016).

Mezirow, J. (1978) *Education for perspective transformation: Women's re-entry programs in community colleges*. New York: Teachers College, Columbia University.

O'Sullivan, E.V., Morrell, A. and O'Connor, M.A. (eds) (2002) *Expanding the boundaries of transformative learning: Essays on theory and praxis*. New York: Palgrave Press.

Reay, D. (2012) 'What would a socially just education system look like?: Saving the minnows from the pike', *Journal of Education Policy*, 27 (5), pp.587–599.

Rogers, C. (1969) *Freedom to learn*. Columbus, OH: Merrill.

Thomas, A. and Pattison, H. (2007) *How children learn at home*. London: Continuum.

Zembylas, M. and Fendler, L. (2007) 'Reframing emotion in education through lenses of parrhesia and care of the self', *Studies in Philosophy and Education*, 26, pp.319–333.

PHILOSOPHY

KEY CONCEPT: *BILDUNG*

Dave Trotman

Concept origins

In the UK, *Bildung* is one of the more obscure educational concepts. In the Continental European tradition of education, *Bildung* is by comparison one of its key ideas (Biesta, 2002a, p.390). Emerging from German philosophical thought, the term *Bildung* is thought to have entered into common usage around the middle of the eighteenth century (Nordenbo, 2002). Although the educational ideas associated with *Bildung* can be traced to the philosophy of ancient Greece, its development was primarily advanced in the theoretical writings of the Prussian philosopher Wilhelm von Humboldt. Most scholars of *Bildung* agree that the term defies singular definition and that it is better to consider the concept as having multiple histories (Biesta, 2002a; Prange, 2004).

Current status and usage

Since the 1960s, *Bildung* has undergone something of a revival in Nordic and Germanic countries. While the exact meaning of the term is notoriously difficult to pin down, due to the twin challenges of translation and its multiple histories, there is a general agreement that *Bildung* concerns the promotion of liberty and human dignity (Prange, 2004, p.502); the inner life of the human soul, mind and humanity (Biesta, 2002b, p.378) and the spiritual and aesthetic aspects of our lives (Prange, 2004, p.503). There is also general agreement that *Bildung* involves formation of the self (Beck *et al.*, 2015, p.445), self-cultivation (Sorkin, 1983) and edification (Masschelein and Ricken, 2003, p.139).

In its contemporary use, *Bildung*'s emphasis on human dignity, self-cultivation and formation underscores the function of education as being something above and beyond the acquisition of basic skills and qualifications. In this sense, *Bildung* aligns with the notion that education is first and foremost a matter of development. This is in contrast to those standpoints that view education and the **curriculum** as serving largely **instrumental** needs, free of value and amenable to measurement (see e.g., Kelly, 2009, on curriculum). One important quality of *Bildung*, then, is the virtue of **autonomous learning** for its own sake (Prange, 2004). At first sight, this concept is fundamentally about self-cultivation and education as a greater good. Hence, notions of educational performance, the measurement of educational outcomes and a curriculum solely for occupational purposes are alien to the principles of *Bildung*. Rather, *Bildung* foregrounds the development of human qualities that are informed and enriched by such things as general knowledge, **creativity**, an appreciation of art and **culture** (European Network of Education Councils, 2011, p.7), the aesthetic and the spiritual (Nordenbo, 2002, p.345; Prange, 2004, p.505).

⚙ The promotion of such things as **creativity**, **culture**, the spiritual and the aesthetic, as part of the wide educational knowledge-base of *Bildung* is echoed in the educational aims of a number of countries (O'Donnell *et al.*, 2010). When aligned with notions of self-cultivation, however, the configuration of culture and cultivation has led to criticism by some scholars of a tendency for self-indulgence and elitism (Adorno, 1962). This tendency towards bourgeois forms of self-education (Løvlie and Standish, 2002) is balanced, however, by *Bildung*'s commitment to human dignity (Prange, 2004, p.502), ethical **behaviour**, moral judgement and critical thinking (European Network of Education Councils, 2011, p.7; Chapman, 2015, p.154). The balancing of self-cultivation with wider moral purpose parallels aspects of ancient Greek philosophy noted in the origins of the concept, in particular of Aristotelean ideas of *phronesis*, involving a moral disposition to act in a truthful and just manner (Carr and Kemmis, 1986, pp.32–33; Furlong, 2013, pp.177–179). This wider moral imperative associated with *Bildung* further points to the socio-cultural and socio-political aspects of the concept.

💡 As part of a changing postmodern landscape, from the 1980s onwards, *Bildung* underwent a resurgence of interest following its virtual disappearance in continental Europe some two decades earlier (Biesta, 2002b, p.379). The challenges associated with **globalisation**, involving migration and mobility, economic change and rapid technological development saw not only rekindled interest in *Bildung* as a response to increasingly **technocratic** forces in education, but the advancement of *Bildung*'s socio-political characteristics in a new orientation to **citizenship**.

This contemporary reading of *Bildung*, emphasising self-determination, freedom and emancipation (Klafki, 1986, p.458) involves transcending a personal adaptation to a singular reality (and the pursuit of personal interests within that reality) to a more objective engagement with cultural histories, social contexts and multiple realities (Biesta, 2002b, p.379). In this revitalisation of *Bildung,* the concept is one that has a strong political and community imperative that is both lifelong and broadly conceived—to the extent that **school**s and the traditions of **schooling** are regarded as problematic.

Questions to consider

1. What aspects of *Bildung* can be found in contemporary education systems?
2. Can *Bildung* be realised as an educational idea and if so how?
3. What aspects of *Bildung* might be problematic or difficult to implement?
4. How might contemporary **school** systems need to be changed in order to enable the principles of *Bildung* to be realised?
5. Is it possible to know when *Bildung* is successful?

References (with recommended readings in bold)

Adorno, T. (1962) 'Theorie der Halbbildung' [The theory of half-Bildung] in Horkheimer, M. and Adorno, T.W. (eds) *Sociologica II. Reden und Vorträge*. Frankfurt am Main: Europäishe Verlagstanstalt, pp.168–192.

Beck E.E., Solbrekke, T.D., Sutphen, M. and Fremstad, E. (2015) 'When mere knowledge is not enough: The potential of *Bildung* as self-determination, co-determination and solidarity', *Higher Education Research & Development*, 34 (3), pp.445–457.

Biesta, G. (2002a) 'Bildung and modernity: The future of Bildung in a world of difference', *Studies in Philosophy and Education*, 21 (4-5), pp.343–351.

Biesta, G. (2002b) 'How general can Bildung be? Reflections on the future of a modern educational ideal', *Journal of Philosophy of Education*, 36 (3), pp.377–390.

Carr, W. and Kemmis, S. (1986) *Becoming critical: Education, knowledge and action research*. London: Falmer Press.

Chapman A. (2015) 'Wellbeing and schools: Exploring the normative dimensions', in Wright, K. and McLeod, J. (eds) *Rethinking youth wellbeing: Critical perspectives.* London: Springer, pp.143–159.

European Network of Education Councils (2011) *'Bildung' in a lifelong learning perspective* (Report of the seminar of the European Network of Education Councils, Budapest, Hungary, 9–10 May 2011). Brussels: EUNEC Secretariat. Available at: www.eunec.eu/sites/www. eunec.eu/files/event/attachments/report_budapest.pdf (accessed 26 October 2016).

Furlong, J. (2013) *Education—An anatomy of the discipline: Rescuing the university project?* Abingdon: Routledge.

Kelly, A.V. (2009) *The curriculum: Theory and practice*, 6th edn. London: Sage.

Klafki, W. (1986) 'Die Bedeutung der klassischen Bildungstheorien für ein zeitgemässes Konzept von allgemeiner Bildung' [The meaning of the classical theory of 'Bildung' for a contemporary concept of general education], *Zeitschrift für Pädagogik*, 32 (4), pp.455–476.

Løvlie, L. and Standish, P. (2002) 'Introduction: Bildung and the idea of a liberal education', *Journal of Philosophy of Education*, 36 (3), pp.317–340.

Masschelein, J. and Ricken, N. (2003) 'Do we (still) need the concept of Bildung?', *Educational Philosophy and Theory*, 35 (2), pp.139–154.

Nordenbo, S.E. (2002) 'Bildung and the thinking of Bildung', *Journal of Philosophy of Education*, 36 (3), pp.341–352.

O'Donnell, S., Sargent, C., Byrne, A. and White, E. (2010) *Thematic probe: Curriculum review in the INCA countries.* Slough: NFER. Available at: http://webarchive.nationalarchives.gov.uk/20130220111733/ http:/inca.org.uk/Curriculum_review_probe_final_01_dec_2010. pdf (accessed 26 October 2016).

Prange, K. (2004) 'Bildung: A paradigm regained?', *European Educational Research Journal*, 3 (2), pp.501–509.

Sorkin, D. (1983) 'Wilhelm Von Humboldt: The theory and practice of self-formation (Bildung), 1791–1810', *Journal of the History of Ideas*, 44 (1), pp.55–73.

KEY CONCEPT: CRITICAL THEORY

Stephen Griffin

Concept origins

Etymologically speaking, the word 'critic' can be traced back to the Latin root 'criticus' meaning 'capable of judging'. Similarly the Greek word 'kritikos', when applied to an individual, describes someone who is 'able to judge or discern'. These foundations provide some insight into the origins of the concept, in that they suggest that critical theory is an active process of enquiry. The modern use of the term 'critical theory' can be traced back to Horkheimer's 1937 description of the work he and others undertook as part of the 'Frankfurt School' Institute for Social Research. This had intellectual roots in German philosophy, particularly the work of Kant and Hegel. Utilising the ideas of Karl Marx, he intended critical theory to be a method of cultural analysis. Building on philosophical, psychoanalytic and sociological techniques, the Institute sought to critique capitalist **society** in order 'to liberate human beings from the circumstances that enslave them' (Horkheimer, 1982, p.244).

Current status and usage

Currently, critical theory can be thought of as a broad range of contemporary, reflexive approaches to academic enquiry that encompass what Sim and Van Loon refer to as a 'theory of everything' (2004, p.3). However, critical theory 'does *not* form a unity' (Held, 1997, p.14). Rather, it encompasses traditions of thought that may differ from one another and from the origins of the movement in the Frankfurt School. Jurgen Habermas, who was a junior member of the Frankfurt School, has come to symbolise the evolution of critical theory. His writing grew from his reflections on the rise of the Third Reich in Germany and as Lovat (2013) explains, his most significant impact has been epistemological: his 'theory of knowing ... impels the kind of reasoned and compassionate reflection and self-reflectivity that issues in benevolent action' (p.70). This, he felt, was imperative, if societies' mistakes of the past were to be avoided in the future. More recently, however, Nikolas Kompridis has suggested that critical theory needs to renew itself (2006). Discussing Habermas's attempts to reformulate the tradition, he suggests this may produce a 'split between new and old critical theory so deep that the **identity** and future of critical theory are at risk' (Kompridis, 2006, p.17).

Modern interpretations of critical theory are often unhelpfully understood as any approach seeking to theorise the **social science**s and **humanities** (Buchanan, 2010). Such understandings can depart from the idea of critical theory as developed by the Frankfurt School and Horkheimer's rules for its usages. In his seminal 1937 essay, 'Traditional and Critical Theory', Horkheimer suggests that critical theory, in order to be effective, must operate on three levels (1972). First, it must explain what is currently wrong with **society**. Second, it needs to provide practical solutions to address the issue that has been identified. Third, clear, supporting, normative statements must be provided, open to criticism and therefore able to enable social change. In this sense, critical theory is a reflexive process requiring the theorist to acknowledge the subjective nature of theory and to recognise that it is bound by a range of sociological and historical factors. In essence then, critical theory identifies and describes what is perceived to be wrong with society: social conflict theories such as Marxism, for example, suggest that **school**s help to reinforce and replicate social divisions in society (Bartlett and Burton, 2012). Thus, values held by the dominant ruling classes are reinforced as are their positions in society, while the lower classes remain socially and economically disadvantaged. Bowles and Gintis (1976) further observed that there is a relationship between the ways in which pupils are treated by schools and the roles that most will have to undertake in later life. They suggested that this 'correspondence' helped to prepare lower-**class** pupils for unskilled labour (see also Willis, 1977). In this manner, critical theories shed light on structures and institutions in society by looking at what might otherwise be taken for granted and subverting such assumptions.

⚙ Another interpretation of critical theory—and in relation to education—can be seen in the work of Bourdieu and Passeron (1990). They suggested inequalities in the education system and wider **society** could be explained in terms of different forms of capital: economic, cultural and social. Economic capital refers to financial resources and the benefits that they bring. Cultural capital refers to cultural resources, such as knowledge of the **culture**, deemed appropriate by the dominant classes. **Social capital** relates to social resources such as networks providing access to influential people. Bourdieu argued that those children who had accrued appropriate amounts of (especially cultural) capital would 'naturally' progress and benefit most from the education system. Utilising Bourdieu's ideas, we might then suggest that the **school curriculum** is a representation of the dominant culture in society and therefore privileges those pupils who speak its language. From a critical and practical perspective, creating a more culturally inclusive curriculum would then become necessary in order to address educational inequality (see also Sullivan, 2002; Grenfell, 2014, 2007).

☺ Critical theory seeks to understand the foundations upon which certain ways of thinking and being have become possible. As such 'its goal is man's emancipation from slavery' (Horkheimer, 1972, p.249), in order that we might determine our own life courses free from the state, its social systems and impositions. Critical theory therefore rejects the idea that modern **society** has resulted from the logical progression of human endeavour. Instead, it acknowledges the impact of cultural, social and psychological influences that assert the dominance of particular groups within **society**. For example, critical feminist perspectives might suggest that society is predicated upon patriarchal value systems. Cixous developed this idea with her deconstruction of binary oppositions, such as Sun and Moon and Mother and Father, claiming they represented women in a negative light (Cixous *et al.* 1976). However, she also proposed the idea of *l'écriture féminine*, suggesting writing can take place in an abstract, in-between space that rejects male hierarchies. In this sense, critical theory offers a challenge to convention. It is unsettling, deliberately disruptive and turns its attention to hidden social structures that limit and subjugate specific groups. As such, it offers a means of peeling back the layers of educational practice to uncover the conditions of possibility that allow certain practices to come into being.

Questions to consider

1. Towards what aspects of education might it be useful to apply critical theory?
2. In what way is the **school curriculum** 'gendered'?
3. What structures exist in wider **society**, and more specifically in school, that limit particular groups' educational achievement?
4. How can critical theory be used to affect social change?

References (with recommended readings in bold)

Bartlett, S. and Burton, D. (2012) *Introduction to education studies*. London: Sage.

Bourdieu, P. and Passeron, J.C. (1990) *Reproduction in education, society and culture*, 2nd edn. London: Sage.

Bowles, S. and Gintis, H. (1976) *Schooling in capitalist America: Educational reform and the contradictions of economic life*. London: Routledge and Kegan Paul.

Buchanan, I. (2010) *Oxford dictionary of critical theory*. Oxford: Oxford University Press.

Cixous, H., Cohen, K. and Cohen, P. (1976) 'The laugh of the Medusa', *Signs*, 1.4, pp.875–893.

Grenfell, M.J. (2007) *Pierre Bourdieu: Education and training*. London: Continuum.

Grenfell, M.J. (ed.) (2014) *Pierre Bourdieu: Key concepts*, 2nd edn. Abingdon: Routledge.

Held, D. (1997) *Introduction to critical theory: Horkheimer to Habermas*. Oxford: Polity Press.

Horkheimer, M. (1972) 'Traditional and critical theory'. Translated by Jeremy J. Shapiro, in Horkheimer, M. *Critical theory*. New York: Herder and Herder.

Horkheimer, M. (1982) Critical theory: Selected essays. New York: Continuum.

Kompridis, N. (2006) *Critique and disclosure: Critical theory between past and future*. London: MIT Press.

Lovat, T. (2013) 'Jurgen Habermas; Education's reluctant hero', in Murphy, M. (ed.) *Social theory and education research: Understanding Foucault, Habermas, Bourdieu and Derrida*. Abingdon: Routledge.

Murphy, M. (ed.) (2013) *Social theory and education research: Understanding Foucault, Habermas, Bourdieu and Derrida.* **Abingdon: Routledge.**

Sim, S. and Van Loon, B. (2004) *Introducing critical theory.* Royston: Icon Books.

Sullivan, A. (2002) 'Bourdieu and education: How useful is Bourdieu's theory for researchers?', *The Netherlands' Journal of Social Sciences*, 38 (2), pp. 144–166.

Willis, P. (1977) *Learning to labor: How working class kids get working class jobs.* New York: Columbia University Press.

KEY CONCEPT: EDUCATIONAL THEORY

Helen E. Lees

Concept origins

Theory starts when we see a difference between a *given* practice and the thinking of and about practice. In order to theorise, we must reflect on what is, what occurs or what could and might occur. Theorisation allows educationists then to know education better or indeed to create education. This is at the heart of things, due to the ways in which education affects people practically: they learn, they come to know, they acquire skills, they develop themselves and others. Theory, thus, is a vital part of what occurs if education is to interact with people in an ethical and moral manner: it fits education to people rather than people to education. In this sense, there is no origin of the concept of educational theory. It is always an integral part of education as social practice and theoretically devised forms of education have always been with us. The word 'theory' is from the Greek *thorós*, meaning spectator: theory looks at the world and tries to explain. In doing so, it can enable change rather than stasis; a perennial feature of the engagement of people with the world and a useful part of education.

Current status and usage

To theorise in education is increasingly recognised as vital for good practices and good thinking about education as well as possibly helpful for **teacher** retention in **school**s (Lees, 2016). McDougall and Trotman suggest an '**Education Studies** student *needs* to do theory' (2009, p.19, emphasis added). However, its necessity in the field of education is in question. A number of publications in recent years deny the need for theory and theorising in **educational research** and practice, suggesting it is too vague, calling it 'junk sculpture' (Thomas, 2007, p.4), saying that 'The domains in which theory has been useful find no congruence in education' (Thomas, 2007, p.20), or seeing it as an 'impossible goal' (Wilfred Carr, 2006, p.147). Others, however, point to the vital role theorising plays in educational work to enrich our understanding of what we do as educators and as educated people. A lack of theorising and a practice–theory divide is seen as 'false and debilitating' (Dimitriadis and Kamberelis, 2006, p.vii) and inconsistent with reality, given that people are 'theorizing creatures' (Rajagopalan, 1998, p.337). A denigration of theory in education by calling those using theory 'The Blob, in thrall to Sixties **ideologies**' (Gove, 2013), enables a move away from serious *study* of education into **teaching**-as-craft, as though teaching only needs to be taught, rather than considered and debated. In the US, educationists must deal with the 'What Works' agenda: a programme designed to find the best practices for teaching and **learning** through a 'clearinghouse', supposedly devoid of any theoretical take on what *might* work (for some but not all). Attention to an a-theoretical 'machinery' of educating is lamented as the difference between mere ignorant, mechanistic instruction and *education* (Nock, 1932). The argument about theory in education is not going away.

In education, there are a range of theories and theorists. Some cover concepts like **behaviour** or **motivation** or **creativity** or **curriculum**. Some theorists, like Michel Foucault or Pierre Bourdieu, offer brave perspectives and ideas to see the given in new ways. There is no concept in this book which won't have some kind of theory to explain it somehow, so theory pervades education. Students are often asked "What theory are you using?" when they attempt educational arguments. The idea is that theory will scaffold empirical data gathering in research projects or support arguments made in essays, making them also often a lot more interesting. While some see theory as 'thinking on steroids' (Thomas, 2007, p.114), 'a conceptual poltergeist' (p.12), 'and a 'security blanket' (p.11), we can question this scepticism. Any suggestion of a 'bricolage' approach (collecting various bits and putting them together to make a whole picture) to educational meaning making (Thomas, 2007) is likely to meet opposition and criticism for its lack of respect for the value of theory: an argument 'against theory may be marked by the very same "looseness" or straying along' being denounced (Rajagopalan, 1998, p.350; Lees and Biesta, 2011). In other words, educationists may *need* theory to not make a mess in their writing. Theory—either borrowed and appropriated or created—gives form and depth to educational argumentation. Outside of education—in international relations, economics or physics, for example—theorists occupy positions of prestige (Mearsheimer and Walt, 2013, p.428), whereas in education the role and status of theory and theorists is, for largely unaccountable reasons, less revered.

Of course, not all theories agree, so within one concept there will be opposing visions and their accompanying theoretical explanations, frameworks or approaches to understanding. Theory and theories can be of a practical kind—for instance, how to understand stages of development in children—or like those of Foucault, mentioned above, which offer the idea that there is not one theory to follow but many. Jean-François Lyotard has suggested, using what one could call a postmodern theory, that we are to have 'incredulity towards metanarratives' (Lyotard, 1984). This means, in essence, that we are not to believe the stories we are told about the world. This is a challenge to a status quo of **epistemology** and **ontology**, restoring control and decision on what we believe to people's *own* thinking. Which is perhaps the core of the matter: theory allows and encourages thinking for oneself. It is an activity not an instruction.

Because of an enthralment with the doing of education as some kind of ritualistic tradition of known and set practices and the **hegemony** of **authoritarianism** as a way of organising educational **behaviour**, thinking through theory for education suffers from a lack of investment (Biesta *et al.*, 2011). Montuori rightly identifies 'there is a danger in what I see as an increasing anti-intellectual tendency to dispose of theory or suggest theory is simply an abstract opinion, as in "it is just a theory"' (Montuori, 2012). Yet as Gasparatou (2009, p.26) argues, we live according to language games which create a stable set of ideas amounting to 'an existing everyday framework', explaining 'how education works'. In other words, the problem in education is **ontotheological** (see **ontology**) conservatism: a common educational sense of things—the shared and shareable world—can also act to stop new ideas. What follows is binary, limited visions reducing the inherent complexity of educational realities to easily digestible, yet false, notions: 'Discussions about theory have often been conducted in terms of unhelpful dichotomies such as theory versus practice, the theoretical versus the **empirical**, or theoretical versus useful' (Biesta *et al.*, 2011, p.226). Education is complicated and theory allows us to show this under a spotlight, as well as making sense of the complexity through a theoretical lens. The result is very often an increase in knowledge for **social justice**. This is why educational theory matters.

Questions to consider

1. What is educational theory?
2. Why theorise in education?
3. How can an educationist use theory to improve their **teaching**?
4. What is the best theory you have come across to explain or inform your preferred approach to education?
5. What does education look like without theory?

References (with recommended readings in bold)

Biesta, G.J.J., Allan, J. and Edwards, R. (2011) 'The theory question in research capacity building in education: Towards an agenda for research and practice', *British Journal of Educational Studies*, 59(3), 225–239.

Carr, W. (2006) 'Education without theory', *British Journal of Educational Studies*, 54(2), 136–159.

Dimitriadis, G., and Kamberelis, G. (2006) *Theory for education*. New York: Routledge.

Gasparatou, Z.R. (2009) 'Education as initiation to a "form of life": Conceptual investigation and education theory', *The International Journal of Learning*, 16(1), 27–33.

Gove, M. (2013) 'I refuse to surrender to the Marxist teachers hell-bent on destroying our schools: Education Secretary berates "the new enemies of promise" for opposing his plans'. Available at: www.dailymail.co.uk/debate/article-2298146/I-refuse-surrender-Marxist-teachers-hell-bent-destroying-schools-Education-Secretary-berates-new-enemies-promise-opposing-plans.html

Lees, H.E. (2016) 'Learn to love theory to find joy in your practice', *TES magazine*, 15 April.

Lees, H.E. and Biesta, G. (2011) 'The necessity of educational theory', British Educational Research Association Conference. London: Institute of Education.

Lyotard, J.-F. (1984) *The postmodern condition: A report on knowledge*. Translated by G. Bennington and B. Massumi. Manchester: Manchester University Press.

McDougall, J. and Trotman, D. (2009) '"Doing theory" on education', in S. Warren (ed.) *An introduction to education studies: The student guide to themes and contexts*. London: Continuum.

Mearsheimer, J.J. and Walt, S.M. (2013) 'Leaving theory behind: Why simplistic hypothesis testing is bad for international relations', *European Journal of International Relations*, 19(3), 427–457.

Montuori, A. (2012) 'Transdisciplinary reflections: Transdisciplinarity as play and transformation'. Available at: http://integralleadershipreview.com/7589-transdisciplinary-reflections-transdisciplinarity-as-play-and-transformation.

Nock, A. J. (1932) '*The theory of education in the United States*'. Available at: https://mises.org/library/theory-education-united-states.

Rajagopalan, K. (1998) 'On the theoretical trappings of the thesis of anti-theory; or, why the idea of theory may not, after all, be all that bad: A response to Gary Thomas', *Harvard Educational Review*, 68(3), 335–352.

Thomas, G. (2007) *Education and theory: Strangers in paradigms*. Maidenhead: Open University Press.

KEY CONCEPT: EPISTEMOLOGY

Nick Peim

Concept origins

Questions concerning how we know what we know, and how we might extend the knowledge that we have, belong to the branch of philosophy usually referred to as epistemology. The word has Greek roots. In recent times, the word 'episteme' has been used to signify an order of knowledge. We are all familiar with the idea that there are different types of knowledge: historical knowledge is different, for example, from mathematical knowledge. But few of us are automatically inclined or trained to think in terms of an order of knowledge that we live within: in other words, an unconscious set of assumptions that determines what counts as knowledge for us in different spheres of life.

Current status and usage

Epistemological questions have been at the forefront of western metaphysics in modernity. This strong emphasis on questions of knowledge coincides with the rise of the idea and practice of science, based on the notion that method—defined and practised rigorously—could somehow guarantee truth (Bacon, 1620); that it could minimise at least the role of ideas and so keep 'metaphysics' away from real, hard, **empirically** acquired knowledge. In fact, recent theories of science are more likely to suggest that science is the product of varieties of practice and that the essence of science, its essential method, is much more elusive once you begin to seriously probe what it is (Feyerabend, 1975). Modern and contemporary science theory is likely to be very modest about claims to truth, preferring to suggest that the quest for knowledge is necessarily incomplete and that the knowledge that we do lay claim to may be subject to complete revision. Such theory is also likely to concede that science can't be strictly separated from metaphysics (Kuhn, 1970).

One big concern with modern epistemology concerns questions of how certain we can be about the knowledge that we have. This epistemological question is dramatically put on the scene by Descartes in the seventeenth century. Descartes (1641) poses the question: How can I know that what I know is in fact the case? Pursuing rigorously all the possibilities of doubt, Descartes faced the rather troubling question: Can I know anything at all with any certainty? Even at the simplest level, Descartes demonstrated quite forcefully that doubt could haunt the most mundane forms of knowledge. In the end, Descartes famously doubted his own existence and wondered what basis could there be from which to construct knowledge. 'I think therefore I am' is Descartes' modest starting point for knowing at least something. Knowing that you exist is a starting point, but it does not guarantee that what you know beyond yourself is certain and true. What is more, theories of a psychological cast (see **psychoanalysis**) that emerged in the latter part of the nineteenth century suggested strongly that knowledge of self is more problematic and difficult than even Descartes realised.

In the work of Immanuel Kant, the Enlightenment explored the limits of reason as grounds for knowledge (Kant, 1781) and found that knowledge of 'things-in-themselves' (or 'noumena') could never be guaranteed. Friedrich Nietzsche pursued this critical logic to the limit (Doyle, 2009). Nietzsche argued that knowledge did not need to justify itself by having a relation to some absolute sense of truth. For Nietzsche, truth is always fraught with illusion and can never be a secure category. For Nietzsche, we may as well collectively live happily with this freedom and actively *create* the kinds of truth that will serve our desire to live well and to live fully. The absence of absolute, external truth (as with the death of God) does not drain the world of meaning and purpose. Rather, it poses a positive question for us: What kind of world are we going to make anew, given that we have been empowered to a new destiny as authors of our own value system? In this view, knowledge will be at the service of our new vision for the future. This is a future that we can—indeed, must—create for ourselves. The pursuit of knowledge is then more an artistic project than an unveiling of what already exists in some as yet unveiled space of truth.

What is the contemporary understanding of our relation to knowledge? On the one hand, we have confidence in techniques for the production of knowledge for delivering data. But there is radical uncertainty in terms of how to make sense of that knowledge and put it to use and on what terms to understand our current condition of being in this time. While approaches epistemologically privileging the speculative (the domain of thinking) may be less in favour than those that privilege the **empirical**, there is much cause to question this hierarchy. Research handbooks in **social science** frequently represent the empirical dimension—fieldwork or data gathering—as the essential element of real research. This is a seriously limiting myth, albeit a powerful one. It somehow suggests we can immediately get hold of the stuff of reality without looking seriously at the conditions we do our research from or the conditions that define the nature of the object of our enquiry. A critical epistemology will seek to call into question what is already fixed and determined. In Jacques Derrida's curious approach to questions of knowledge, the archive must be guarded against the intrusion of improper elements (Derrida, 1996). Knowledge here supposedly belongs to what is established and needs to be protected against unruly or wayward disturbances. These 'archons' (perhaps another name for universities in the modern era) protect not only the store of received knowledge but also protect the rituals of entry into the world of knowledge. The archons, for example, guard over the form of the doctoral thesis. They decide what is publishable and what is not. On this view, the production of really new knowledge is a struggle against the prevailing order. This is an idea echoed by modern theories of science particularly in the work of Thomas Kuhn and Paul Feyerabend. On this view, knowledge, science and research are all beset by conflict between the existing order and the threat of something new and as yet unknown.

Questions to consider

1. How can we reflect on and reconsider our understanding of knowledge and its status?
2. What different types of knowledge are there?
3. What is the role of knowledge in contemporary social structures?
4. Why does knowledge change and what are the driving forces of such changes?
5. What is the relation between knowledge and the **curriculum**?

References (with recommended readings in bold)

Bacon, F. (1620) *The new organon.* Edited by Lisa Jardine and Michael Silverthorne. Cambridge: Cambridge University Press, 2003.

Derrida, J. (1996) *Archive fever.* Chicago: Chicago University Press.

Descartes, R. (1641) *Meditations of first philosophy.* Translated by J. Cottingham. Cambridge: Cambridge University Press, 1996.

Doyle, T. (2009) *Nietzsche on epistemology and metaphysics: The world in view.* Edinburgh: Edinburgh University Press.

Feyerabend, P. (1975) *Against method.* New York: Humanities Press.

Kant, I. (1781) *The critique of pure reason.* New York: Dover, 2003.

Kuhn, T. (1970) *The structure of scientific revolutions.* Chicago: Chicago University Press.

KEY CONCEPT: ETHICS

Roger Willoughby

Concept origins

A part of moral philosophy, ethics may be understood as 'the attempt to formulate codes and principles of moral **behaviour**' (Honderich, 1995, p.586). Discussion can be traced back to the fifth century BC, when the Greek Sophists propounded ethical relativism, arguing morality was only a social construction useful for a better life. Subsequent Greek philosophy, particularly that emanating from Plato (380BC) and Aristotle (350BC), radically challenged these views. In *The Republic*, for example, Plato (380BC) argued that a good life consists of harmony of the soul, each of its supposed parts (reason, spirit and appetite) performing its 'proper' function, with traditional virtues being part of this balanced economy. Seen as conducive to happiness and development, the moral life is—Plato argues—the best life. Relatedly, Plato argued that the just **society** was a direct extension of the proper functioning of its constituent parts. These arguments would ultimately influence the emergence of **functionalism** and in Britain the development of the highly flawed '**Tripartite**' system, following the 1944 Education Act.

Current status and usage

Skipping forward over the intervening two millennia of ethical thinking (see MacIntyre, 1998, for an accessible introduction) since Plato, the second half of the twentieth century witnessed a substantial return to and development of classic ethical theorising. Arguing for the universalisability of ethical pronouncements, R.M. Hare (1981) saw this as entailing a variety of utilitarianism (an ethical theory, which crudely speaking argues the morally justified act is that which produces the greatest happiness for the greatest number). In his theory of justice, John Rawls

(1999) proposed basing its principles on a notional contract (a contractarian theory); collective assent here offered some security of individual interests from the potential risks of utilitarianism. The relevance of such views for educational policies and practices (e.g., around **inclusion**, **exclusion**, **pastoral welfare** issues, **diversity**, **performativity**, the **curriculum**, and possibilities of **pedagogy**) is significant. The rise of medical ethics and bio-ethics, which address ethical questions in the biological sciences, medical research and health **care**, has reinvigorated the broader discipline and had profound effects on practice among the medical **profession**s. Questions raised therein (e.g., confidentiality and trust in the doctor–patient relationship, problems of paternalism and choice, and the allocation of resources) have influenced analogous debates in education (Haynes, 1999, 2015) and other human sciences. Applied ethics has exercised a similarly invigorating function (Singer, 1986), debating vital questions from the justifiability of war, through **special educational needs**, up to debates on racial and sexual **equality**. The penetration of ethics into routine educational practice is particularly formalised in relation to research (Brooks *et al.*, 2014).

Ethics permeates education in multiple ways, from its very concept, through its functions, **curriculum** and methods, to its **politics** (Peters, 1966; Haynes, 2015; Arthur *et al.*, 2016). All involve controversial topics. With education commonly regarded as being as much about initiation, socialisation, and the transmission of cultural values, as it may be about imparting content knowledge, essentially ethical questions immediately arise about what counts as a good life, one's **relationships** to others and more broadly to **society**, the correctness of actions, etc. With responses to such questions often drawing on Plato's (380BC) ideas, much of the ethical discussion in education has had a strong **functionalist** bent. This supports existing **power** relations, adjusting people to set positions in society, where each performs their 'proper' function, this 'harmony' being equated to the good life. Of course, such perspectives can be criticised as conservative orthodoxies or **discourses** of **hegemony** (Gramsci, 1971; Hoerder, 2014) that support a select powerful few while limiting social mobility for many. Progressive—**alternative education**—approaches, classically associated with Rousseau (1762) and Dewey (1897, 1899, 1916), propose more **child-centred** educational regimes, emphasising **liberal** varieties of ethical naturalism. While such approaches are problematic (apart from for a select few) in developed market economies, later proposals that emphasise the development of personal **autonomy** (Callan, 1988, 1994), well-being and **care** (Gilligan, 1982; Noddings, 2002, 2013) have wider though still contested applicability. Often threaded throughout the curriculum, in England these initiatives are perhaps most visible in PSHE. Given the dominance of normative approaches in education, two further ethical initiatives may be noted here: the widespread use of student **behaviour** contracts and analogous codes of conduct for staff. Arising out of Hobbesian-type views (Hobbes, 1651) that depict self-interest and the pursuit of power as typifying human nature, the excesses of which are held in check through forms of social contract and state power, akin to contractarian views (Rawls, 1999), these encourage and police behaviour if not always actual values.

⚙ As is evident in even a brief consideration of the history of ethics, much of the territory is disputed. With secular theorising dominating **mainstream** ethical debate in Western academic contexts, its ideas (e.g., promoting **autonomy** rather than custom) can sit uncomfortably at times with both religious education and diverse **ethnic** and cultural traditions. The position is further complicated with histories of **colonialism**, with control being often sustained through narratives of greater ethical, cultural and intellectual virtue, as much as through force. Internalisation of such narratives (Fanon, 1952), perpetuates and problematises ethical **identity** and integrity. In post-colonial and multi-cultural contexts addressing such effects is vital, especially given the weight of evidence of racialised bias (Mac an Ghaill, 1988; Andrews, 2013), which can contaminate ethical sense. This engagement promotes empathy and can deepen understanding of the ethical dimensions of **diversity**, identity and **race** issues. Similar arguments pertain to the insidious role of patriarchy and its negative **gender-**related effects, especially on women and girls.

🙂 As a disciplinary concept, ethics is primarily a branch of philosophy. Yet, as seen above, ideas from other areas, such as sociology, **politics**, post-colonial theory, **gender** studies and psychology, may all also legitimately critique its arguments. This **interdisciplinary** process is usefully illustrated in the evolution of thinking about the ethics of **care.** The neo-Piagetian psychological studies of moral development by Kohlberg (1984; Kohlberg and Hersh, 1977), suggested a three-level model of its evolution (termed pre-conventional, conventional and post-conventional morality), culminating in a rarely attained ethical outlook incorporating abstract reasoned self-chosen principles on individual rights and justice. Among the various critiques of this work, Gilligan (1982) challenged the skewed (all-male) nature of Kohlberg's initial sample and what she perceived as the devaluation of traditional female virtues around contextual caring and relational qualities. The latter observations would prove more influential, inaugurating an ethics of care perspective in addition to Kohlberg's emphasis on justice. Hume (1751) had, of course, previously emphasised the crucial role of sympathy or fellow-feeling in the promotion of ethical action, but Gilligan's work gave this a gender emphasis. This was substantively taken up by Noddings (2002, 2013), who positions **care** as an educational goal and as a foundation for pedagogic practice. Although rather **essentialist** in flavour and potentially reinforcing of traditional gender roles, such an ethic may usefully inform **education research**, promoting in particular the importance of the researcher–participant relationship (Brooks *et al.*, 2014).

Questions to consider

1. What is the 'good life' and is it attainable through education?
2. Ethics may be seen as a constraint on action. Is this justified and if so why?
3. Which three ethical principles are most important in conducting educational research?
4. Can ethics be distinguished from ideological forms of social control and, if so, how and why?
5. Do we need ethics?

References (with recommended readings in bold)

Andrews, K. (2013) *Resisting racism: Race, inequality and the black supplementary school movement*. London: Trentham Books.

Aristotle (350BC) *Nicomachean ethics*. Translated by D. Ross. Oxford: Oxford University Press, 2009.

Arthur, J., Kristjánsson, K., Harrison, T., Sanderse, W. and Wright, D. (2016) *Teaching character and virtue in schools*. Abingdon: Routledge.

Brooks, R., te Riele, K. and Maguire, M. (2014) *Ethics and education research*. London: Sage.

Callan, E. (1988) *Autonomy and schooling*. Kingston, ON: McGill Queen's University Press.

Callan, E. (1994) 'Autonomy and alienation', *Journal of Philosophy of Education*, 28, pp.35–53.

Dewey, J. (1897) 'My pedagogic creed', *The School Journal*, 54, pp.77–80.

Dewey, J. (1899) *The school and society*. New York: Cosimo Classics, 2008.

Dewey, J. (1916) *Democracy and education*. New York: Cosimo Classics, 2005.

Fanon, F. (1952) *Black skin white masks*. Translated by Charles Lam Markmann. London: Pluto Press, 1986.

Gilligan, C. (1982) *In a different voice*. Cambridge, MA: Harvard University Press.

Gramsci, A. (1971) *Selections from the prison notebooks of Antonio Gramsci*. Translated and edited by Q. Hoare and G. Norwell-Smith. London: Lawrence & Wishart.

Hare, R. M. (1981) *Moral thinking: Its levels, method, and point*. Oxford: Clarendon Press.

Haynes, F. (1999) 'Ethics and education', in Peters, M.A. (ed.) *Encyclopaedia of educational philosophy and theory*. Available at: http://eepat.net/doku.php?id=ethics_and_education (accessed 2 November 2016).

Haynes, J. (2015) 'Moral reasoning, ethics and education', in Haynes, J. Gale, K. and Parker, M. (eds) *Philosophy and education: An introduction to key questions and themes*. Abingdon: Routledge, pp.93-105.

Hobbes, T. (1651) *Leviathan*. Edited by N. Malcolm. Oxford: Oxford University Press, 2012.

Hoerder, D. (2014) 'Education for a transcultural life-world or for a hegemonic nation? Schooling in the British empire, in France, and in Canada, 1830s–2000s', *Studia Migracyjne—Przeglad Polonijny*, 40 (3), pp.17–32.

Honderich, T. (ed.) (1995) *The Oxford companion to philosophy*. Oxford: Oxford University Press.

Hume, D. (1751) *An enquiry concerning the principles of morals*. Edited by T.L. Beauchamp. Oxford: Oxford University Press, 1998.

Kohlberg, L. (1984) *The psychology of moral development*. New York: Harper.

Kohlberg, L. and Hersh, R.H. (1977) 'Moral development: a review of the theory', *Theory into Practice*, 16, pp.53–59.

Mac an Ghaill, M. (1988) *Young, gifted and black: Student–teacher relations in the schooling of black youth*. Milton Keynes: Open University Press.

MacIntyre, A. (1998) *A short history of ethics*. London: Routledge.

Noddings, N. (2002) *Educating moral people: A caring alternative to character education*. Williston, VT: Teachers College Press.

Noddings, N. (2013) *Caring: A relational approach to ethics & moral education*, 2nd edn. Berkeley: University of California Press.

Peters, R.S. (1966) *Ethics and education*. London: Allen & Unwin.

Plato (380BC) *Republic*. Translated by R. Waterfield. Oxford: Oxford University Press, 2008.

Rawls, J. (1999) *A theory of justice*, rev. edn. Cambridge, MA: Harvard University Press.

Rousseau, J.J. (1762) *Émile, or on education*. Translated by A. Bloom. New York: Basic Books, 1979.

Singer, P. (ed.) (1986) *Applied ethics*. Oxford: Oxford University Press.

KEY CONCEPT: LITERACY

Nick Peim

Concept origins

Literacy, at its most basic, signifies being able to operate in the domain of reading and writing. It is usually assumed that literacy is a relatively recent historical phenomenon. The emergence of what we refer to as writing dates from not much more than 8000BC. What has come to be called literacy is thought to have arisen independently in Mesoamerica, China, Mesopotamia and in Egypt, in early civilisations that had developed writing systems. Literacy in this sense is strongly associated with the development of writing and is assumed to be an essential element in the development of highly regulated, organised societies, including their complex technological competences. For us today— 'we contemporaries'—literacy is so much a part of our form of life and of our understanding of things that it is a difficult topic to 'uncover'. In education, familiar clichés refer first of all to the benefits of literacy for social competence and sometimes also for personal fulfilment. These commonly held ideas have been challenged from a number of perspectives, so that literacy can be understood as a contested field although one dominated by **mainstream** educational values (Street, 1984).

Current status and usage

Literacy is particularly relevant to our understanding of education and of the role of education in the contemporary world. The conventional wisdom is that education confers the gift of literacy upon its subjects. In the educational field, an expanded sense of literacy incorporates a range of areas of competence: historical literacy, media literacy, visual literacy and so on. All of these modes of literacy involve some idea of being able to 'read' the world and to make sense of and to participate in the reception and production of signs in meaningful sequences. Modern forms of education are predicated on the idea that forms of literacy both can be and should be taught and that there can be objective standards—including timescales for attainment—that the competence of those who are positioned as learners of literacy can be judged against set criteria. This relatively new dimension of education and literacy has far-reaching implications (Peim, 2009).

As education emerged in northern Europe, in Japan and North America as a necessary means for shaping the substance of new mass populations, **learning** to read and write competently was understood as an essential attribute for a modern industrial labour force. Education systems in industrially developed countries aimed at ensuring that literacy was universal. At the same time, academics and politicians became concerned with the language and **culture** of the masses and developed means of state intervention. Later, concerns with the preservation of a dominant model of the language (especially in written form) to maintain the idea of a national culture expressed through its literature emerged (Doyle, 1989). This created the notion of national literature as cultural heritage, an idea still to be found in national curricula. English in the UK, for example and ironically perhaps, was born in India, where the British sought to encourage a subaltern Indian middle **class** with the values of English culture. Literacy in this sense can be seen as an instrument of **imperialism** (Viswanathan, 1989). In industrial Britain, working-class mass populations experienced English **teaching** embedded in universal elementary education. The effects of such a subject that touched on intimate dimensions of language and culture meant that it could reach into the hearts and minds of its subjects.

Starting with the Newbolt Report of 1921, a **school** offers literacy at least partly in terms of correcting and improving the literacy of certain social groups. Thus, promotion of literacy through **schooling** could be considered as being about empowerment, yet some contemporary thinking suggests otherwise. Literacy can be seen more as the ground for dispute about what relevant cultural knowledge is, who determines what forms of reading and writing are significant and who determines what passes for good writing, good speech and even good listening. All of these things have been part of a **curriculum** that children are tested against. In our time, we are also used to the idea of multiple literacies with clear differences between being media-literate and being literate in a more canonical sense (Peim, 1995). Critiques from sociology, sociolinguistics, cultural studies and media studies have challenged the dominant model of literacy but have not been able to shift its **power** very much (Holderness, 1988; Lapsley and Westlake, 1988; Fiske, 1989). These critiques have suggested that people with different social and cultural affiliations will engage differently with literacy and its objects, even arguing that its objects and its preferred practices can differ from group to group. An important dimension of this work has been concerned with **gender**. The literary canon, for example, has been critically revisited and redefined in relation to women's writings (Belsey, 1980; Moi, 1985).

The modern history of literacy is bound up with the history of the social division of labour and maintenance of social hierarchies determined by occupation (Donald, 1989). There is a dark side to this: formal literacy promotion via **schooling** involved making judgements about the quality of language used by whole groups of people (Bernstein, 1971; Bourdieu, 1991). Such judgements have now been shown to be arbitrary, classist and prejudicial. In effect, they seemed to deny the value of certain forms of **culture** and the language that informed their characteristic modes of being. New technologies have introduced an element of uncertainty into the field of literacy. The rise of powerful visual media after the invention of cinema (1895) and developments with radio and television introduced what became known as mass communications. Sorting out what was worthy and what was not might require some kind of media literacy knowledge and training, as with media studies. Some have argued that the new field of 'semiotics' changed the way we might think about literacy—especially in relation to understanding how texts work and what they might mean, enabling sifting between worthwhile texts of whatever form (Barthes, 1973). The contemporary scene is very interesting. Educational practices remain tied to a literary model of literacy, yet social practices involve a far greater range of text types and textual practices, including the vast range of electronic media that we all engage with through **technology** (Easthope, 1991). The future will determine what model of literacy prevails.

Questions to consider

1. What is the history of literacy as it relates to the rise of modern education systems?
2. What might you understand by the social dimension of literacy?
3. Is it possible to define the characteristics of a literate person in our time?
4. What is the **politics** of literacy? And what different positions might be held in relation to this idea?

References (with recommended readings in bold)

Barthes, R. (1973) *Mythologies*. London: Paladin.
Belsey, C. (1980) *Critical practice*. London: Methuen.
Bernstein, B. (1971) *Class, codes and control, volume 1: Theoretical studies towards a sociology of language*. London: Routledge and Kegan Paul.
Bourdieu, P. (1991) *Language and symbolic power*. Cambridge: Polity Press.
Donald, J. (1989) 'Beyond our ken: English, Englishness, and the national curriculum', in Brooker, P. and Humm, P. (eds) *Dialogue and difference*. London: Routledge, pp.13–30.
Doyle, B. (1989) *English and Englishness*. London, Routledge.
Easthope, A. (1991) *Literary into cultural studies*. Routledge: London.
Fiske, J. (1989) *Understanding popular culture*. London: Unwin Hyman.
Holderness, G. (ed.) (1988) *The Shakespeare myth*. Manchester: Manchester University Press.
Lapsley, R. and Westlake, M. (1988) *Film theory: An introduction*. Manchester: Manchester University Press.
Moi, T. (1985) *Sexual/textual politics*. London: Methuen.
Peim, N. (1995) 'Key Stage 4: Back to the future', in King, P. and Protherough, R. (eds) *The challenge of English in the national curriculum*. London: Routledge, pp.164–181.
Peim, N. (2009) 'English and the government of language and culture', in Hill, D. and Helavaara Robertson, L. (eds) *Equality in the primary school: Promoting good practice across the curriculum*. London: Continuum.
Street, B. (1984) *Literacy in theory and practice*. Cambridge: Cambridge University Press.
Viswanathan, G. (1989) *Masks of conquest: Literary study and British rule in India*. New York: Columbia University Press.

KEY CONCEPT: ONTOLOGY

Nick Peim

Concept origins

Ontology derives its meaning initially from a Greek word for being. Ontology signifies a concern with being, 'nature' or essence. When we ask what something is, we are engaging in an ontological quest. When we ask about the meaning of being we are thinking ontologically. Ontology is not really a common sense idea and yet some claim that its significance in western thinking and in our general understanding of things cannot be overstated. Ontology is concerned with 'being', concerned that is with questions of the very nature of things, whether that be all things taken together ('Being') or with particular things ('beings') (Internet Encyclopedia of Philosophy, n.d.).

Current status and usage

In the field of education, for example, where research abounds and is funded to significant levels in the name of improvement, it is frequently the case that research will by-pass the ontological dimension. **Education research** and knowledge seem to take it for granted that we know already what education is; or that we know what knowledge is; or what research itself is; or what a **school** is; or that we know what a classroom is. These, after all, are the fundamental components of the huge apparatus that we know as education and, in particular, the school, as its most significant social manifestation. And yet these basic phenomena—objects and ideas—cry out for understanding. Just because they are familiar doesn't mean that we have exhausted their meaning (Hunter, 1994). Some would argue that the contrary is the case. Martin Heidegger, for instance, the great ontologist of modern philosophy, claimed that what is nearest to us is hardest for us to

understand. For Heidegger, ontology was of the utmost importance. He claimed ontology had been forgotten by western philosophy, to the detriment of our thinking and our knowledge of
things (Internet Encyclopedia of Philosophy, n.d.).

The significance of ontology, or of the ontological dimension, resides
in its fundamental nature. Classically, ontology is first philosophy. In
other words, it belongs to what must be considered first in philosophical engagements. Sometimes ontological questions can appear
banal or absurd: 'What is a table?' The question seems irrelevant and
to belong to a parody of what philosophy is. To ask the question
seems to suggest a merely indulgent desire to problematise what
doesn't need to be scrutinised. After all, it is blindingly obvious, isn't
it, what a table is? The apparent absurdity of the question belongs to
the mundane nature of the object in question. Also to the fact that
asking such a question seems to serve no useful purpose whatsoever.
On the whole, we live in the world without troubling the objects
that we encounter with questions about their **identity** or their provenance. Heidegger refers to this mode of engagement with things in
terms of those things being ready-to-hand. We don't ask what a table
is very often because most of the time we are using it, putting things
on it, writing on it, manoeuvring round it, cleaning it, polishing it. It
is both deeply familiar and deeply obvious what it is. But there are
times when things puzzle or bemuse us. Sometimes these are relatively trivial things, like tables, but sometimes they are more important,
less obvious and sometimes powerfully complex things that we still
don't fully grasp, in spite of the fact that they are familiar features of
our everyday world and experience.

If we think of some of the complex objects that inhabit the world of
education, their **identity** is not necessarily given. Although a great deal
of **educational research** does treat such objects as though their ontological status can be taken for granted, occasionally ground-breaking
work can be achieved by going back to basics and asking fundamental
questions about fundamental objects. In my own experience, everyday complex components of education—the classroom, the **school**, the
playground, **literacy**, **learning,** for example—will all bear the kind of
scrutiny that ontological interrogation will offer (Foucault, 1977). The
meaning and identity of these things, after all, cannot be said to have

finally been settled, in spite of our common-sense impulses to think the contrary. This openness in the identity of things is a very common property of key entities that are addressed by **social science** research. It can be understood as a basic ontological property of the nature of things: that what anything is is not and cannot be given once and for all, that there is a certain openness about the very nature of things (Derrida, 1976). The awareness of this openness can be exciting to experience, as it suggests the possibility of changes in both ourselves and in the very nature of the world that can sometimes seem beyond the reach of change. Ontological thinking can remind us that the relations between how we think and how things are in the world is more dynamic and more interesting than we might ordinarily expect when we give in to some dull form of realism that says 'That's just the way it is'.

☺ We tend to develop a more-or-less systematic way of understanding the nature of things based on **culture** and education: on assumptions that are roughly 'knotted into a system'. Most of the time the system and the way it shapes our understanding of the nature of things operates at an unconscious level: working in terms of 'unknown knowns' to borrow Donald Rumsfeld's famous **epistemology**. It is in the realm of the unknown knowns that we are most likely to be in the grip of what Heidegger sometimes referred to as onto-theology. Ontotheology refers to the kind of thinking that is so deeply and so strongly embedded in us, in our language and in our habits and everyday practices that we no longer interrogate its meaning. Ontotheology is the realm of powerful, often unconscious, but almost always unchallenged beliefs that stabilise our thinking and that often persuades us that our knowledge can be complete and beyond the reach of the question (Derrida, 1976, 1978, 1982, 1987). Education is perhaps the greatest possible example of ontotheology at work. It is generally assumed in our world, in our culture and certainly in our political **discourses**, that education is generally a good thing and that education is also an important feature of democracy, that education is a gift that potentially grants all sorts of benefits on those who receive its blessings. And yet there is a powerful counter-story that has been presented to us for many decades by the sociologists of education. According to this alternative view, education as we know it does not by any means benefit all equally. In fact, education displays the kinds of prejudices based on social factors such as social **class**, **ethnicity** and **race** that a democratic **society** and a society based on the idea of **equality** of opportunity would find fault with. At a fundamental level, we might challenge the ontological status of education as an unquestioned 'good'. What is education in its overpowering modern form, where it takes hold of life from an earlier and earlier point and where it seeks also to become a lifelong principle?

Questions to consider

1. Why have ontological questions been foreclosed or neglected in **education studies**?
2. What might be gained by subjecting key categories of education—**school**, university, **curriculum**, for instance—to ontological interrogation?
3. Why has education become such a powerful idea in modern times?
4. What is the dominant 'ontotheology' in the field of education?
5. What is a school if we do not take it for granted as a given?

References (with recommended readings in bold)

Derrida, J. (1976) *Of grammatology*. London: The Johns Hopkins University Press.

Derrida, J. (1978) *Writing and difference*. London: Routledge and Kegan Paul.

Derrida, J. (1982) *Margins of philosophy*. Brighton: Harvester.

Derrida, J. (1987) *Positions*. London: Athlone.

Foucault, M. (1977) *Discipline and punish*. London: Allen Lane.

Hunter, I. (1994) *Rethinking the school*. Sydney: Allen and Unwin.

Internet Encyclopedia of Philosophy (n.d.) 'Martin Heidegger (1889–1976'. Available at: www.iep.utm.edu/heidegge.

PRACTICE

KEY CONCEPT: ALTERNATIVE EDUCATION

Helen E. Lees

Concept origins

There has always been an alternative *to something* in education: whether it was **school** as the alternative to children running around the streets unsupervised or **learning** to steal in Victorian times, or a child learning a musical instrument instead of learning equations for a maths test. In this sense, the phrase 'alternative education' signifies merely options to the assumption of the school as a **hegemony**. However, the idea is developing a stronger sense than this: it pertains as a concept mostly to significant forms of education, rather than curricula choices or attendance. Alternative education evolves as an educational concept in response to needs of **teacher**s, parents and most of all children, seeking for and needing something *different*: while this could be a **schooling** away from a given school (such as a **special educational needs** school or a **pupil referral unit**) **child-centred** education tends to characterise alternative education. This is a style different from **authoritarian** forms, expecting freedoms rather than any imposed, coercive structure. The concept for alternative education as a movement in the 21st century can be attributed to pioneering educational projects in the UK such as A.S. Neill's Summerhill School, or the Sudbury Valley schools in the US. A 'movement' for alternatives began, however, with 'progressive education' (see, e.g., Darling, 1994; Röhrs and Lenhart, 1995), which here is subsumed under the term 'alternative', closely aligned to **child-centred**—see below). Thus, alternatives as outlined have a history as long as education has been viewed as the school.

Current status and usage

In the past 30 or so years, alternative education has become common in two separate domains, although both have commonalities. In America, alternative education often means a setting outside of **mainstream schooling**—where children who have been removed as an **exclusion** from mainstream **school**s go to receive some form of education. The second kind of alternative is education done differently from a mainstream approach, with regard to its core educational philosophies for freedom and choice for children. Often this is **democratic education** or **elective home education**. Education of the freedom, **child-centred** kind as we see in alternative/progressive education (Darling, 1994; Howlett, 2013; Eryaman and Bruce, 2015; Lees and Noddings, 2016) is acting as an alternative to unacceptable—for some—**culture**s and **politics** of mainstream education. It is still, however, subject to significant ignorance in the face of the **hegemony** of the idea of schooling as custodian of the common good, a normative (e.g., around **gender** identities) and some say 'foreclosing' force (Flint and Peim, 2012). While new schools are being set up around the world to develop educational change (see e.g., www.eudec.org or www.democraticeducation.org or www.educationrevolution.org) and journals such as *Other Education* (www.othereducation.org) and *Journal of Unschooling and Alternative Learning* (https://jual.nipissingu.ca) are aiming to condense and advance alternative education scholarship, alternative education is fashionable for some and is in development, but it remains marginal in terms of numbers and is poorly understood by the public and **policy** makers.

⏻ Why do we need an alternative? Some scholars claim that 'common **schooling**' is the most important way for education to occur in **society**, but ask for alternative ways for this to happen within a system (Apple, 2000; Fielding and Moss, 2011; Reay, 2012). Others such as Ivan Illich have argued schooling needs 'disestablishment': a reconfiguration of relations between the passive taught by the powerful, towards loving communities where **learning** is shared and co-developed (Bruno-Jofré and Zaldívar, 2012). Critiques of schooling abound, focused on more areas than one can mention—indeed, sometimes it is easy to think there is nothing right about schooling in the **mainstream** and only an alternative to this will do. However, this is to negate the deep complexity inherent in why we have **school**s in the first place, as well as the positive role they can take. The first point perhaps of the alternative is to hold schools to account and to be a form of 'opposition party'. The idea of having alternatives within education writ large instead of just the **school** is linked to **politics**, **power**, **society**, **hegemony** and so much more. It is a key idea in education because it is about a human right to self-determine instead of a potentially non-benign state doing it for us on their terms, not ours. Educational alternatives are about freedoms, but not licence (as A.S. Neill, 1966, pointed out) to do whatever we might please: they are always necessarily within a community of others and this is a key idea in relevant work on student and staff **voice**, such as within the **democratic education** meeting (Fielding, 2013).

✿ Are there any major differences between 'alternative', 'progressive', **'child-centred'**, **'holistic'** or even 'natural' education? The answer is 'Not really', at this time: they all stand for a sense of freedom, **equality** and respect for individuality in and through education. As the **educational research** field of this somewhat nascent area develops further, we may see significant ideological splits emerge and **school**s of thought coalesce around distinct ideas that challenge this commonality. Those key foci are, however, hard to unimagine: they characterise an alternative. This is because, some say, the school as the **mainstream** is systemically and organisationally not characterised by freedom, equality or particular respect for individuality (Meighan, 2005; Harber, 2004, 2009b; Flint and Peim, 2012), on account of both the scale of the system as well as its undemocratic manners. Another way to put this is that any alternative to the **mainstream** dogmas of education has a common 'enemy' (an unfortunate phrase, but sometimes it seems like that, in the reception of the **mainstream** to alternative's interests and approaches) with other alternatives. This does not mean that differences between practices are not to be found, because alternatives, in respecting freedoms and individuality, behave according to local circumstances: as a product of small community engagements and agreements (see e.g., Röhrs and Lenhart, 1995). There is no boss or pre-set agenda of such education. Practices are iterative and involve flexible arrangements between people in democratically inclined **schooling** or home-educating families. Perhaps on account of this flexibility, people who have experienced alternative education report happiness, independence of thought, community sensibilities and enterprising attitudes (Sheffer, 1995; Miedema, 2016). Such outcomes are, unfortunately, in stark contrast to *some* reports of the students emerging from schooling outcomes, which indicate low achievement of self potentials, poor mental health and low **motivation** to societally contribute. Problems or questions about practices do pertain to alternative education (see e.g., Tsabar, 2014) and the picture is incredibly varied, so this poses challenges: Steiner schools, as one example, can follow strict ideas of Rudolf Steiner's sometimes strange writings, but are seen to be within the umbrella of alternative education despite, or perhaps because of, unusual ideas such as peach-blossom-coloured walls being optimal in certain classroom settings.

Alternative education has surprising features which set it apart from **mainstream schooling**, and on account of our interest in education as (we hope) a force for social good, these deserve mention. First, the field is replete with consistent and widespread testimonies of joy in having control over one's life and the experiences of **learning** that go with it (e.g., Sheffer, 1995; Neuman and Avriam, 2003; Lees, 2011), which is sometimes not the case with the more **authoritarian** forms of education (see, e.g., Harber, 2004, 2009a, 2009b). Not only that, but outcomes from an education experienced in alternative 'mode' are widely self-reported by students (past and present) as effective for their upbringing and learning, such that the young people are enabled to take a full part in **society** (Goodsman, 1992; Greenberg and Sadofsky, 1992; Gray and Riley, 2015). The point here is that something curiously 'good' is occurring through forms of education that respect self-determination and **voice**, and it behoves a student of education to study with **care** where good outcomes emerge. Yet, seen in the light of the history of the formation of education as a social 'good', we see a lack of appreciation or interest in such education with **autonomy** and **voice**. Why? The answer for some lies in perversion of the good (Bruno-Jofré and Zaldívar, 2012) or a deliberate foreclosing of possibilities for autonomy by powerful elites in order to control populations for the ends of elites, not of the people (Foucault, 1977; Flint and Peim, 2012; Reay, 2012).

Questions to consider

1. Do we need alternatives to a common **school** system?
2. What might be deficient or wrong with educational alternatives?
3. How can an alternative offer and mean ways to be free?
4. What does an alternative do?
5. What does an alternative look like?

References (with recommended readings in bold)

Apple, M.W. (2000) 'Away with all teachers: The cultural politics of home schooling', *International Studies in Sociology of Education,* 10 (1), pp.61–80.

Bruno-Jofré, R. and Zaldívar, J.I. (2012) 'Ivan Illich's late critique of deschooling society: "I was largely barking up the wrong tree"', *Educational Theory,* **62 (5), pp.573–592.**

Darling, J. (1994) *Child centered education and its critics.* London: Paul Chapman Publishing.

Eryaman, M.Y. and Bruce, B.C. (eds) (2015) *International handbook of progressive education.* New York: Peter Lang.

Fielding, M. (2013) 'Whole school meetings and the development of radical democratic community', *Studies in Philosophy and Education,* 32(2), 123–140.

Fielding, M. and Moss, P. (2011) *Radical education and the common school: A democratic alternative.* **London: Routledge.**

Flint, K.J. and Peim, N. (2012) *Rethinking the education improvement agenda: A critical philosophical approach.* London: Continuum.

Foucault, M. (1977) *Discipline and punish: The birth of the prison.* London: Penguin.

Goodsman, D. (1992) 'Summerhill: Theory and practice', unpublished PhD thesis, University of East Anglia.

Gray, P. and Riley, G. (2015) 'Grown unschoolers' evaluations of their unschooling experiences: Report I on a survey of 75 unschooled adults', *Other Education,* 4 (2), pp.8–32.

Greenberg, D. and Sadofsky, M. (1992) *Legacy of trust; Life after the Sudbury Valley School experience.* Framingham, MA: Sudbury Valley School Press.

Harber, C. (2004) *Schooling as violence: How schools harm pupils and societies.* London: RoutledgeFalmer.

Harber, C. (2009a) '"Revolution, what revolution?": Contextual issues in citizenship education in schools in England', *Citizenship, Social and Economics Education,* 8 (1), pp.42–53.

Harber, C. (2009b) *Toxic schooling: How schools became worse.* Nottingham: Educational Heretics Press.

Howlett, J. (2013) *Progressive education: A critical introduction.* London: Bloomsbury.

Lees, H.E. (2011) 'The Gateless Gate of home education discovery: What happens to the self of adults upon discovery of the possibility and possibilities of an educational alternative?', unpublished PhD

thesis, University of Birmingham, Birmingham. Available at: http://
etheses.bham.ac.uk/1570.

Lees, H.E., and Noddings, N. (eds) (2016) *The Palgrave international handbook of alternative education*. **London: Palgrave.**

Meighan, R. (2005) *Comparing learning systems: the good, the bad, the ugly, and the counter-productive*. Nottingham: Educational Heretics Press.

Miedema, E.L. (2016) *Exploring moral character in everyday life: Former democratic school student's understandings and school experiences.* Brighton: University of Brighton.

Neill, A.S. (1966) *Freedom: Not license!* New York: Hart Publishing Company, Inc.

Neuman, A. and Avriam, A. (2003) 'Homeschooling as a fundamental change in lifestyle', *Evaluation and Research in Education*, 17(2/3), 132–143.

Reay, D. (2012) 'What would a socially just education system look like?: Saving the minnows from the pike', *Journal of Education Policy*, 27 (5), pp.587–599.

Röhrs, H. and Lenhart, V. (eds) (1995) *Progressive education across the continents*. Frankfurt am Main: Peter Lang.

Sheffer, S. (1995) *A sense of self—Listening to home schooled adolescent girls*. Portsmouth, NH: Boynton/Cook Publishers.

Tsabar, B. (2014) 'Resistance and imperfection as educational work: Going against the "harmony" of individualistic ideology', *Other Education*, 3 (1), pp.23–40.

KEY CONCEPT: ASSESSMENT

Parminder Assi

Concept origins

The term 'assess' derives from the Latin verb 'assidere', which means 'to sit by', thereby implying the integral role of assessment (the making of judgements) is to support **learning** and **teaching**. Historically, the process of testing has dominated assessment practice, initially introduced in England to promote meritocracy, as prior to this the certification of learning and entry into occupations was largely by patronage (Black, 1998). In the 1920s, for example, the Moray House Tests of Edinburgh University were widely used in pursuit of this aim across the UK as a popular (and profitable) means of attempting to measure children's verbal reasoning ability and English and Maths competencies (SITC, 2007). This was one of the first early examples of systematic, 'to-order' assessment.

Current status and usage

Assessment (mainly through testing) is globally important in terms of discussion around *what* is assessed (in terms of knowledge understanding and skills), *how* and *when* this assessment is done and *why* (the purpose). Assessments may be constructed in a variety of ways for a range of purposes, depending on who decides the nature and content of the assessment (Stobart, 2008). The outcomes of assessment are important in terms of what these are used for and what these mean for learners, **teacher**s and other stakeholders. Increasingly, qualifications arising from assessments are deemed vital for career progression. Despite concerns raised about tests not accurately measuring aspects of **learning** which involve analysis, critique and synthesis (Gardner, 2006), these continue to dominate education, leading to an outcomes driven **curriculum** (Patrick, 1996). The current centrality of the assessment debate in England can be seen in concerns expressed about baseline assessment and 'readiness' of the youngest of students, even at age four. Here, a singular assessment is proposed to be administered to all, irrespective of the pupil's date of birth and irrespective of the diverse experiences of the learner to provide 'reliable' data (Bradbury and Roberts-Holmes, 2016). Such moves of **policy** and government meet with strong opposition from **educational research** quarters while the **teaching profession** appears unable to offer an alternative response due to the performative demands of targets and funding. In a sense, such imposed testing of four-year-olds is a sign of the ill-health of the system caused by assessment.

 There are numerous types of assessment in education, which we will start to look at here. We will begin with summative assessment. This describes the overall evidence of the achievement of an individual at a point in time (generally at the end of a period of **learning**), and this is often used to evaluate **teaching**, institutions and policies. This is often contrasted with formative assessment, which is integral to teaching and learning, being used often informally throughout the school day to check progression and provide feedback to the student. Alongside the variety of assessments, there are also different purposes these serve. Is the assessment designed to support the learning process? Is the assessment valid or reliable? Was the assessment designed for the purposes of **selection** by specific criteria? Is the assessment norm referenced? One English example of a norm-referenced, selective assessment can be seen in the testing process (11+ resulting from the 1944 Education Act). This test was promoted as being 'highly accurate' for predicting learning potential and became the principal means of allocating pupils to differing **school**s. With such tests students are placed in rank order and often pre-determined proportions are placed in various grade categories. This differs from criterion-referenced assessment, where the grade is based on the quality reached, irrespective of the performance of others, or *ipsative* assessment, where the performance is compared to the same pupil's previous achievement (Boud, 1988). With the growth in educational testing has come the creation of different sets of international comparisons, including Progress in International Reading Literacy Study (PIRLS), Trends in Mathematics and Science Study (TIMSS) and Programme for International Student Assessment (PISA). These tests globally compare the performance of diverse groups through common assessment tools. There are concerns raised on their methodological and statistical limitations and how these tests oversimplify complex global educational phenomena into relatively crude league tables (Grek, 2009). **Globalisation** and economic competition between nations has inevitably had an impact on assessment practices, and international assessment tables are predicated on supposed links between high 'standards' in assessments, employability and national economic growth. The range and scope of assessment processes centres on the debate about exactly what assessment is for: to support progression or for judging 'quality' (Gipps and Stobart, 1997; Black and Wiliam, 1998).

There are concerns that assessment has become de-theorised and disconnected from the **learning** process because of the dominance of *summative* assessment practices and attempts to raise standards. In response to this, the Assessment Reform Group, headed by Black and Wiliam (1998) promoted a '**paradigm** shift' in educational assessment, by focusing on ways in which assessment could help to advance learning rather than merely measure learning. This *formative* view of assessment (assessment *for* rather than *of* learning) reflects the ways learning is constructed in the social context of classroom interactions. Use of techniques such as questioning and discussion, enable **teachers** to gain an understanding of what pupils can do and how to guide their progression, and at the same time reflect on the effectiveness of their own **teaching.** This '**constructivist**' view of learning facilitates an equally active role for both learner and teacher in learning and teaching interactions and thereby places assessment as integral to the learning–teaching process.

While the summative purpose of assessment has raised concerns in that normative assumptions are made about the progress and maturation of unique individuals (Delandshere, 2001), there is also concern about how **power** is concealed in assessment and how assessment is implicated in the reproduction of inequality in educational experience and outcome. Reay and Wiliam (1999) explore how assessment leads to **labelling**, where the already 'successful' thrive and others 'under-achieve', leaving lasting effects on learner **motivation,** confidence and self-esteem. The use of assessment can be seen as contributing to an arbitrary notion of 'standards', reinforcing ideological representations of prescribed 'theory' of 'knowledge' and the 'roles' of **teacher** and learner. Foucault's work (1991) can be seen to place assessment as a site of power and authority in education as it regulates individuals. Assessment thus serves as surveillance, self-regulation and administrative control through associated processes, such as monitoring, tracking and levelling (Broadfoot, 2007; Gipps, 2012). Bourdieu's work (Bourdieu and Passeron, 1990) on the concept of **social capital** illustrates how assessment practices conceal power in terms of the **selection** of specific assessment content and process. This serves to reproduce inequality by making failure inevitable (by imposing a particular language in a broad sense) that is more accessible for some than others (Reay, 2001).

Questions to consider

1. Why is formative assessment difficult to implement in traditional classroom contexts?
2. Look at a standardised assessment tool (for example a reading test): what are your thoughts on the language, content and expectations represented?
3. Is testing fair?
4. Can we assess meaningfully across different individuals?
5. Why test?

References (with recommended readings in bold)

Black, P.J. (1998) *Testing, friend or foe?: The theory and practice of assessment and testing.* London: Falmer Press.

Black, P.J. and Wiliam, D. (1998) *Inside the black box: Raising standards through classroom assessment.* London: Kings College London.

Boud, D. (1988) *Developing student autonomy in learning.* London: Kogan Page.

Bourdieu, P. and Passeron, J. (1990) *Reproduction in education, society and culture.* London: Sage.

Bradbury, A. and Roberts-Holmes, G. (2016) *The introduction of reception baseline assessment: 'They are children ... not robots, not machines'.* London: ATL and NUT. Available at: www.teachers.org.uk/files/baseline-assessment–final-10404.pdf (accessed 28 November 2016).

Broadfoot, P. (2007) *An introduction to assessment.* London: Continuum.

Delandshere, G. (2001) 'Implict theories, unexamined assumptions and the status quo of educational assessment', *Assessment in Education*, 8 (2), pp.113–133.

Foucault, M. (1991) *Discipline and punish: The birth of the prison.* London: Penguin.

Gardner, J. (ed.) (2006) *Assessment and learning.* London: Sage.

Gipps, C. (2012) *Beyond testing: Towards a theory of educational assessment.* Abingdon: Routledge.

Gipps, C. and Stobart, G. (1997) *Assessment: A teacher's guide to the issues.* London: Hodder and Stoughton.

Grek, S. (2009) 'Governing by numbers: The PISA 'effect' in Europe', *Journal of Education Policy*, 24 (1), pp.23–37.

Patrick, H. (1996) 'Comparing public examination standards over time', BERA conference, Birkbeck College, London.

Reay, D. (2001) 'Finding or losing yourself?: Working-class relationships to education', *Journal of Education Policy*, 16 (4), pp.333–346.

Reay, D. and Wiliam, D. (1999): '"I'll be a nothing": Structure, agency and the construction of identity through assessment', *British Educational Research Journal*, 25 (3), pp.343–354.

SITC (2007) 'Test construction and the Moray House tests'. Available at: www.ces.ed.ac.uk/old_site/SSER/about/test.html (accessed 22 June 2017).

Stobart, G. (2008) *Testing times: The uses and abuses of assessment.* Abingdon: Routledge.

KEY CONCEPT: CARE

Gill Hughes

Concept origins

Exploring the origins of care as idea, van Manen stated 'the etymology of the term sorrow derives from the Danish, Swedish, Dutch, and German equivalents of *sorge/zorg* meaning anxiety and worry. [Thus] "I'm sorry" [translates to] "I care"' (2002, p.266). Petrie (2003, p.62) similarly identifies Old Teutonic and Old English 'care' as 'referr[ing] to anxiety, burden and concern (compare careworn and carefree)'. Petrie moves on to suggest that care developed into 'a charge or duty ... oversight of someone or something, surveillance with a view to protection, preservation or guidance (*Shorter Oxford English dictionary*)'. Foucault, exploring public health during the French revolution, saw care, in the work of Frank (1779), as having concern for 'wholesome food, good housing, health care, and medical institutions which the population needs to remain healthy, in short to foster the life of individuals' (Foucault *et al.*, 1988, p.147). It was here that 'care' became a 'duty for the state'. Thus, Foucault and Petrie's identification of the notion of duty underpins the current requirements within **schools**—that staff, *in loco parentis*, have a 'duty of care', a governmental responsibility to manage and care for the **school** population (Foucault, 2009). Foucault also remarked on ancient Greek notions of 'care for oneself' in his work on sexualities (1986).

Current status and usage

Current discussions on care emanate from the development of the **ethics** of care in the 1980s in the US, attributed to Gilligan (1982) and Noddings (2003). By foregrounding the role and contribution of women, the ethics-of-care sought to counter the reliance on what they saw as a more masculine objectivity and universalism in traditional deontological ethical thinking derived from Kant (1724–1804). Held explicates the difference: '[a]n ethic of justice focuses on questions of fairness, **equality**, individual rights, abstract principles, and the[ir] consistent application. An ethic-of-care focuses on attentiveness, trust, responsiveness to need, narrative nuance, and cultivating caring relations' (Held, 2006, p.15). In the UK at the same time, the women's movement challenged the **essentialist** alliance of women with care, which undermined **equality** of opportunities (Finch and Groves, 1983). Ruddick (1995, p.217) contended a merger was necessary; 'justice is always seen in tandem with care'. Thus, despite critiques, the ethics-of-care influenced contemporary theorists, offering permission to deconstruct care, within context and in relation to others; '[the] ethics of care provide a different way of thinking about care ... [it] moves us from care as a task performed by adults on children, to care within relational encounters of all forms' (Moss, 2003, p.39).

Rogers and Webb posit that 'our knowledge of caring is tacit; it is implicit in action. In other words, although we have difficulty defining it, we know it when we see it' (1991, p.177). Years on, Moss concluded that '[c]are ... is one of those words ... much used ... less often examined' (2014, p.422). Fine offers the old adage of 'apple pie and motherhood' as a means of suggesting care's eminent 'goodness' (2007, p.23). Noddings said '[s]tudents in a given high **school** say that they want **teacher**s to care for them, but "nobody cares". Their teachers make a convincing case that they *do* care ... Through a relational perspective, we are encouraged to study the conditions that make it possible for caring relations to flourish' (Noddings, 2003, p.xiv). If connection to school relies on young people feeling cared about as individuals and their **learning**, then it is necessary to understand the subjective and contested construct of care and how it might manifest in relation to the 'duty' applied in education. Identifying a 'relational' model is key: care must be offered and acknowledged to work and be indeed care (Fischer and Tronto, 1990; Noddings, 2002). The circularity represents a process: the carer recognises that the caree is in need of care. This is referred to as 'receptive attention' (Noddings, 2002, p.17). The carer offers care—'motivational displacement'—the carer's 'motive energy begins to flow to' the caree, and if the caree acknowledges the receipt of the gesture as care, this connotes the exchange of care has taken place. If the caree does not acknowledge the gesture as care, the encounter has faltered (Noddings, 2002). As one person's care might be another's control, it is precarious, so care needs to be defined and negotiated and is dialogic. Noddings posits that where care does not seem to have taken place despite good intentions, '[t]he teachers may or may not be at fault, and the same can be said of the students. Both may be blameless, and the fault may lie in the situation—in the structures and routines of their school' (Noddings, 2003, p.xiv). Practices under **neo-liberal** education systems can constrain the relational process of care (see **democratic education**, **alternative education** and **unschooling** for discussion of other settings).

So how can care be conceptualised in practice? Noddings draws out 'listening and responding', 'humour' and 'curiosity' as ways of demonstrating care (2003, p.244). Tronto offers 'attentiveness, responsibility, competence and responsiveness' (1993, p.127). Later, Tronto stated importantly 'care expresses **relationships**', and can demonstrate 'deepest convictions … I care about' (Tronto, 2013, p.x). Hughes (2016) undertook **empirical** research with young people and adult students to understand how care played out in practice within **school**s in their experience and identified feelings of being 'Looked after, bothered about, listened to, safe, belonging, warmth, being known and understood [context], being interested, funny [also banter/laugh/teasing], firm but fair, constructive, honest, consistent/stability, interesting and creative **teaching**, being human, respect, environment, time, being nice' (Hughes, 2016, p.183). With no firm definition of care, these responses can be designated as signifiers-of-care (Hughes, 2016). Such signifiers suggest that understanding context and knowing young people will underpin relational care.

To explore further layers of care in practice, Hughes (2016) offers three domains-of-care for exploration: the personal, considered more intimate and non-conditional associated with familial care; the private domain, where care can be a commodity, a care package—a monetary unit of social care; and the public, where a **profession**-led practitioner might be charged with a duty to care. Natural care would be associated with the personal domain. In practice, it is important to be mindful of crossing boundaries—a professional cannot offer unconditional care, but equally if the signifiers-of-care illuminate how care might be experienced, 'actions or dispositions' (Tronto, 2013) must go further than formal duties enshrined within health and safety policies. Thus, 'ethical caring [which] derives its strength from natural caring' (Noddings,

2013, p.xvi), but halts before intimacy, may be called upon where natural care is inappropriate, or as Noddings (2013, p.xvi) posits, when it is required in 'difficult' and 'complicated' situations, where a connection is not apparent between practitioner and young person. Ethical care draws from the memory of when 'we are at our caring best. And through this challenging process of reflection, we decide what to do, how to respond' (Noddings, 2013, p.xvi). Noddings' 'relational ontology' (2013, p.206) suggests care as a way of being in the world, requiring negotiated care before personal/intimate, to delineate inappropriate crossing of professional boundaries, and beyond public/duty of just fulfilling legal requirements to reach the nexus of relational-care. Tronto posits care is 'a practice rather than a set of rules or principles ... It involves particular acts of caring and a 'general habit of mind' to care that should inform all aspects of moral life' (Tronto, 1993, p.127). Thus, utilising a 'lens of care' (Barnes, 2012, p.5) could influence any decisions and practices within education.

Questions to consider

1. How would you define care?
2. How could you know whether a **teacher** cared about you or your **learning**?
3. Did relational connections impact your engagement with staff, **curriculum** and more generally with **school**?
4. How could school practices encompass care at the centre of decision making?

References (with recommended readings in bold)

Barnes, M. (2012) *Care in everyday life: An ethic of care in practice.* Bristol: Policy Press.

Finch, J. and Groves, D. (eds) (1983) *A labour of love: Women, work, and caring.* London: Routledge and Kegan Paul.

Fine, M.D. (2007) *A caring society? Care and the dilemmas of human service in the twenty-first century.* Basingstoke: Palgrave Macmillan.

Fischer, B. and Tronto, J. (1990) 'Toward a feminist theory of caring', in Abel, E.K. and Nelson, M.K. (eds) *Circles of care: Work and identity in women's lives.* Albany, NY: State University of New York Press, pp.35–62.

Foucault, M. (1986) *The care of the self: The history of sexuality, volume 3.* London: Penguin.

Foucault, M. (2009) *Security, territory, population: Lectures at the Collège de France 1977-1978*, vol. 4. Basingstoke: Palgrave Macmillan.

Foucault, M., Martin, L.H., Gutman, H. and Hutton, P.H. (1988) *Technologies of the self: A seminar with Michel Foucault*. Amherst, MA: University of Massachusetts Press.

Gilligan, C. (1982) *In a different voice: Psychological theory and women's development*. Cambridge MA: Harvard University Press.

Held, V. (2005) *The ethics of care: Personal, political, and global*. Oxford: Oxford University Press.

Hughes, G. (2016) 'The construct of care and its place in school connectedness', PhD thesis, University of Hull.

Moss, P. (2003) 'Getting beyond childcare: Reflections on recent policy and future possibilities', in Brannen, J. and Moss, P. (eds) *Rethinking children's care*. Milton Keynes: Open University Press, pp.25–43.

Moss, P. (2014) 'The social protection floor: What place for care?', *Global Social Policy*, 14 (3), pp.422–431.

Noddings, N. (2002) *Starting at home: Caring and social policy*. Berkeley: University of California Press.

Noddings, N. (2003) *Caring: A feminine approach to ethics and moral education*, 2nd edn. Berkeley: University of California Press.

Noddings, N. (2013) *Caring: A relational approach to ethics and moral education*, 2nd edn. Berkeley: University of California Press.

Petrie, P. (2003) 'Social pedagogy: An historical account of care and education as social control', in Brannen, J. and Moss, P. (eds) *Rethinking children's care*. Milton Keynes: Open University Press, pp.61–79.

Rogers, D. and Webb, J. (1991) 'The ethic of caring in teacher education', *Journal of Teacher Education*, 42(3), pp.173–181.

Ruddick, S. (1995) *Maternal thinking: Toward a politics of peace*. Boston, MA: Beacon Press.

Tronto, J.C. (1993) *Moral boundaries: A political argument for an ethic of care*. London: Routledge.

Tronto, J.C. (2013) *Caring democracy: Markets, equality, and justice*. New York: New York University Press.

van Manen, M. (2002) 'Care-as-worry, or "don't worry, be happy"', *Qualitative Health Research*, 12 (2), pp.262–278.

KEY CONCEPT: CURRICULUM

Dave Trotman

Concept origins

In the lexicon of education, curriculum is one of the well-established concepts. From the Latin root *currere,* to run the racecourse, the origins of the term reveal this concept as fluid, unpredictable and indeterminate. In the UK, the work of Hirst (1975) is well known for promoting the idea of curriculum being concerned with 'forms of knowledge'. Bernstein (1971) meanwhile notes that the **selection**, classification, distribution, transmission and evaluation of educational knowledge by **society** through a curriculum reflect both the distribution of **power** and also principles of social control. For other scholars of curriculum (see Schubert, 1986; Slattery, 1995), *currere* emphasises the capacity of the individual to reflect upon and reconceptualise their own lifecourse.

Current status and usage

In much of its contemporary usage, curriculum in its verb form of *currere* has been obscured by a version that favours 'fixed objects' of content, subjects, programmes of study and syllabi for **school** settings. In England and much of the UK, the concept of curriculum has become synonymous with the idea of a National Curriculum, involving centrally prescribed content, structures and **assessment**, as well as a given world view of what matters. This view of the curriculum as national and uniform is something of a misnomer, in that while each nation of the UK under devolved government has responsibility to design its own programme content, the prescribed subjects in fact only account for part of the total curriculum experience encountered by children and young people. Common usage of the term typically reduces curriculum to that which is visible, static and subject to external control.

Much of the literature on curriculum reveals this concept as complex and somewhat indeterminate. Among the many definitions, Marsh (1997, p.3) includes the following: That which is taught in **school**; a set of subjects; content; a set of materials; performance objectives; that which is taught both inside and outside of school and directed by the school; that which an individual learner experiences as a result of **schooling**; everything that is planned by school personnel. In attempting to make sense of the complexity of curriculum, one popular approach is to categorise it in terms of the official, the informal and the hidden. The official curriculum can be regarded as publicly stated contents, subjects and intended outcomes, such as a national curriculum that may then be subject to legal enforcement. This then is a public and clearly defined framework of intention and content. The inference here is that a curriculum is something residing exclusively in schools. While the official curriculum is a programme of study or activity designed and endorsed by a school or other external bodies, the informal curriculum, as the name suggests, embraces aspects of experience and **learning** that arise through other means: not officially prescribed or directed. Among school-based examples are informal **teacher**-student conversations, school clubs, or aspects of curriculum enrichment such as off-site visits and field trips. The **hidden curriculum** involves those aspects of school learning and experience that while not publicly expressed are nonetheless often powerfully communicated to children and young people. Among examples of this are subjects that appear to be deemed more important than others in the hierarchy of curriculum, how teacher **behaviour**s affect (positively and negatively) the experiences of pupils, the values schools seek to advance and how communities or groups are represented and valued. Recent research reported in the field of **elective home education** offers a different perspective by advancing a cultural curriculum: enacted through casual, often lengthy and in-depth conversations within families and among friends about how the world is experienced and the nature of successful learning (Pattison and Thomas, 2016).

In Kelly's (2009) writing on curriculum, he proposes its **relationship** with education can be understood in three ways: curriculum as content and education as transmission; curriculum as product and education as **instrumental**; curriculum as process and education as development. In the first of these ways, the curriculum is concerned with the transmission of specifically determined content deemed of importance for future participants in **society**—education then is principally a matter of transmission. In the framing of curriculum as product, curriculum is a matter of assessable objectives which are largely value-free. Drawing on the traditions of behavioural psychology, an objectives-led curriculum sees education as an instrumental enterprise amenable to the measurement of effectiveness and efficiency. In Kelly's third example, curriculum is viewed as a process through which individuals are 'assisted towards the highest levels of **autonomous** human functioning' (Kelly, 1989, p.112). A curriculum involving processes of exploration, discovery and guided **learning** then offers the possibility of an education that is both developmental and a basis for future independent learning. This account is useful because it makes an explicit connection between the curriculum and the wider educational ambitions and purposes of those who have responsibility for curriculum design.

⌣ While each of the above approaches offers a helpful introduction to ways in which we might delineate the curriculum in terms of how it functions and its educational purposes, the concept, as the origins of the term suggests, is complex. As Goodson (1994, p.111) has noted, the curriculum is 'a multifaceted concept, constructed and negotiated at a variety of levels and in a variety of arenas'. Apple (1993) has argued that any curriculum is not a neutral assemblage of knowledge, but rather part of a selective tradition: 'someone's **selection**, some group's vision of legitimate knowledge', telling us important things about who has **power** in **society**. While there has been a common adoption in many developed countries of a curriculum built on 'forms of knowledge' (see e.g., the work of Paul Hirst, 1975)—in which prescribed subjects are afforded hierarchies of privilege on **school** timetables—postmodern readings of the curriculum return to it as *currere*. Doll's (1993) postmodern view of the curriculum sees this as an open and fluid phenomenon, not closed or static, but one where principles of chaos and emergence can allow knowledge **transformation**. In this sense, postmodern approaches conceptualise curriculum as socially constructed and knowledge as provisional and contested. Combined with a global context in which contemporary electronic media contribute to rapid changes and re-shaping of knowledge (Bartlett and Burton, 2012, p.101), postmodern perspectives of the curriculum underscore personal journeys, narratives and uncertainties.

Questions to consider

1. Who decides the **school** curriculum?
2. Who should decide a curriculum?
3. What forces affect the design and experience of curricula?
4. How does the curriculum relate to what school pupils experience and learn?
5. Can/should a curriculum be prescribed as a national programme?

References (with recommended readings in bold)

Apple, M.W. (1993) 'The politics of official knowledge: Does a national curriculum make sense', *Teachers College Record*, 95 (2), pp.222–241.

Bartlett, S. and Burton, D. (2012) *Introduction to education studies*, 3rd edn. London: Sage.

Bernstein, B. (1971) 'On the classification and framing of educational knowledge', in Young, M.F.D. (ed.) *Knowledge and control: New directions for the sociology of education*. London: Routledge.

Doll, W.E. (1993) *A post-modern perspective on curriculum*. New York: Teachers College Press.

Goodson, I.F. (1994) *Studying curriculum*. New York: Teachers College Press.

Hirst, P.H. (1975) *Knowledge and the curriculum*. London: Routledge and Kegan Paul.

Kelly, A.V. (1989) *The curriculum: Theory and practice*, 3rd edn. London: Paul Chapman Publishing.

Kelly, A.V. (2009) *The curriculum theory and practice*, 6th edn. London: Sage.

Marsh, C.J. (1997) *Perspectives: Key concepts for understanding curriculum*. London: Falmer Press.

Pattison, H. and Thomas, A. (2016) 'Great expectations: Agenda and authority in technological, hidden and cultural curriculums', in Lees, H.E. and Noddings, N. (eds) *The Palgrave international handbook of alternative education*. London: Palgrave, pp.129–144.

Schubert, W.H. (1986) *Curriculum: perspectives, paradigm, possibility*. New York: Macmillan.

Slattery, P. (1995) *Curriculum development in the post modern era*. New York: Garland Publishing.

KEY CONCEPT: DEMOCRATIC EDUCATION

Helen E. Lees

Concept origins

'Democratic education' means many things to many people, but there are two clear directions. On the one hand are those who see **mainstream** **school** itself as a form of 'common', democratically and politically inclined education, with organisational and pedagogical aspirations to be free and accessible to all, on equal terms (Fielding and Moss, 2011; Reay, 2012). On the other hand, 'democratic education' is a **pedagogy** and form of organisation in presently a few **alternative education** schools, where **voice** and choice for students at every level of their education matters and occurs—from what they wear, to what they study. A relationship to the democratic state or **society** is an important element of such education, but that relationship to the state is ultimately *secondary* to personal feelings of *democratic interpersonal* outcomes. Such an education is said by A.S. Neill, as one famous exponent, to involve 'freedom not licence' (Neill, 1966, 1968). Historically, democratic education starts perhaps with the polis of ancient Greece and, in particular, Socrates' manner of dialogue to develop the critical thought of philosophical interlocutors. However, this form of education was democratic for only an elite group, whose role it was to run the demos. More recently John Dewey (1916) is considered a key developer of the concept of democratic education for all because of his ideas about the school as a place in which democracy is learnt. Whether that does occur in reality or not is debatable.

Current status and usage

In contemporary **society**, increases in testing, **assessment**, competition, **authoritarian** tropes and other anti-democratic elements, mean that **school**, around the world, struggles to be democratic in any meaningful way (Harber, 2004, 2009; Harber and Mncube, 2012). In a small number of carefully considered schooling projects—e.g., Summerhill and Sands in the UK (see Gribble, 2001), Sudbury Valley schools in the US (Schwartz and Maher, 2006) and schools in Israel, Germany, the Netherlands, Japan and elsewhere—reports are of a viable and flourishing sector of the educational landscape. There is a rise in the creation of such schools being reported in informal ways. A shift in appreciation and understanding of beneficial outcomes from democratic education among **policy** makers and the general public is, however, still in process. **Neoliberal, mainstream** preoccupations with inspection for standards are a constant threat to the approach of such schools because their ideas and practices still struggle with foreclosures of possibilities due to the relationship of education with the state and its socio-economic-political imperatives (Flint and Peim, 2012) as well as strengthened governance by neoliberal forces (Ball, 2007).

At the most basic level, democratic education is considered in two ways: the concern of parents (and a particular kind of **teacher**) for their children in terms of a type of equal-and-**voice**-led educational experience, and the business of the state for **society**. Those who see it as education linked to the socially political consider education's role to be extremely powerful: 'issues of democratic education raise general questions about democracy and democratic **citizenship**' (Gutmann, 2008, p.xii). On the other hand—and we could also call it the other side—some parents are focused on children feeling free to be and express themselves without undue pressure from **mainstream school** as an organ of the state. Given that the state has the bigger social picture in mind than the particularities of individual children and their families, parents may be right to question what the state stands for and can 'do' to their children through its educational formation. Others, however, question the removal of children from state education on the grounds of anti-democratic (in the state sense) sentiments (Apple, 2000).

Of course, achieving *personal* democratic interactions of any kind is a long haul and a specialist project. There are organisations such as the Phoenix Trust (UK) aiming to develop on-the-ground democratic **behaviour**s within a **mainstream school**'s organisational principles—through forums for **voice** and **equality**. These kinds of endeavours may achieve some success as dedicated consultants for lessened **authoritarianism.** Others go for a 'good enough' approach to **power** and its **relationality** involving fairness and respect for individuality (Bingham, 2008). As research into the democratisation of school environments through '**citizenship**' initiatives shows (Hannam, 2001; Harber, 2009), the **learning** curve is a steep one: voluntariness and capacity for democratic voice-led interactions of **teachers** trained to fit the mainstream system is largely absent. Most teachers are trained to be in charge of their environment, which conditions their perspective on any interactions needing a firm hand: they were trained to be in charge and are judged as 'good' teachers on account of their ability to seem in charge with unequal authority. Voice for students continues to be largely tokenistic, except for teachers who find this relational dynamic uncomfortable and anti-child. Many of these teachers seem to struggle to remain within school environments that do not agree with their democratic views. For students to *experience* schooling democratically (instead of being taught *about* democracy or being part of a democratic state project), such a release and change is required on the part of the **teaching** staff first. The **dissonance** between rhetoric and reality about democratic education (as experience and as curricula object) is an international issue affecting schools around the world because a **colonial** mentality of the master–slave dynamic persists in schooling, under the guise of needful authority (Harber, 2004, 2012). Many children suffer greatly from the maintenance of unequal **power** in school and 'exit' into **elective home education**, **alternative provision** or school refusal as a result of having no voice (Yoneyama, 1999; Fortune-Wood, 2007; Lees, 2014; Lees and Noddings, 2016).

Emerging research data from small democratic schools is encouraging. In considering dimensions such as moral development and entrepreneurial spirit (Miedema, 2016), happiness across the life-span (Lucas, 2011), and the development of trust in education (Goodsman, 1992; Greenberg and Sadofsky, 1992), such studies broadly support the efficacy of democratic interactions. They do not breed chaos or cause a loss of **power**, but can instead promote an often-gradual shift towards fair dealings for all. Thus, the fostering of student voice through personalised relational **pedagogy** and formalised 'Meetings' (Fielding, 2013) is good for children, developing their skills for negotiation, listening and tolerance. Conversely, deficits in these areas can be positively detrimental for many children (Pilkington and Piersel, 1991; Carlen et al., 1992). In sum, all educationists have a responsibility to ask: 'From whence comes a desire to dominate others and be anti-democratic at the personal level in education?' Responses to this question might highlight a variety of factors, such as a lack of knowledge about the role of **consent** in promoting human well-being, to assumptions that unequal power and a lack of 'educational mutuality' is appropriate. Elsewhere (Lees, 2016), I have argued that a lack of consent-seeking may actually signal an inherently anti-child attitude. To have an education system where democracy is its ethos and organising principle (see e.g., Neary and Winn, 2015), would be a radical change in how education works. Already we see some of this with the rise of a technological democratisation of knowledge, for example with Massive Open Online Courses (MOOCs) being made available to anyone with internet access and through alternatively styled pedagogy (Rix and McElwee, 2016). The idea of allowing people to choose for themselves how and what to learn opens up a Pandora's box: there is not a single concept in this book unaffected by such a change.

Questions to consider

1. What is a democratic **school** environment?
2. What happens to **teacher**s and children in education when they listen and heed each other?
3. What does following one's own interests do to our concept of education?
4. What outcomes do real-life experiences of having **power** as a child have on personal and social formation, in the short and long term?
5. Who is democratic?

References (with recommended readings in bold)

Apple, M.W. (2000) 'Away with all teachers: The cultural politics of home schooling', *International Studies in Sociology of Education*, 10 (1), pp.61–80.

Ball, S.J. (2007) *Education plc: Understanding private sector participation in public sector education*. Abingdon: Routledge.

Bingham, C. (2008) *Authority is relational*. Albany: State University of New York Press.

Carlen, P., Gleeson, D. and Wardhaugh, J. (1992) *Truancy: The politics of compulsory schooling*. Buckingham: Open University Press.

Dewey, J. (1916) *Democracy and education.* New York: Free Press, 1944.

Fielding, M. (2013) 'Whole school meetings and the develop-ment of radical democratic community', *Studies in Philosophy and Education*, 32 (2), pp.123–140.

Fielding, M. and Moss, P. (2011) *Radical education and the common school: A democratic alternative.* London: Routledge.

Flint, K.J. and Peim, N. (2012) *Rethinking the education improvement agenda: A critical philosophical approach.* London: Continuum.

Fortune-Wood, M. (2007) *Can't go won't go: An alternative approach to school refusal.* Blaenau Ffestiniog: Cinnamon Press.

Goodsman, D. (1992) 'Summerhill: Theory and practice', unpublished PhD thesis, University of East Anglia.

Greenberg, D. and Sadofsky, M. (1992) *Legacy of trust; Life after the Sudbury Valley School experience.* Framingham, MA: Sudbury Valley School Press.

Gribble, D. (2001) *Worlds apart.* London: Libertarian Education.

Gutmann, A. (2008) *Democratic education.* Princeton, NJ: Princeton University Press.

Hannam, D. (2001) *A pilot study to evaluate the impact of the student partici-pation aspects of the citizenship order on standards of education in secondary schools.* London: Independent report to the DfEE.

Harber, C. (2004) *Schooling as violence: How schools harm pupils and socie-ties.* London: RoutledgeFalmer.

Harber, C. (2009) '"Revolution, what revolution?": Contextual issues in citizenship education in schools in England', *Citizenship, Social and Economics Education*, 8 (1), pp.42–53.

Harber, C. and Mncube, V. (2012) 'Democracy, education and develop-ment: Theory and reality', *Other Education*, 1 (1), pp.104–120.

Lees, H.E. (2014) *Education without schools: Discovering alternatives.* Bris-tol: Policy Press.

Lees, H.E. (2016) 'Educational mutuality', in Lees, H.E. and Noddings, N. (eds) *The Palgrave international handbook of alternative education.* London: Palgrave MacMillan, pp.159–175.

Lees, H.E. and Noddings, N. (eds) (2016) *The Palgrave international handbook of alternative education.* London: Palgrave Macmillan.

Lucas, H. (2011) *After Summerhill: What happened to the pupils of Britain's most radical school?* Bristol: Pomegranate Books.

Miedema, L.E. (2016) '*Exploring moral character in everyday life: Former democratic school students' understandings and school experiences',* unpub-lished MPhil thesis, University of Brighton, Sussex.

Neary, M. and Winn, J. (2015) 'Beyond private and public: A model for co-operative higher education', *Krisis: Journal for Contemporary Philosophy*, 2, pp.114–119.

Neill, A.S. (1966) *Freedom: Not license!* New York: Hart Publishing.

Neill, A.S. (1968) *Summerhill*. Harmondsworth: Penguin.

Pilkington, C.L. and Piersel, W.C. (1991) 'School phobia—a critical analysis of the separation anxiety theory and an alternative conceptualization', *Psychology in the Schools*, 28 (4), pp.290–303.

Reay, D. (2012) 'What would a socially just education system look like?: Saving the minnows from the pike', *Journal of Education Policy*, 27 (5), pp.587–599.

Rix, S. and McElwee, S. (2016) 'What happens if students are asked to learn Geography content, specifically population, through SOLE?', *Other Education*, 5 (1), pp.30–54.

Schwartz, J. and Maher, T. (eds) (2006) *Trusting children: A look at Sudbury education around the world*. Salt Lake City, UT: Sego Lily School.

Yoneyama, S. (1999) *The Japanese high school: Silence and resistance*. London: Routledge.

KEY CONCEPT: DIVERSITY

Parminder Assi

Concept origins

The concept of diversity is used as an addition to the concept of **equality** in education. It is about recognising individual as well as group differences, treating people as individuals and placing *positive* value on differences. The term is linked to the 1948 UN Universal Declaration of **Human Rights**, which recognises and stipulates basic human rights, including civic, political, economic, social and cultural rights and the right to protection from abuse and exploitation. Since the end of the Second World War immigration from the former colonies of Western European nations to places such as the UK, France and Germany has increased **ethnic**, cultural, linguistic and religious diversity in societies and has raised discussions about how to make the most of human potential. The concept of diversity is integral to discussions around global **citizenship**, the promotion of pluralistic values and provision of just educational provision. Due to the ways in which places like the US and Australia were largely created in more recent history by immigration, such societies are incredibly multicultural. This has, however, not meant that indigenous population issues and historical concerns with **race** have not been serious matters. The history of diversity is diverse and dependent on national as well as international stories.

Current status and usage

Diversity includes all the ways in which people differ, such as **race**, **ethnicity** and **gender**, but also age, national origin, religion, **disability**, sexual orientation, socio-economic status, educational need, marital status, language and physical appearance. In terms of education, diversity is thus centred on these characteristics in individuals as they can affect the **learning** and development process. Current usage of diversity as a concept in education is focused on **inclusion** of provision in order to investigate how characteristics of diversity may be linked to differing educational experience and outcomes for groups and individuals. Promoting diversity in educational settings involves the interrogation of ideas, perspectives, structures and values, as well as political realities which may serve to disempower individuals and limit their participation. Educational provision for students with English as an additional language (EAL) is one area in **school**s in the UK where diversity plays itself out. Multiple issues thus surface connected to fairness, expectations and geography (some areas of a country having greater numbers of immigrant and refugee children), as well as issues to do with **teacher** training and the idea of diverse learners as posing problems for classrooms (Butcher *et al.*, 2007).

Cole (2012) notes that the concept of diversity relates to **human rights** and **equality** and refers to the importance of recognising difference and ensuring equity in terms of access and participation in the community and workforce. Historically, educational services have ignored certain differences such as cultural, **ethnic**, linguistic, religious and socioeconomic. One example is the way in which monolingual **discourses** have been privileged, and needs of speakers of languages other than 'dominant' languages have been omitted from **policy** and practice. Here **assimilationist** beliefs have held sway, with the assumption being that immigrant groups have to forsake their original **culture** and language in order to 'fit' in (Safford, 2003). Speakers of other languages have thus been seen as 'deficient' and their possible value has been sidelined by discourses of problems caused by their diversity (Butcher *et al.*, 2007). Often educational provision has been inappropriate (i.e., integration of foreign language speakers into groups with pupils having a **learning** difficulty, echoing the assumption that not speaking English equals no *ability*), which can cause issues for children's self-esteem (Siraj-Blatchford and Clarke, 2000). The adherence to a 'universal' age-related model of language development and **assessment** has further exacerbated disadvantages faced by diverse language speakers. More recent approaches evidence a recognition of diversity, for example, implementation of initiatives to monitor experiences of different groups to see how provision may need adjusting to cater to both individuals and groups. However, these initiatives stem from an economically driven, **performativity** agenda to raise educational standards (DfE, 2012), rather than address needs of individuals. Therefore, they may fail to make any meaningful change to practice.

⚙ **Policy** and legal frameworks in England are examples of attempts to address diversity issues through fair dealing. These frameworks include the Equality Act 2010, which makes it unlawful for public-, private- and voluntary-sector providers of goods and services to treat employees and/or service users less favourably on the grounds of actual or assumed difference for 'protected characteristics' (EHRC, 2015). This one piece of legislation combines previous **law**s such as the Equal Pay Act 1970, Sex **Discrimination** Act 1975, Race Relations Act 1976 and **Disability** Discrimination Act 1995. This was a way of 'simplifying legislation and harmonising protection for all of the characteristics covered [and] will help Britain become a fairer **society**, improve public services, and help business perform well' (EHRC, 2015). Tatchell (cited in Cole, 2012) identifies a range of discussions which argue that the Equality Act does *not* address all characteristics and that there are a number of compromises within the categories, including economic and social rights. Although the law and legislative frameworks can effectively tackle forms of inequality, it can be argued that a **culture** of compliance may promote an approach to **equality** and diversity that is driven by legal duties, at the expense of real and meaningful equality. Banks (2016) suggests that adherence to policy initiatives without a meaningful dismantling of hierarchy, structured along lines such as **class**, **race** and **gender**, are doomed to failure. Taking the example of the perceived 'failure' of **multicultural** education, he argues that when multiculturalism is viewed solely as change in **curriculum** content (rather than the dismantling of attitudes, beliefs and entrenched **institutional** practices), the celebration of diversity is impaired.

☺ Fundamental to the promotion of diversity is the recognition of **power** imbalances that exist at a micro and macro level in education: treating individuals fairly does not mean treating all in the same way. Nor does a rhetoric of **equality** equal a system that behaves equally (Reay, *et al.*, 2008; Reay, 2012). Educators have a responsibility to recognise such issues and acknowledge their existence, so that perpetuation of power imbalances and inequality in the face of diversity do not cause detriment to some. At a time when increased global migration poses opportunities to enrich **society** with increased diversity, the challenge of promoting unity in the context of pluralistic values necessitates that effective safeguards are in place to ensure that diversity is valued (Osler and Starkey, 2010; Wilkinson and Pickett, 2009). With a rise in global migration, the post-Second World War 'return' of the political right and a rejection of open borders in some countries, such 'welcoming' attitudes are proving hard to maintain.

Questions to consider

1. Which areas of education do you think diversity has most impact on and how?
2. What areas of **equality** and diversity within **education** do you think require improvement?
3. What works well in education regarding a respect for diversity?
4. Who can influence policies towards diversity?
5. Is diversity an educational issue or primarily a political or social one?

References (with recommended readings in bold)

Banks, J.A. (2016) *Cultural diversity and education: Foundations, curriculum and teaching*, 6th edn. London: Routledge.

Butcher, J., Sinka, I. and Troman, G. (2007) 'Exploring diversity: Teacher education policy and bilingualism', *Research Papers in Education*, 22 (4), pp.483–501.

Cole, M. (2012) *Education equality and human rights: Issues of gender, 'race', sexuality, disability and social class*, 3rd edn. Abingdon: Routledge.

DfE (2012) *Including all learners*. London: Department for Education.

EHRC (2015) *Equality Act Guidance*. Equality and Human Rights Commission. Available at: www.equalityhumanrights.com/en/advice-and-guidance/equality-act-guidance (accessed 20 November 2016).

Equality Act 2010. Available at: www.legislation.gov.uk/ukpga/2010/15/pdfs/ukpga_20100015_en (accessed 27 October 2016).

Osler, A, and Starkey, H. (2010) *Teachers and human rights education*. London: David Fulton.

Reay, D. (2012) 'What would a socially just education system look like?: Saving the minnows from the pike', *Journal of Education Policy*, 27 (5), pp.587–599.

Reay, D., Crozier, G., James, D., Hollingworth, S., Williams, K., Jamieson, F. and Beedell, P. (2008) 'Re-invigorating democracy?: White middle class identities and comprehensive schooling', *The Sociological Review*, 56 (2), pp.238–255.

Safford, K. (2003) *Teachers and pupils in the big picture: Seeing real children in routinised assessment.* Watford: NALDIC.

Siraj-Blatchford, I. and Clarke, P. (2000) *Supporting identity, diversity and language in the early years.* Buckingham: Open University Press.

Wilkinson, R. and Pickett, K. (2009) *The spirit level: Why more equal societies almost always do better.* London: Penguin Books.

KEY CONCEPT: EDUCATION RESEARCH

Dave Trotman

Concept origins

From the late 16th century, obsolete French: *recerche* (noun) and *recercher* (verb) 'to search'. In their introduction to *Research methods in education*, Cohen *et al.* (2011) assert that humankind has a long-standing concern to make sense of its environment and to 'understand the nature of phenomena' as it is revealed to the senses. Drawing on the work of Mouly (1978), they contend that this 'search for truth' can be classified into three categories: experience, reasoning and research. The origins of research, then, can be considered to range from enquiry (to ask about phenomena) to inquiry as a formal investigation.

Current status and usage

In describing the current usage of the concept, it is helpful to turn first to those research associations that make explicit declarations about the nature of educational research and its primary purpose. The American Educational Research Association, for instance, describes education research as 'the scientific field of study that examines education and **learning** processes and the human attributes, interactions, organisations, and institutions that shape educational outcomes' (AERA, n.d.). The British Educational Research Association, in turn, asserts that the aim of educational research is to 'extend knowledge and understanding in all areas of educational activity' (BERA, n.d.). The Australian Association for Research in Education reflects the ambitions of many in its pursuit of 'educational research to enhance the public good' (AARE, n.d.). Acknowledging the multidisciplinary interests of those undertaking educational research, BERA reflects a well-recognised position that 'truth' and 'reality' are contested ideas and that different research standpoints generate important creative tensions for the enhancement of intellectual capital (BERA, 2011, p.4). For AERA, rigorous research also involves the development of new tools and methods. Hence, in the current usage of the term educational (or education) research, we should recognise, first and foremost, that the conduct of research is neither fixed nor uniform, but fluid and dynamic.

To get a better understanding of the concept, we should first think about the essential difference between 'finding out' and conducting research. Often the term 'research' is applied as a general shorthand for *finding things out*—where to go on holiday, which is the best gadget to buy, who was the leading actress in a film, which countries make up NATO, etc. Finding out can be driven by a particular need, problem, interest or simple curiosity. Often, this will involve the searching out of basic information, most commonly these days through the internet, social media, or simply by asking someone who is more knowledgeable. Like 'finding out', *researching* frequently begins on the basis of a particular concern, problem, interest, curiosity or speculation. Where this progresses differently is with the need to understand research as a *systematic inquiry* (Merriam, 2009, p.1); this involves the person or people undertaking the research to consider carefully why they wish to conduct the research, what they are going to do and how they intend to do it in a methodical, considered and rigorous manner (Kellett, 2005, p.10). Often this manner is acquired by virtue of specialist research methods courses. The ways in which a question, assertion or interest might be researched will depend upon the nature of the phenomenon or area to be researched. This can involve the collection of statistical information, e.g., the number of students receiving free **school** meals, or the comparison of results achieved in public examinations between girls and boys. It might, however, involve eliciting the viewpoints of school-leavers about their experience of school, or inviting young children to draw pictures of their ideal school. Each of these requires the researcher to give careful thought about the *methods* of collecting *data* and the *ethical* implications of doing so. Numbers, percentages, interviews and pictures are all different forms of data collected through different methods that might include surveys, cohort analysis, interrogation of data-sets, interviews, focus groups, video diaries, and visual representation. At its most basic level, research that involves focusing on statistical data is generally described as **quantitative** research, while the latter, typically concerned with meanings, interpretations, **behaviour**s, personal ideas and so forth is termed **qualitative** research.

⚙ Adopting a systematic approach requires that we think carefully about the design of our research. This involves the relationship between the research problem and the questions we are seeking to address, the methods of data collection that we intend to use and the **ethics** of our chosen approach. In this regard, as Denscombe points out, there is no right or wrong approach, rather it is a matter of 'horses for courses', involving the researcher making strategic decisions aimed at putting themself in the best possible position to gain the best outcome from their research, based upon suitable approaches for specific kinds of problems (Denscombe, 2003, p.3). This might involve a **quantitative** approach, in which statistical data can be analysed using available software packages designed for this purpose, or the researcher undertaking an interpretive analysis of **qualitative** data collected through methods that might include interviews, focus groups, narratives and poetry. In both cases, the materials, statistics, conversations and poems become research data when they are made the subject of systematic collection, construction, analysis and interpretation. In other instances, a research study might involve a large-scale quantitative survey combined with qualitative focus group discussions, designed using a *mixed* methods approach (Teddlie and Tashakkori, 2011). This brings us to one of the crucial distinctions in research practice; between research methods outlined above and *methodology*. In asking the questions: 'Why interview?' 'Why use questionnaires?', Clough and Nutbrown assert that methodology is fundamentally a matter of justifying selected research methods that 'carry very deep, often unarticulated implications based on values and assumptions which influence the study' (Clough and Nutbrown, 2012, p.25). Hence, methodology is about explaining our research decisions, choices of approach and philosophical dispositions that legitimise the research design.

˙ᵕ˙ In addition to ensuring a systematic approach and making informed methodological and design choices, one of the cornerstones of research is the development of a theoretical framework. Sometimes also known as a conceptual framework, Atkins and Wallace explain this as a 'model, or set of ideas, which is used as a way of understanding or explaining something' (Atkins and Wallace, 2012, p.51); it is essential for ensuring rigorous and credible research. Another way of thinking about this is that the theoretical/conceptual framework is the lens through which we observe the world (Merriam, 2009, p.67) and would involve a variety of concerns from **epistemology** and **ontology.** Different disciplinary orientations and traditions offer divergent ways in which we observe and make sense of the world, e.g., the problem of student disaffection in **school**s is likely to be approached differently from the perspective of behavioural psychology, philosophy, economics or sociology, for instance, or from alternative positions involving approaches to **politics**, **attachment** and **relationships**. An important distinction between these lenses and approaches is further made by Merriam, who notes that in qualitative research, enquiries typically involve inductive processes in which researchers gather data in order to 'build concepts, hypotheses or theories rather than deductively testing hypotheses' (Merriam, 2009, 15). This then leads us to consider the question: 'What makes research educational?' As Pring (2000) has persuasively argued, research that claims to be educational necessarily involves forms of moral purpose and value in which theory and practice are profoundly interconnected.

Questions to consider

1. British educationalist Lawrence Stenhouse famously described research as 'systematic enquiry made public' (Stenhouse 1981, p.104). What does this mean in practice and how might it be achieved?
2. What is the difference between a research method and methodology?
3. In what ways can we think of research as being educational research?
4. What makes theory in educational research *educational* theory?

References (with recommended readings in bold)

AARE (n.d.) *Australian Association for Research in Education.* Available at: www.aare.edu.au/pages/about-aare.html (accessed 21 June 2017).

AERA (n.d.) *What is education research?* American Educational Research Association. Available at: www.aera.net/AboutAERA/WhatisEducationResearch/tabid/13453/Default.aspx (accessed 20 May 2016).

Atkins, L. and Wallace, S. (2012) *Qualitative research in education.* London: Sage.

BERA (2011) *Ethical guidelines for educational research*. British Educational Research Association. Available at: www.bera.ac.uk/wp-content/uploads/2014/02/BERA-Ethical-Guidelines-2011.pdf (accessed 20 May 2016).

Clough, P. and Nutbrown, C. (2012) *A students guide to methodology*, **3rd edn. London: Sage.**

Cohen, L., Manion, L. and Morrison, K. (2011) *Research methods in education*, **7th edn. London: Routledge.**

Denscombe, M. (2003) *The good research guide*, 2nd edn. Maidenhead: Open University Press.

Kellett, M. (2005) *How to develop children as researchers: A step-by-step guide to teaching the research process*. London: Paul Chapman Publishing.

Merriam, S. (2009) *Qualitative research: A guide to design and implementation*. **San Francisco: Jossey-Bass.**

Mouly, G.J. (1978) *Educational research: The art and science of investigation*. Boston, MA: Allyn and Bacon.

Pring, R. (2000) *Philosophy of educational research*, 2nd edn. London: Continuum.

Stenhouse, L. (1981) 'What counts as research', *British Journal of Educational Studies*, 29 (2), pp.103–114.

Teddlie, C. and Tashakkori, A. (2011) 'Mixed methods research: Contemporary issues in an emerging field', in Denzin, N.K. and Lincoln, Y.S. (eds) *The Sage handbook of qualitative research*, 4th edn. London: Sage, pp.285–300.

KEY CONCEPT: ELECTIVE HOME EDUCATION

Helen E. Lees

Concept origins

Elective home education is, it could be argued, the original educational form (Gaither, 2008). Before **schooling** existed as an option or assumption for children's formation in youth, the home was the obvious *main* place of a child's formative and summative education. This varied from hired governesses **teaching** within the nursery settings of the wealthy, to the homes of the poor where living and getting by became the way to acquire various skills, although not necessarily the formal ones of numeracy and **literacy**. As formal education legislation has been adopted by countries around the world towards compulsory *education* mostly undertaken in **school**s, home education became an *elective* option, distinct and distant from schooling or education in the home (on account of ill health, for example), organised and sanctioned by authorities. Thus, elective home education (EHE)—or home schooling as it is better known in the US (and simply home education outside of the UK)—was originally a significant yet tacit educational concept. Nowadays, the origins of the idea are linked to a minority choice which leads parents and children away from school attendance. In other words, millions of children around the world go to school at home based on their parent's decision (and circumstances), rather than state compulsion.

Current status and usage

Within a short span of time (especially since 2000), elective home education has become an alternative educational pathway *option*, distinct from **school** attendance, for around 2–3 million children globally—from Ireland to Kenya to Colombia and anywhere in-between. This is anecdotally (using a variety of sources) said to be a number on the increase (Mansell and Edwards, 2016). The role of media coverage has much to do with it, as does the fluidity of the internet for sharing of information about this option (Wheeler, 2012). Some question such rises as part of natural flow and flux captured at 'high tide', and point out the lack of reliable data on numbers (Lees and Nicholson, 2016). The option for education without school is maintained and is (currently) legally secure in all English first-language countries. Elsewhere, such as in Germany, it is entirely outlawed (Spiegler, 2003). In Sweden and Spain, it is very difficult to pursue. The number of home-educated children we imagine exists may be many more, as state registration is not always required, but 'elective' is the key—this option must be chosen to be deemed home educating rather than lacking school provision. A wide variety of parents opt, by using their human right (Article 26, 3: UN Declaration of **Human Rights**) and national education **law**, to educate their children according to their own philosophical and religious beliefs, without knowledge or involvement of the state. However, **safeguarding** conflations with education continually threaten this freedom (Lees, 2014). Research on EHE is developing continually. It consistently (if not unilaterally) suggests that this option is viable and successful as a suitable, efficient education (Rothermel, 2015), although what suitable and efficient means depends on national interpretations and case law (Davies, 2015).

Home educating is a contested educational concept. A **neoliberal** foreclosing of educational ideas (Flint and Peim, 2012) renders the idea of education without **school**s subject to **dissonance**: people find it hard to accept as a notion. Many cannot believe that *not* attending a school is right or good for children. Can it work? 'Yes' is the answer from a wide variety of research. Surprisingly for some, academic outcomes from elective home education indicate comparative status with school attendance (Kunzman and Gaither, 2013). Entrance to higher education does not seem a barrier for children who have never attended a school (Gray and Riley, 2015). The essence of the matter seems to be that children able to **play** (whatever 'games') and self-determine are natural learners (Gray, 2016). Home educating often works very differently from school; using casual conversation (Thomas and Pattison, 2007), a deliberate lack of structure, self-direction and adult facilitation, rather than **didactic teaching**, EHE can enable **learning** to flourish (Kunzman and Gaither, 2013). While research indicates home educators do well by their children to equip them for a secure future, this involvement is reported as hard work due to a lack of state support (Rothermel, 2015). To home educate is to opt for 'a fundamental change in lifestyle', according to a number of studies leading to greater political, environmental, social–community and interpersonal sensibilities, as well as to activism (Neuman and Avriam, 2003, p.132; Stevens, 2003; Morton, 2010; Lees, 2014).

⚙ Instead of following the **school** year, or constraining features of timetable and **assessment** criteria, home educators have complete free choice to do as they see fit, according to age and aptitude of the child/ren. As mentioned above, these freedoms are nation-state-dependent. In the UK, they are complete so long as it appears an education of some kind is in progress and there is no cause for concern. This kind of freedom has an impact on how home educators live: for some this freedom for self and **family** means more travel or unusual pursuits like a concentration on a particular musical or science **curriculum** focus, with a great deal of time dedicated to these interests (and other curricula items emerging from this). Some home educators and educatees like to have a structured routine and take a 'school at home' approach. Others drop any idea of **schooling**, and daily, weekly or monthly follow their interests and inclinations without long-term planning, based on the wish to go with the flow and see what emerges that feels right to pursue. This latter approach is known as 'unstructured', '**autonomous** home education' or **unschooling** (Gray and Riley, 2015), with the beginning phase of losing or getting past a school mentality known as **deschooling** (McKee, 2002). This kind of home educating through informal **learning** involves a 'cultural curriculum', rather than predetermined ideas of what constitutes desirable or valid knowledge (Thomas and Pattison, 2013; Pattison and Thomas, 2016).

☺ National **law**s vary as to their demands on what *kind* of education is required in and through elective home education, but a child should be fitted by their home education to contribute as an adult successfully to a wider **society**. They should also be enabled to exit their community for another, should they wish, as with a community such as the Pennsylvanian Amish (McAvoy, 2012). The responsibility in law for providing an education for children in the UK rests with individual parents. The state does not have a legal responsibility to provide **school** education, although it does do so (Lees and Nicholson, 2016). Why do some parents choose home education? **Motivation**s vary (Rothermel, 2003; Morton, 2010; Spiegler, 2010). Often the situation at a school is proving intractable in adequately meeting the specific or special needs of a child (Parsons and Lewis, 2010). Parents, then, consider perhaps they can do better. Otherwise, it might be an emergency measure to give a traumatised child respite in the face of bullying (see, e.g., Wray and Thomas, 2013). Some parents never send their children to school, not being interested in the offer from the state. There is a sense within home educating communities that if *a child* did wish to go to school, this would be enabled by the parents, informed by **child–centred** philosophies. Socialisation outside of school education is fluid and might include smaller children and older people. While sufficient for some, critics suggest the issue of socialising children demands a more complex response (Monk, 2004). Conservative Christians in North America form a large home-educating population, where socialisation is more limited to their own social group (Kunzman, 2009), raising questions about the idea of a **democratic education** (Apple, 2000).

Questions to consider

1. Why is elective home education not legal everywhere?
2. How do home-educated children flourish and succeed as adults?
3. What do home educators and educatees do?
4. How do they socialise?
5. Why do home-educated children not go to **school**?

References (with recommended readings in bold)

Apple, M.W. (2000) 'The cultural politics of home schooling', *Peabody Journal of Education*, 75, pp.256–271.

Davies, R. (2015) 'A suitable education?', *Other Education*, 4, pp.16–32.

Flint, K.J. and Peim, N. (2012) *Rethinking the education improvement agenda: A critical philosophical approach*. London: Continuum.

Gaither, M. (2008) *Homeschool: An American history*. New York: Palgrave Macmillan.

Gray, P. (2016) 'Mother nature's pedagogy: How children educate themselves', in Lees, H.E. and Noddings, N. (eds) *The Palgrave international handbook of alternative education*. London: Palgrave Macmillan, pp.49–62.

Gray, P. and Riley, G. (2015) 'Grown unschoolers' evaluations of their unschooling experiences: Report I on a survey of 75 unschooled adults', *Other Education*, 4, pp.8–32.

Kunzman, R. (2009) *Write these laws on your children: Inside the world of conservative Christian homeschooling*. Boston, MA: Beacon Press.

Kunzman, R. and Gaither, M. (2013) 'Homeschooling: A comprehensive survey of the research', *Other Education*, 2 (1), pp.4–59.

Lees, H.E. (2014) *Education without schools: Discovering alternatives*. Bristol: Policy Press.

Lees, H.E. and Nicholson, F. (2016) 'Home education in the UK', in Gaither, M. (ed.) *Wiley handbook of home education*. New York: Wiley, pp.303–328.

Lees, H.E. and Noddings, N. (eds) (2016) *The Palgrave international handbook of alternative education*. London: Palgrave Macmillan.

McAvoy, P. (2012) '"There are no housewives on Star Trek": A reexamination of exit rights for the children of insular fundamentalist parents', *Educational Theory*, 62 (5), pp.535–552.

McKee, A. (2002) *Homeschooling our children unschooling ourselves*. Madison: Bittersweet House.

Mansell, W. and Edwards, P. (2016) 'DIY schooling on the rise as more parents opt for home education'. *Guardian*, 12 April.

Monk, D. (2004) 'Problematising home-education: Challenging "parental rights" and "socialisation"', *Legal Studies*, 24 (4), pp.568–598.

Morton, R. (2010) 'Home education: Constructions of choice', *International Electronic Journal of Elementary Education*, 3 (1), pp. 45–56. Available at: https://www.pegem.net/dosyalar/dokuman/138520-2014010417471-5.pdf (accessed 26 October 2016).

Neuman, A. and Avriam, A. (2003) 'Homeschooling as a fundamental change in lifestyle', *Evaluation and Research in Education*, 17 (2–3), pp.132–143.

Parsons, S. and Lewis, A. (2010) 'The home-education of children with special needs or disabilities in the UK: Views of parents from an online survey', *International Journal of Inclusive Education*, 14 (1), pp.67–86.

Pattison, H. and Thomas, A. (2016) 'Great expectations: Agenda and authority in technological, hidden and cultural curriculums', in Lees, H.E. and Noddings, N. (eds) *The Palgrave international handbook of alternative education*. London: Palgrave, pp.129–144.

Rothermel, P. (2003) 'Can we classify motives for home education?', *Evaluation and Research in Education*, 17 (2–3), pp.74–89.

Rothermel, P. (ed.) (2015) *International perspectives on home education: Do we still need schools?* Basingstoke: Palgrave Macmillan.

Spiegler, T. (2003) 'Home education in Germany: An overview of the contemporary situation', *Evaluation and Research in Education*, 17 (2–3), pp.179–190.

Spiegler, T. (2010) 'Parents' motives for home education: The influence of methodological design and social context', *International Electronic Journal of Elementary Education*, 3 (1), pp.57–70. Available at: http://iejee.com/index/makale/135/parents-motives-for-home-education-the-influence-of-methodological-design-and-social-context (accessed 26 October 2016).

Stevens, M. (2003) *Kingdom of children: Culture and controversy in the homeschooling movement.* Princeton, NJ: Princeton University Press.

Thomas, A. and Pattison, H. (2007) *How children learn at home.* London: Continuum.

Thomas, A. and Pattison, H. (2013) 'Informal home education: Philosophical aspirations put into practice', *Studies in Philosophy and Education*, 32 (2), pp.141–154.

Wheeler, B. (2012) 'Home schooling: Why more black US families are trying it', *BBC News Magazine*, 15 March. Available at: www.bbc.co.uk/news/magazine-17224662 (accessed 26 October 2016).

Wray, A. and Thomas, A. (2013) 'School refusal and home education', *Journal of Unschooling and Alternative Learning*, 7 (13), pp.64–85.

KEY CONCEPT: EXCLUSION

John Bayley

Concept origins

Arguably there are two major areas of exclusion in an educational context. First, there is unauthorised absence from formal education (truancy) which is 'organised' by the student themselves; the second area is formal exclusion from **school**, whereby pupils are excluded by the school, usually for reasons linked to some kind of disruptive **behaviour**. Both are strongly connected with pupil disaffection, alienation and disconnectedness rather than a wish to dispatch with schooling per se.

Current status and usage

Statistics from the Department for Education reveal that, in 2013–2014, 4,950 pupils were permanently excluded from **school**s in England, with 'persistent disruptive **behaviour**' accounting for 32.7 per cent of these. In the same year, 142,850 fixed-term exclusions were given (DfE, 2015). Only school headteachers are able to issue such exclusions. Government guidance states that the most serious of exclusions (fixed-term is a less serious, albeit severe option) is permanent exclusion, which 'should only be used as a last resort' and that any exclusions cannot discriminate against pupils on the basis of protected characteristics, such as **race** or **disability** (DfE, 2012). In terms of non-authorised pupil absence, the government identifies a category of 'persistent absence', which is defined as a pupil missing 10 per cent or more of possible attendances, though over 50 per cent of these are accounted for by illness. There are a number of groups that are over-represented in formal school-decision exclusion statistics. Boys are three times more likely to be excluded than girls. Pupils with **Special Educational Needs** (SEN) are, overall, around nine times as likely to receive both permanent and fixed-term exclusions than those with no SEN. Pupils who are eligible for free school meals are around four times more likely than those without. Two **ethnic** groups are disproportionately represented—Gypsy/Roma/Traveller pupils, and pupils of Black Caribbean heritage at a rate three times more likely than pupils without these heritages (DfE, 2015).

 Not all countries have systems to exclude pupils from **school**; for example, in Sweden and Denmark, young people cannot be excluded from school (Riley and Rustique-Forrester, 2002, p.11). The statistics in England make for stark reading in terms of a number of vulnerable groups, especially as those students who are excluded from education, for whatever reason, will be at risk of social exclusion, subject to higher levels of poverty and unemployment, criminal activity, as well as connected physical and mental ill health and **relationship** breakdowns throughout their life course (Bynner, 2000). Exclusion is a **social justice** issue and has far-reaching implications: 'permanent exclusion tended to trigger a complex chain of events which served to loosen the young person's affiliation and commitment to a conventional way of life' (Berridge *et al.*, 2001, p.vi). Schools are required to set and mark work for pupils who are excluded for a fixed term for the first five days, and then should make **alternative provision** from day six (DfE, 2012). There is evidence that some schools are making 'illegal exclusions', with some pupils being placed on extended study leave, some being coerced into leaving their current school for **elective home education** or other destinations under threat of permanent exclusion, etc. (Office of the Children's Commissioner, 2012). Local authorities must find another placement for pupils who are permanently excluded, and this frequently involves alternative provision (e.g., a 'managed move' to a different school, referral to a special school, etc.). There were around 400 **Pupil Referral Units** (PRUs) in operation by 2013 (DfE, 2015). These are alternative provision for excluded pupils, which should provide pupils with a more flexible **curriculum** and support with **behaviour** issues, although Ofsted (2016), found that in a quarter of such settings, the curriculum was too narrow. The Taylor Report, *Improving Alternative Provision* (2012), highlighted that academic outcomes for pupils who go into PRUs are poor, in part accounted for by the fact that most such pupils have had a history of behavioural and **teaching relationship** difficulties, which impede academic progress.

⚙ As mentioned, if outcomes are poor for the excluded, then there are implications for **society**. Educational underachievers (who may become disaffected from **school**) are likely to progress to poorly paid jobs, are more likely to be engaged in criminal activities, and are less likely to lead healthy lifestyles (Williams and Pritchard, 2006). This, of course, has both economic and social implications for society, as well as, obviously, the costs to the individual, and is a **policy** issue. In much of the research (e.g., Riley and Rustique-Forrester, 2002), the children themselves are identifying a range of issues that they perceive as potentially leading to disaffection, and therefore exclusion. Among these factors are relationships, the nature, purpose and relevance of the **curriculum**, **labelling** of pupils, and feelings disavowed or disregarded. As Klein (2000) points out, the curriculum, consisting of a 'crowded', increasingly 'academic' set of prescribed subjects, predicated upon attaining specific targets, is likely to alienate certain pupils, causing disconnectedness, which may explain the high proportion of excluded children with **special educational needs**. The National Curriculum, especially since its revision in 2010, has less time for creative expression, particularly in the non-core subjects, where many less academic children may achieve (and enjoy their studies of this kind), and it may cater less to the cultural history and interests of many pupils from **ethnic** minorities. Riley and Rustique-Forrester (2002) found that many of the pupils they interviewed found few connections between what they learned in school, and its relevance to their 'real' worlds. Carlen *et al.* identified truancy as a signifier of a sane response by absconding—self-excluding—students to a schooling that caused them harm (Carlen *et al.*, 1992).

☺ So, how might cycles of alienation and disaffection causing forms of self-styled or **school** determined exclusions be disrupted? National **policy**, on, for example, **curriculum**, school structure, and exclusion, in England is unlikely to change in the near future, so it may be up to schools themselves to create more social and educational **inclusion**. They can begin by listening more carefully to the **voice**s of their pupils, and 'acknowledging the reality of their lives' (Klein, 2000, p.73). This equates to respect for pupils, which is seen, by them, as extremely important, and which many perceive that they are not sufficiently getting from schools. **Teacher**s need to look beyond what they might perceive as 'disruptive' **behaviour**, and listen to pupils in order to understand, consider possible adjustments, and give more explanation and support (Parker *et al.*, 2016). Education systems around the world do not, it seems, bother much with those at risk of exclusion in order to keep them held within the system.

The price of 'letting them go' is, as we can see above, a heavy one for all in **society**.

Questions to consider

1. How can the tensions between a relatively inflexible **curriculum** and the needs of pupils vulnerable to exclusion be resolved?
2. What provisions should be made in **school**s to support pupils at risk of exclusion?
3. What kind(s) of **alternative provision** would be desirable for excluded pupils?
4. What is exclusion from school?
5. Who decides whether exclusion works?

References (with recommended readings in bold)

Berridge, D., Brodie, I., Pitts, J., Porteous, D. and Tarling, R. (2001) *The independent effects of permanent exclusion from school on the offending careers of young people*. RDS Occasional Paper No. 71. London: The Research, Development and Statistics Directorate, Home Office.

Bynner, J. (2000) *Risks and outcomes of social exclusion: Insights from longitudinal data*. London: OECD Reports. Available at: www.oecd.org/edu/school/1855785.pdf (accessed 28 November 2016).

Carlen, P., Gleeson, D. and Wardhaugh, J. (1992) *Truancy: The politics of compulsory schooling*. Buckingham: Open University Press.

DfE (2012) *Exclusion guidance, updated April 2012*. Available at: www.spexe.org/wp-content/uploads/2014/01/DFE-Exclusion-Guidance-2012.pdf (accessed 21 June 2017).

DfE (2015) *Permanent and fixed-period exclusions in England: 2013 to 2014*. Department for Education. Available at: www.gov.uk/government/statistics/permanent-and-fixed-period-exclusions-in-england-2013-to-2014 (accessed 21 June 2017).

Klein, R. (2000) *Defying disaffection*. Stoke-on Trent: Trentham Books.

Office of the Children's Commissioner (2012) '*They never give up on you*': *Office of the Children's Commissioner school exclusions inquiry*. London: Office of the Children's Commissioner.

Ofsted (2016) *Alternative provision: The findings from Ofsted's three-year survey of schools' use of off-site alternative provision (160011)*. London: Ofsted.

Parker, R., Rose, J. and Gilbert, L. (2016) 'Attachment aware schools: An alternative to behaviourism in supporting children's behaviour?', in Lees, H.E. and Noddings, N. (eds) *The Palgrave international handbook of alternative education*. London: Palgrave Macmillan, pp.463–483.

Riley, K. and Rustique-Forrester, E. (2002) *Working with disaffected students*. London: Paul Chapman Publishing.

Taylor, C. (2012) *Improving alternative provision*. London: Department for Education.

Williams, R. and Pritchard, C. (2006) *Breaking the cycle of educational alienation*. Maidenhead: Open University Press.

KEY CONCEPT: INCLUSION

John Bayley

Concept origins

The provenance and growth of the use of the term inclusion is difficult to locate. In the UK, the term is frequently cited in government **policy**-making, regardless of the difficulties of establishing specific meaning. So, for example, in a number of policy documents inclusion appears to be cited as an opposition to **exclusion**, particularly in an educational context (e.g., in DfES, 2001), while in a global context inclusion is typically aligned to issues of **equality** and **human rights** (e.g., see the work of the Centre for Studies in Inclusive Education: www.csie.org.uk).

Current status and usage

The Salamanca Statement on Special Needs Education (UNESCO, 1994), is widely regarded as a trigger for the **policy** development of inclusion in the UK and elsewhere, in response to the assertion that children with **special educational needs** (SEN) are most effectively educated in a 'regular' **school** rather than those specifically dedicated to children and young people with identified SEN. In the UK, the Code of Practice for SEN of 1996 and its revised version of 2001 suggested that the majority of pupils with identified SEN should have their needs met in **mainstream** schools. Adopting the term 'Inclusive Schooling', the UK's Department for Education and Skills stated that 'with the right training, strategies and support nearly all children with special educational needs can be successfully included in mainstream education' (DfES, 2001). More recently, in England, the concept of inclusion has been extended from special educational needs to encompass **disability** (SEND), but this designation is to embrace the needs of *all* so-called 'vulnerable groups', among children, young people and adults. This reflects a view

> that properly inclusive approaches involve moving away from a deficit model of learners with special educational needs and disabilities as 'problems', in favour of a model where differences between children and between adults are celebrated as resources for **learning** (Booth and Ainscow, 2011).

Among the competing perspectives on the nature and implementation of inclusion, so-called 'full inclusionists' would contend that all children should be educated together, with no segregation by location (Hodkinson, 2016), and that this is an issue of children's rights and **social justice**. Others would agree with Warnock (2005, p.1) that the special **school** sector should be seen as providing an effective education for those children and their parents who see this as a more 'productive and creative' alternative. Equally, the benefits of inclusion can be eclipsed where schools see a tension between, on the one hand, their obligation to meet externally imposed performance measures and, on the other, an ethical commitment to addressing the **special educational needs** of pupils. This is recognised in the revised Code of Practice for Special Educational Needs and **Disability** (2014), which specifies that the wishes of children and their parents must be taken into consideration. In other countries, SEN is complicated by national attitudes and histories, just as in the UK. In Romania, although moves are being made towards a more inclusive school system, Ghergut notes that 'a tradition of rigid curricula and **pedagogy**, creates an atmosphere that is not favourable towards children who experience difficulties of any kind' (2011, p.595). This extends to inclusion of minorities such as Roma gypsies struggles to gain ground due to historical prejudicial **race** issues. In Germany, inclusion is a key and enforceable principle, which involves a **law** against **elective home education**, such that there is the suggestion that German inclusion law around education is too strict and thereby goes against human interests (Spiegler, 2003). In some rural schools in Scotland, inclusion of lesbian, gay and bisexual (LGB) pupils in schools on the grounds of their **sexuality** saw students 'depicted as victims in need of specialist support', rather than as included on terms of **equality** (McIntyre, 2007, p.2). As we can see, the issue of inclusion is far-reaching and multi-dimensional.

As we can see, inclusive education goes much further than the education of children with SEN and disabilities in **mainstream school**s. In itself, inclusion can stop at mere 'integration' due to attitudinal barriers, as identified by Glazzard (2011), who suggests some pupils may, in effect, be taught separately from their peers although co-located in a shared school. In line with the Equality Act 2010, it is illegal for schools to **discriminate**, on the grounds of **disability**, over issues of admission or participation. However, this does not necessarily allow for fuller integration—here understood as proper inclusion—of pupils with SEND: some schools **teach** such pupils in spaces set away from others, often in sessions led by under-qualified **teaching** assistants. Based on deficit models of children and young people with **learning** difficulties, such **policy** attempts to 'normalise' learners fails to address essential ideas of encompassing **diversity** (Lloyd, 2008) and **equality**, and smacks of **perfomativity**. The assumption that educators can bridge a so-called 'learning gap' is problematic—it privileges **instrumental** forms of academic achievement at the expense of other aspects of personal development, e.g., social **relationships** development might be more significant and relevant as learning for some children with autism. Armstrong summarises the problems involved when inclusion policy is 'aimed not at promoting equity … but at establishing narrow cultural parameters of normality to which all have the opportunity to conform' (Armstrong, 2005, p.147).

Although issues throughout the world have already been highlighted, in many continental European countries, inclusion is regarded as an extension of a comprehensive approach to education, in which children's rights and **social justice** are positioned at the forefront of educational thinking; one that goes beyond tolerance and compensating for pupils' perceived 'disabilities'. In Finland, for example, pupils with **special educational needs** are included in **mainstream** schooling, underscoring a philosophy that all students will need support at some point in their lives (Sahlberg, 2015). Rieser (2012)—himself disabled—for instance, takes a **human rights** perspective on inclusion, arguing that every child has the right to belong to her/his local mainstream school and to be provided with all the support s/he needs to thrive. In observing the negative connotations of much of the language used about **disability** ('handicapped', 'sufferer', etc.), he asserts that: 'we wish to be known as "disabled people" in recognition of the common oppression we face' (Rieser, 2012, p.202). By implication, terms such as 'disabled' and 'disability' (as negatives of 'abled' and 'ability') serve to perpetuate negative stereotypes of the needs of children, young people and adults that demand to be challenged and realigned in order to enable authentic inclusive educational practice. Gibson and Haynes

(2009), citing Freire's (1985) work on the '**culture** of <u>**silence**</u>', suggests that neoliberalist **ideology** has stifled the **voice**s of disabled children and young people by hijacking the language of inclusion to serve **neoliberal** agendas, rather than allowing 'authentic voices' to be heard. Despite a strong leaning within inclusion matters towards issues of SEND inclusions, to imagine that including children is only about special circumstances is to misunderstand the matter: it is a vast concern touching on most concepts in this book. Without the idea of inclusion at the heart of education, fairness fails and *all* children (in particular) are failed in numerous ways.

Questions to consider

1. Is it possible to define inclusion?
2. What might be the key features of an inclusive **school**?
3. Does some of the language of inclusion reinforce possible stereotypes?
4. Is a segregated system of schooling desirable?
5. Who includes, and what does including mean?

References (with recommended readings in bold)

Armstrong, D. (2005) 'Reinventing "inclusion": New Labour and the cultural politics of special education', *Oxford Review of Education*, **31 (1), pp.135–151.**

Booth, T. and Ainscow, M. (2011) *Index for inclusion: Developing learning and participation in schools.* Bristol: Centre for Studies on Inclusive Education.

DfES (2001) *Code of practice for special educational needs.* London: Department for Education and Skills.

Freire, P. (1985) *The politics of education: Culture, power and liberation.* Westport, CT: Greenwood Publishing.

Ghergut, A. (2011) 'Education of children with special needs in Romania: Attitudes and experiences', *Procedia—Social and Behavioral Sciences*, 12, pp.595–599.

Gibson, S. and Haynes, J. (2009) *Perspectives on participation and inclusion.* London: Continuum.

Glazzard, J. (2011) 'Perceptions of the barriers to effective inclusion in one primary school: Voices of teachers and teaching assistants', *Support for Learning*, **26 (2), pp.56–63.**

Hodkinson, A. (2016) *Key issues in special educational needs and inclusion*. London: Sage.

Lloyd, C. (2008) 'Removing barriers to achievement: A strategy for inclusion or exclusion?', *International Journal of Inclusive Education*, 12 (2), pp.221–236.

McIntyre, E. (2007) 'The silence: Barriers and facilitators to inclusion of lesbian and gay pupils in Scottish schools', DEdPsych thesis, University of Newcastle upon Tyne.

Rieser, R. (2012) *Implementing inclusive education: A Commonwealth guide to implementing Article 24 of the UN Convention on the Rights of Persons with Disabilities*. London: Commonwealth Secretariat.

Sahlberg, P. (2015) *Finnish lessons 2.0*. New York: Teachers College Press.

Spiegler, T. (2003) 'Home education in Germany: An overview of the contemporary situation', *Evaluation and Research in Education*, 17 (2–3), pp.179–190.

UNESCO (1994) *The Salamanca Statement on Principles, Policy and Practice in Special Needs Education*. Paris: UNESCO. Available at: http://portal.unesco.org/education/en/ev.php-URL_ID=10379&URL_DO=DO_TOPIC&URL_SECTION=201.html.

Warnock, M. (2005) *Special educational needs: A new look*. London: Philosophy of Education Society of Great Britain.

KEY CONCEPT: LEARNING

Stephen Griffin

Concept origins

The concept of learning can be traced back to the old English word *Leornian*, meaning to 'acquire knowledge or skill as a result of study, experience or **teaching**' (OED, 1989). This emphasises the active, participative nature of learning and the need for a person to engage positively with their own learning through study. However, in educational settings, learning has also historically been linked with the idea of instruction, whereby **teacher**s impart approved knowledge in designated contexts. There are parallels here with the idea of religious instruction, e.g., the production of the *Ratio Studiorum* or plan for Jesuit education in 1599 emphasised the importance of memory and recitation for effective learning (O'Donnell, 1984). In particular, this has connotations of **didactic** instruction and 'rote' learning: learning through drill, repetition and memorisation, sometimes without comprehension. This interpretation of learning has its ideological roots in classical humanism and traditionalism and the emphasis placed upon formal, absolute knowledge and 'tried and tested methods' of tuition (Bartlett and Burton, 2016, p.27). However, Romantic interpretations of education stemming from the Enlightenment movement, such as those espoused by Locke (1689) and Rousseau (1762), accentuate the importance of the individual child and their innate skills and potentials. The role of the teacher here becomes a guide rather than an instructor and the importance of first-hand experience becomes a prerequisite for effective learning.

Current status and usage

In contemporary educational usage, learning is often assumed to be that which takes place in a formal institution such as a **school**, college or university. In these contexts, it is important to acknowledge that learning is therefore subject to the specific **epistemology**, **ontology** and related **curriculum** ideas favoured by each setting, or those directly mandated by an external body. From a governmental perspective, it might be argued, then, that learning is inextricably linked with the **assimilation** of knowledge found in official approved curricula favoured by school types, linked to political **ideologies**. As Apple (2004) explained: 'Schools do not only control people; they also help control meaning' (p.63). Currently in the UK, curriculum programmes and syllabi have a preference for linear curricula, where understanding is assessed by endpoint examination as opposed to modular ongoing **assessment** (e.g., Ofqual, 2016; Bartlett and Burton, 2016). Learning in schooling is therefore increasingly constructed as an educational product, as opposed to a process, leading to Kelly's concern that 'the assessment (and evaluation) tail will always wag the curriculum dog' (2009, p.148). Moreover, Biesta (2009) has raised concerns about the 'learnification' of educa- tion, where education is reduced to discussions of learners and learning at the expense of a consideration of values.

To understand the concept of learning, we need to see how its related processes have been explained by different theoretical traditions. Draw- ing on experimentation with animals, **behaviourism**, which has its roots in psychological enquiry, looks at externally observable **behav- iour**. In this sense, behaviourism seeks to explain learning in terms of visible, external responses as opposed to internal, mental processes. In particular, the work of Thorndike (1911) and Pavlov (1927) has attempted to explain how animals, and by association humans, learn. Pavlov, for instance, observed that dogs could be trained to salivate by associating the sound of a metronome, buzzer or other such stimuli with the arrival of food. Such classical conditioning involves the asso- ciation of a neutral stimulus with a reward. Watson (1913) and Skinner (1953) developed behaviourism further: they recognised that rewards and punishments could reinforce desirable behaviours and diminish undesirable traits. This relies on the existence of 'operants' or deliberate actions impacting on the learner's environment. In an educational set- ting, positive 'reinforcers', such as **teacher** praise or reward points, can then be seen as encouraging good learning behaviours, while nega- tive reinforcers or 'punishers', such as detention, may decrease poor behaviour. Significantly, Skinner found that intermittent rather than continuous reinforcement was more effective in consolidating learning and negative reinforcement could be counterproductive. These learning models of behaviour, however, largely depict learners as passive respondents to environmental stimuli, problematically situating them not as agents engaged in a collaborative enterprise but as mere subjects to be shaped (Parker *et al.*, 2016).

In stark contrast with behavioural learning models, **cognitive** theories are expressly focused on the internal mental processes that take place during learning. Here, the learner is seen as an active constructor of knowledge, within specific stages, each of which has its own distinct modes of structuring and expression. Cognitivists largely depict the mind as an information-processing system, with thought as a form of computation. Jean Piaget was perhaps the best-known proponent of **cognitivism**. In his theory of cognitive development, Piaget (1983) highlighted the importance of learning as a process of *adaptation* between the learner and their environment. Piaget saw learning as predicated upon *schemas* (or schemata): these are cognitive frameworks that organise information and thus a learner's thoughts and beliefs. These may, of course, be erroneous and contribute to forms of prejudice, as well as providing foundations for more evidenced knowledge and pro-social attitudes. Learning (*or* adaptation) then takes place when new concepts or ideas are *assimilated* into the existing schema. Furthermore, schemas may be modified to take account of new circumstances through a process of *accommodation*. As a 'stage theorist', Piaget proposed that there are four stages to cognitive development: the *sensori-motor, pre-operational, concrete-operational,* and *formal-operational* stages, each spanning ages 0–2, 2–7, 7–12, and 12-plus, respectively (Wadsworth, 1996). Despite problems with Piaget's research methods, his downplaying of background or contextual factors, and his stage theory model (for critiques, see e.g., Donaldson, 1978; Sternberg and Williams, 2010), many **school** programmes have been influenced by the latter, as have discovery learning and **constructivist** approaches.

More recent theories of learning (e.g., Illeris, 2009), while incorporating varying elements of **behaviourist** and **cognitivist** theories, often build on varieties of **social constructivism** (Pritchard and Woollard, 2010). This proposes that learning takes place and knowledge is produced as the result of interactions between the learner, their prior experiences, other more experienced individuals and the environment. In this sense, learning is an active process: we construct, rather than acquire, new knowledge. Vygotsky (1934; Daniels *et al.*, 2007) is most closely associated with this socio-cultural approach to **cognitive** development. He suggested learning can be culturally mediated and social interaction is essential for cognitive development to occur. Vygotsky also proposed children operate at two developmental levels: independently and collaboratively with the support of more experienced others. Vygotsky (1978, p.86) referred to this space as the Zone of Proximal Development (ZPD). This **educational theory** suggests that optimal learning occurs within this zone alone and that supporting learning, through interaction with a more capable other, facilitates cognitive development. Bruner (1966; Wood *et al.*, 1976) further emphasised the importance of social interaction for learning, coining the term 'scaffolding' to describe the support of more experienced others. New information or knowledge, Bruner suggested, is effectively attained by personal discovery. This kind of thinking about learning has been picked up in recent times by **alternative education** theorists, whose **empirical** research is showing that conversation alone can serve to scaffold effective learning (Thomas and Pattison, 2007, 2013). Furthermore, this chimes with Alexander's (2008) conception of dialogic **teaching** that encourages greater pupil–**teacher** interaction. Contemporary interest in *theories* of learning has spawned a growing and theoretically diverse literature (Hattie, 2009; Illeris, 2006, 2009). Within this, the work of Dweck (2012) has attracted considerable though sometimes uncritical attention. Her 'mindsets' model of learning highlights 'fixed' and 'growth' mindsets, the former depicting learners holding potentially restrictive (**essentialist**) views of their capabilities, while those in the latter category regard themselves as having qualities which can be developed and thus may be more enthusiastic towards learning. Relatedly, Dweck argues that praise focused on supposed **intelligence** or talent, rather than hard work, can be counterproductive. While clearly not a comprehensive theory of learning (Rustin, 2016), Dweck's work illustrates the ongoing theorisation of the concept.

Questions to consider

1. How might learning theories be useful in **school**s?
2. Is **constructivism** right?
3. What factors govern learning in and out of school?
4. Are there other ways to learn than through being taught?
5. How is learning connected to **teaching**?

References (with recommended readings in bold)

Alexander, R. (2008) *Essays on pedagogy.* Abingdon: Routledge.

Apple, M. (2004) *Ideology and the curriculum.* London: RoutledgeFalmer.

Bartlett, S. and Burton, D. (2016) *Introduction to education studies,* 4th edn. London: Sage.

Biesta, G.J.J. (2009) 'Good education in an age of measurement: On the need to reconnect with the question of purpose in education', *Education, Assessment, Evaluation and Accountability,* 21, pp.33–36.

Bruner, J.S. (1966) *Toward a theory of instruction.* Cambridge, MA: Belknap Press.

Daniels, H., Cole, M. and Wertsch, J.V. (2007) *The Cambridge companion to Vygotsky.* New York: Cambridge University Press.

Donaldson, M. (1987) *Children's minds.* London, Fontana Press.

Dweck, C. (2012) *Mindset: How you can fulfil your potential.* London: Robinson.

Hattie, J. (2009) *Visible learning: A synthesis of over 800 meta-analyses relating to achievement.* Abingdon: Routledge.

Illeris, K. (2006) *How we learn: Learning and non-learning in school and beyond.* Abingdon: Routledge.

Illeris, K. (ed.) (2009) *Contemporary theories of learning: Learning theorists … in their own words.* Abingdon: Routledge.

Kelly, A.V. (2009) *The curriculum theory and practice,* 6th edn. London: Sage.

Locke, J. (1689) *Some thoughts concerning education.* London: Awnsham and John Churchill.

O'Donnell, J. (1984) 'The Jesuit *Ratio Studiorum*', *Philippine Studies,* 32 (4), pp.462–475.

OED (1989) *Oxford English dictionary.* Oxford: Clarendon Press.

Ofqual (2016) *Summary of changes to AS and A levels from 2015.* Available at: www.gov.uk/government/publications/as-and-a-level-changes-a-summary (accessed 11 November 2016).

Parker, R., Rose, J. and Gilbert, L. (2016) 'Attachment aware schools: An alternative to behaviourism in supporting children's behaviour?', in Lees, H.E. and Noddings, N. (eds) *The Palgrave international handbook of alternative education.* London: Palgrave Macmillan, pp.463–483.

Pavlov, I. (1927) *Conditioned reflexes: An investigation of the physiological activity of the cerebral cortex.* Translated and edited by G.V. Anrep. London: Oxford University Press.

Piaget, J. (1983) 'Piaget's theory', in Kessen, W. (ed.) *Handbook of child psychology,* vol. 1. New York: Wiley, pp.103–128.

Pritchard, A. and Woollard, J. (2010) *Psychology for the classroom: Constructivism and social learning.* Abingdon: Routledge.

Rousseau, J.J. (1762) *Émile, or on education.* Translated by A. Bloom. New York: Basic Books, 1979.

Rustin, S. (2016) 'New test for "growth mindset", the theory that anyone who tries can succeed', *Guardian*, 10 May. Available at: www. theguardian.com/education/2016/may/10/growth-mindset-research-uk-schools-sats (accessed 20 November 2016).

Skinner, B.F. (1953). *Science and human behaviour.* London: Collier-Macmillan.

Sternberg, R.J. and Williams, W.M. (2010) *Educational psychology*, 2nd edn. Upper Saddle River, NJ: Merrill.

Thomas, A. and Pattison, H. (2007) *How children learn at home.* London: Continuum.

Thomas, A. and Pattison, H. (2013) 'Informal home education: Philosophical aspirations put into practice', *Studies in Philosophy and Education*, 32, pp.141–154.

Thorndike, E. (1911) *Animal intelligence: Experimental studies.* London: Macmillan.

Vygotsky, L.S. (1934) *Thought and language.* Translated by A. Kozulin. Cambridge, MA: MIT Press, 1986.

Vygotsky, L.S. (1978) *Mind in society: The development of higher psychological processes.* Cambridge, MA: Harvard University Press.

Wadsworth, B.J. (1996) *Piaget's theory of cognitive and affective development: Foundations of constructivism*, 5th edn. White Plains, NY: Longman.

Watson, J.B. (1913) 'Psychology as the behaviorist views it', *Psychological Review*, 20, pp. 158–177.

Wood, D.J., Bruner, J.S. and Ross, G. (1976) 'The role of tutoring in problem solving', *Journal of Child Psychiatry and Psychology*, 17 (2), pp.89–100.

KEY CONCEPT: PASTORAL WELFARE

Stanley Tucker

Concept origins

According to Best (2000, p.3) pastoral welfare is a uniquely British **school** concept and while practitioners and academics have struggled to meaningfully define its epistemic field, they have also had to resolve criticisms over its problematic historical roots in religious hierarchy and paternalism (Best, 2000, p.4). Pastoral welfare as a **curriculum** concern has, then, tended to coalesce around imperatives of **care**, personal and social development and civic responsibility. Michael Marland, however, is widely credited with attempting to define both the concept of care and the importance of it as a central function of school activity. He argued that 'the core of a school's work is the disciplinary, educational, vocational, and personal guidance; and the pupils' real situation must contribute to the formulation of school **policy**' (Marland, 1974, p.12, cited in Best, 2014, p.177).

Current status and usage

The **inclusion** of spiritual and cultural development as part of what was to become a government strategy for the promotion of spiritual, moral, social and cultural (SMSC) education in the **curriculum** in England in the mid-1990s has added more complexity to problems of definition. In reviewing the way in which the provision of pastoral **care** is now being organised and delivered within **school**s, it is possible to detect significant changes both in its priorities and responses to pupil need. Crucially, there appears to be a move away from the delivery of universal provision to targeted pastoral interventions aimed specifically at meeting the needs of those who are defined as the most needy, 'at risk' and vulnerable (Tucker, 2013; Tucker *et al.*, 2015).

What kind of pastoral **care** and support should **school**s provide for children and young people? An appropriate place to begin to answer this question lies in the pages of the seminal text *Pastoral care*, written by Michael Marland in 1974. Published at a time of considerable educational change, following the restructuring of secondary education and comprehensive school reorganisation (DES, 1965) and the raising of the school leaving age (ROSLA) to 16 in 1972, Marland attempted to define both the concept of pastoral care and the importance of it as a central function of school activity. Hence, pastoral care was seen as an essential aspect of educational provisional for both primary and secondary school pupils, i.e., universalistic provision that should be available to all. For Marland, focus needed to be placed on the affective dimension of development, provision of counselling and guidance to promote decision making, and opportunities to develop an individual 'lifestyle' and 'individual enrichment'. In turn, the concept of pastoral care was influential in shaping the school **curriculum**: it created the emergence in both primary and secondary education of elements of pastoral care and support emerging through the development of tutorial-based systems, programmes of study in personal, social and health education (PSHE) and the use of cross-curricular themes to explore aspects of children and young people's lives. In tracing the historical roots of pastoral care, we are in a position to understand the factors that have influenced its subsequent development.

 Recent government policies in the UK have seen a shift in emphasis in pastoral **care** away from universal provision to the allocation of targeted provision for those deemed as needy, 'at risk' and vulnerable. This has involved the allocation of specific resources, through, for example, the provision of an individual pupil premium, to respond to 'the potential links between free **school** meals (as an indicator of social and educational disadvantage) and risk of **exclusion**' (Ofsted, 2012, p.17). Indeed, it can be argued that we have witnessed what Smith *et al.* (2007) describe as the emergence of a 'deficit agenda' **discourse** used to describe and explain educational failure, poor classroom **behaviour** and school exclusion as being the product of dysfunctional behaviours, negative peer group **relationships**, life styles, etc.; a discourse based in negative perceptions of **class**, **family**, **ethnicity** and community values. As a result, a range of pastoral interventions are now utilised that bring together elements of therapy, behaviour modification, social group work, mentorship and advice and counselling. Alongside this, those leading and managing pastoral care in schools point towards the need to engage with external social care and health agencies and professionals to deliver the most effective forms of pastoral care to the most vulnerable children and young people (Tucker, *et al.*, 2015).

☺ **Discourse** as a way of verbally describing and promoting ideas and beliefs, or communicating through a variety of texts, assists in creating 'objects of knowledge', i.e., ways of organising institutions, arranging their work priorities or approving and endorsing particular forms of **behaviour** (Foucault, 1991). Ball, writing in 2008, argues that government-sponsored discourse has been used to promote the importance of a **performativity** agenda for **school**s. This, in turn, has forced some schools to concentrate on developing targets, delivering outcomes and measuring performance, rather than pastoral and pedagogical practices to enable all young people to achieve their potential; what Kenway (1990) terms a 'discourse of derision' based on political expediency and the creation of market **relationships** that set schools in opposition to each other. In this climate, the language of pastoral **care** and support has also been influenced by Smith *et al.*'s (2007) deficit agenda, as well as an overriding concern with pupil failure as it impacts on national and international league tables. In one sense, the competing discourses are utilised to advance particular views concerning the values and priorities of education, such 'commentary' inevitably extending to the position occupied by and the work undertaken in the name of pastoral care.

Questions to consider

1. Will pastoral welfare be dominated by an increasing risk-averse approach to **safeguarding** and child protection?
2. How do inspection regimes judge pastoral welfare?
3. Can pastoral welfare be about a **holistic** approach to welfare prioritising literacy and children's **voice**?
4. Why does pastoral welfare matter?
5. Who does the caring?

References (with recommended readings in bold)

Ball, S. (2008) *The education debate.* Bristol: Policy Press.
Best, R. (2000) 'Concepts in pastoral care and PSE', in Best, R., Lang, P., Lodge, C. and Watkins, C. (eds) *Pastoral care and personal social education: Entitlement and provision.* London: Continuum, pp.3–18.

Best, R. (2014) 'Forty years of pastoral care: An appraisal of Michael Marland's seminal book and its significance for pastoral care in schools', *Pastoral Care in Education,* 32 (3), pp.173–185.

DES (1965) *The organization of secondary education on comprehensive lines.* Department of Education and Science Circular 10/65. London: HMSO.

Foucault, M. (1991) *Discipline and punish: The birth of the prison.* London: Penguin Books.

Kenway, J. (1990) 'Education and the right's discursive politics: Private versus state schooling', in Ball, S. (ed.) *Foucault and education: Disciplines and knowledge.* London: Routledge.

Marland, M. (1974) *Pastoral care.* London: Heinemann.

Ofsted (2012) *The pupil premium: How schools are using the pupil premium to raise achievement for disadvantaged pupils.* Manchester: Ofsted.

Smith, C., Stainton-Rogers, W. and Tucker, S. (2007) 'Risk', in Robb, M. (ed.) *Youth in context: Frameworks, settings and encounters.* London: Sage, pp.219–250.

Tucker, S. (2013) 'Pupil vulnerability and school exclusion: Developing responsive pastoral policies and practices in secondary education in the UK', *Pastoral Care in Education,* 31 (4), pp.279–291.

Tucker, S., Trotman, D. and Martyn, M. (2015) 'Vulnerability: The role of schools in supporting young people exposed to challenging environments and situations', *International Journal of Education Development,* 41, pp.301–306.

KEY CONCEPT: PEDAGOGY

Dave Trotman

Concept origins

From the Greek *paidagōgia*, meaning 'to lead or tend to the child', the term pedagogy can be traced to early Greek times, where its (now obsolete) meaning related to the oversight of a child or 'an attendant leading a boy to **school**' (Mortimore, 1999, p.1). While the concept remains both undeveloped and underused in England and the wider UK, in continental Europe its use became widespread but broadly defined, embracing things as diverse as health and bodily fitness, social and moral welfare, **ethics** and aesthetics (Marton and Booth, 1997, p.178).

Current status and usage

In English and UK contexts, the term *pedagogy* is often idiosyncratically used as a form of shorthand to describe a **teaching** approach or form of instruction in **school**s. In continental Europe, however, pedagogy is a well-established concept in university education programmes as well as in the **discourses** of school, but it is, nonetheless, subject to differing interpretations. Often aligned, or used interchangeably, with the term **'didactics'** (embracing strategies and approaches employed in the teaching of specific subjects in schools), pedagogy is primarily, but not exclusively, concerned with the inter-**relationships** of theories of **learning**, educational philosophy, **curriculum** and methods of **teaching**, mentoring and facilitating. Unlike in the UK, pedagogy in a European context is also applied to a broad range of services that can typically include childcare and early years education, youth work, parenting and **family** support services, secure units for young offenders, residential **care** and **play** work (Petrie *et al.*, 2009). More recently, pedagogy has been subject to renewed interest in continental Europe where the twin concepts of social pedagogy and relational pedagogy have evolved.

The former, social pedagogy, has emerged in the fields of social work and youth work as an alternative to a **school**-based pedagogy that instead focuses on more **holistic** and group-centred approaches to education. The latter, relational pedagogy, places particular emphasis on the value of student knowledge and experience while promoting an orientation to knowledge and **learning** processes based on **constructivism**. One of the most vivid uses of the concept of pedagogy, however, comes in the form of Paulo Freire's (1970) seminal text *Pedagogy of the oppressed,* in which Freire illustrates the problems of a 'banking' concept of education, where people are cast as objects of education (accounts to be filled) rather than sentient subjects. In response, he advances the possibilities of education as cultural education and, in turn, lays the foundations for a critical pedagogy of social action.

Often pronounced with a hard rather than soft second 'g', pedagogy is one of the staple terms in the lexicon of education studies. In English contexts, and in its most rudimentary use, pedagogy is often used as shorthand for the process of **teaching**. Hence, pedagogy, at first sight, might be regarded as being to do with the mechanics of **teaching** as distinct from the 'what' of **curriculum** content and 'ways' of understanding in the process of **learning**. **Teaching** strategies, **teaching** styles, approaches, instruction and methods can all then be considered to come under the umbrella of pedagogy. As an aspect of **teaching**, to refer to pedagogy in one sense is to direct our attention to the skills and techniques of **teaching**; what has often been described as the craft of **teaching**. Inevitably, there are a number of factors that we need to be cautious about when we first encounter the concept of pedagogy. First, we should not make the mistake that pedagogy is a practice that relates only to **schools**. Education, **teaching** and **learning** can all effectively take place outside formal **school** systems; it follows that this is also true of pedagogy. A broader reading of pedagogy also sees this concept extending beyond the ambit of craft (skills and techniques) to simultaneously embrace pedagogy as a science (underpinned by research and theory), and as an art (embracing intuition, **creativity** and **imagination**). Third, in this introduction we should remember that the Greek origins of the term *paidagōgia,* meaning 'to lead or tend to the child', may only be appropriate with regard to education in **childhood**, and hence inappropriate for teaching in any other stage of the lifecourse.

Taking up this latter problematic, there has been a move by some educators to develop new concepts in thinking about the craft, science and art of **teaching** with particular regard to adults. Most notably among these has been the work of Malcolm Knowles on *andragogy* (from the Greek *andre*—meaning man), in which he developed and popularised the notion of a 'gogy' (*agogos*—to lead) for adults as opposed to children (*paid*). This is premised on the (in some ways problematic) notion that adult learners are different from children as learners in a number of key aspects. These include a view of adults as: self-directed; possessing a fund of **learning** experiences; having a readiness to learn in a social context that is problem-centred; and being intrinsically motivated (Knowles, 1984, p.12). Adding to the lexicon, more recently the term *heutagogy* has also entered the field of education. Derived from the Greek representation of 'self', heutagogy positions the learner as both self-determined, grounded in personal experience and valuing self-efficacy (Hase and Kenyon, 2007). While each of these offers a different conception of learner disposition, it is less clear how this might inform the teaching, instruction or facilitation of adult learning as a counterpoint to pedagogy. While both andragogy and heutagogy have sought to offer adult-appropriate alternatives, pedagogy (as a craft, science and art) nonetheless remains undeveloped in the UK. In contrast, Brian Simon (1981) in his seminal paper 'Why no pedagogy in England?' notes the 'honoured place' of pedagogy in continental Europe, where it has developed from the writings of the seventeenth-century philosopher Comenius and a century later through the work of Herbart. In this European tradition, pedagogy and **didactics** (attention to the methods of instruction) continue to provide the backbone of university programmes in **teacher** education.

Pedagogy, it would seem then, is an evolving concept to which a number of interested fields of educational work have contributed or laid claim to. In his text dedicated to the subject, Alexander (2004) offers the following definition:

> Pedagogy is the act of **teaching** together with its attendant **discourse**. It is what one needs to know, and the skills one needs to command, in order to make and justify the many different kinds of decisions of which teaching is constituted.
>
> (Alexander, 2004, p.11)

Social pedagogy and relational pedagogy have offered further reorientations to the concept, notably in the province of youth work and social work as a means of more effectively addressing the integration of the intrapersonal, interpersonal and the communal, while actively promoting learner agency and shared experience. The emphasis on agency and structure as an issue for pedagogy has been powerfully expressed and hugely popularised in Freire's (1970) *Pedagogy of the oppressed* and has, in turn, generated extensive scholarship in the field of Critical Pedagogy. In this affiliation, the imperative of pedagogy is to expose and make sense of the contexts, causes, **ideologies** and discourses that lie beneath surface impressions, dominant myths and received wisdom in contemporary **society** (Shor, 1992). In advancing the principles of critical pedagogy, Giroux (2004) views teaching as a theoretical resource that is both determined and motivated by the problems that emerge in the 'in-between spaces/places/contexts that connect classrooms with the experiences of everyday life' (Giroux, 2004, p.37). Echoing van Manen's (1990) earlier reading of a postmodern pedagogy, we are encouraged *not* to think of pedagogy as process or content, medium or end, but something that operates powerfully and constantly in the realm of the 'in-between', what might otherwise be termed liminal, transitional or transactional space.

Questions to consider

1. How might pedagogy be regarded as a craft, science or art?
2. Can pedagogy be regarded as different to **teaching**?
3. What makes for a good enough or effective pedagogy?
4. How can pedagogy be viewed as an ethical matter?
5. Is a collective pedagogy possible?

References (with recommended readings in bold)

Alexander, R. (2004) 'Still no pedagogy? Principle, pragmatism and compliance in primary education', *Cambridge Journal of Education*, **34 (1), pp.7–34; also available in Alexander, R. (2008)** *Essays on pedagogy.* **Abingdon: Routledge, pp.43–71.**

Freire, P. (1970) *Pedagogy of the oppressed.* **London: Continuum.**

Giroux, H. (2004) 'Critical pedagogy and the postmodern/modern divide: Towards a pedagogy of democratization', *Teacher Education Quarterly*, Winter 2004, 31 (1), pp.31–47.

Hase, S. and Kenyon, C. (2007) 'Heutagogy: A child of complexity theory complicity', *International Journal of Complexity and Education*, 49 (1), pp.111–118.

Knowles, M.S. *et al.* (1984) *Andragogy in action: Applying modern principles of adult education*. San Francisco: Jossey-Bass.

Marton, F. and Booth, S. (1997) *Learning and awareness*. Mahwah, NJ: Lawrence Erlbaum.

Mortimore, P. (1999) (ed.) *Understanding pedagogy and its impact on learning*. London: Paul Chapman.

Petrie, P., Boddy, J., Cameron, C., Heptinstall, E., McQuail, S., Simon, A. and Wigfall, V. (2009) *Pedagogy—A holistic, personal approach to work with children and young people, across services: European models for practice, training, education and qualification*. London: Thomas Coram Research Unit, Institute of Education, University of London Briefing Paper—Update 2009.

Shor, I. (1992) *Empowering education: Critical teaching for social change*. Chicago: University of Chicago Press.

Simon, B. (1981) 'Why no pedagogy in England?' in Simon, B. and Taylor, W. (eds) *Education in the eighties: The central issues*. London: Batsford, pp.121–145.

van Manen, M. (1990) *Researching lived experience: Human science for an action sensitive pedagogy*, 2nd edn. London, ON: Althouse Press.

KEY CONCEPT: PLAY

Helen E. Lees

Concept origins

'Play is older than **culture**', says Huizinga (1950) in *Homo ludens: A study of the play element in culture*. In essence, play precedes humanity. Playing, a play or to play could be confused with theatre as well as a number of other domains. In education, to play and playing are linked often to forms of **learning**, despite play being non-**instrumental**. Playing in the educational sense is, according to children, about 'having fun, being outdoors, being with friends, choosing freely, not working, pretending, enacting, fantasy and drama, and playing games' (Sutton-Smith, 1997, p.49). Children have historically played substantially in lieu of the provision of formalised schooling, but with the rise of industrial **society** and its 'compulsory' (see **elective home education**) education systems, playing has been continually squeezed out of **mainstream schools** (Smith, 2013), and in particular in secondary stage education, to the point where in East Asia, the dominant traditions of **teacher**-led instruction, combined with a disregard for the educational value of play, has led to serious concerns for the well-being of children as they grow (see, e.g., Yoneyama, 1999; Kan, 2016).

Current status and usage

Play is different from games: 'In contrast to games, play **behaviour** is more disorganized, and is typically done for its own sake' (Smith, 2013, p.4). Increasingly, play is seen psychologically as the most developmentally vital aspect of children's **learning**, capable of equalling—sometimes exceeding—formalised instruction as an education (Gray, 2016). The implications of such research findings challenge formalised **school** education's dominance as the ultimate 'best' way to become an educated person. Limited attention to and valuing of children's playfulness in today's global school systems means that while 'Curiosity, playfulness and sociability are the engines of natural learning. Sadly, these are precisely the drives that are most likely to get children into trouble in school' (Gray, 2016, p.61). In schools across the world play is often, relative to **teacher**-directed instruction, overlooked in importance as 'childish' with playgrounds as 'forgotten spaces' (Burke and Grosvenor, 2003, p.45). In **Education Studies**, attention on play is often seen as an early years-stage concern, the idea being that children grow out of a need to play. While this is in some respects true, linked to types and expressions of play, play and playing itself is a life-long need, involving **adult education** and well-being: it enables cultural coherence (Huizinga, 1950). For children at least, there is a global attempt to instigate the right to play (United Nations, 1990, p.14), even if child labour and hardship remain a widespread issue.

A need for play inhabits diverse areas of development and self-expression: children can, through playing freely, express and 'develop pre-literacy skills, problem solving skills and concentration ... social **learning** experiences ... express possible stresses and problems' (Smith, 2013, p.4). In other words, play is both educational and emotionally beneficial. Indeed, research suggests that children who are deprived of play by being kept in a classroom to study afterwards play more vigorously than usual; an indication of their innate need. Furthermore, play is common as voluntary action and instinctual drive among children. All children, except those with restrictive circumstances, play and do so for anything up to 20 per cent of their time, with those more privileged to do so extending play beyond this (Smith and Pelligrini, 2013). Play is seen by some practitioners as 'a biological drive' and a repression of play as abusive (Waters, 2013). Through differing forms of play, children exercise their growing abilities and creatively explore the world and their own potentials in it, as well as the potentials of others. Various types of play include: locomotor play (exercise play), social play (interactions involving children and parents or caregivers), parallel play (in company or alone but not involving others), object play (using objects), language play, pretend play, and sociodramatic play (pretend narrative-based play with others) (Smith and Pelligrini, 2013, p.8). Wood (2010, p.14) writes 'it is not just play, but the capacity to play that has significance for human development and learning'. She considers that children without play in their lives will find **relationships** and new opportunities more difficult to successfully grasp.

⚙ Howard *et al.* (2006) suggest that children see an activity as play if it is enjoyable, takes place somewhere other than at a table, and does not include adults but does include peers. This links with the suggestion that children—including those of secondary **school** age—learn very well from computers when linked to the internet if they are free to have fun with the **technology** without adults interfering, work together, not alone, and do the work outside of a formalised, 'talk-chalk' environment (Mitra *et al.*, 2016; Rix and McElwee, 2016). This suggests that play is possible as a **life-long learning** activity and tool for all ages, under certain conditions. Indeed, in advertising firms and creative organisations such as Google, play-based working is a key process for excellence (Stewart, 2013). Recent work on alternative forms of '**curriculum**' suggests that playing around with ideas and impressions through conversational analysis at home is an efficient driver of educational attainment (Thomas and Pattison, 2007; Pattison and Thomas, 2016). In sum: if children (and adults) are left free to use their own innate curiosity and playfulness, education and sustained meaningful outcomes emerge. Naturally, such a conclusion questions the school as currently configured and gives more scope to **alternative education** approaches.

☺ Returning to Huizinga (1950), play 'is a significant function–that is to say, there is some sense to it. In play there is something "at play"' (p.i). This is significant if we consider **psychoanalysis** and its insistence that there is more to the surface of life than we can know at first glance. We know that children are able to work through emotional difficulties via play and specific techniques of 'Theraplay', 'sand play therapy', 'CLAY-therapy', narrative therapies and many others, which are in common usage with children manifesting issues such as **attachment** problems and relational traumas, as well as those who have experienced social, environmental, migrant or war-related trauma. These techniques are 'Widely practiced across the world, [and] expanding at an exponential rate' (Schaefer and Kaduson, 2006, p.xi). This, ironically, might be partly because too many children are not enabled (due to adult concerns) to access their human right to play. Nor are they getting sufficient quality access to play opportunities, time and spaces in a **neoliberal** world, where structure and goal-based achievement equals meaning.

Questions to consider

1. Why is play and playing forgotten?
2. What can be done to improve the quality and extent of playing for children throughout formalised education?
3. Who plays?
4. Why play?
5. Is playing always fun or can it sometimes take on different meanings?

References (with recommended readings in bold)

Burke, C. and Grosvenor, I. (2003) *The school I'd like*. London: Routledge.

Gray, P. (2016) 'Mother nature's pedagogy: How children educate themselves', in Lees, H.E. and Noddings, N. (eds) *The Palgrave international handbook of alternative education*. London: Palgrave Macmillan, pp.49–62.

Howard, J., Jenvey, V. and Hill, C. (2006) 'Children's categorisations of play and learning based on social context', *Early Child Development and Care*, 176 (3–4), pp.379–393.

Huizinga, J. (1950) *Homo ludens: A study of the play element in culture*. Boston, MA: Beacon Press.

Kan, W. (2016) 'Exploration and rethinking: Student-voice studies in China', in Lees, H.E. and Noddings, N. (eds) *The Palgrave international handbook of alternative education*. London: Palgrave Macmillan, pp.323–338.

Mitra, S., Kulkarni, S. and Stanfield, J. (2016) 'Learning at the edge of chaos—Self-organising systems in education', in Lees, H.E. and Noddings, N. (eds) *The Palgrave international handbook of alternative education*. London: Palgrave Macmillan, pp.227–239.

Pattison, H. and Thomas, A. (2016) 'Great expectations: Agenda and authority in technological, hidden and cultural curriculums', in Lees, H.E. and Noddings, N. (eds) *The Palgrave international handbook of alternative education*. London: Palgrave Macmillan, pp.129–144.

Rix, S. and McElwee, S. (2016) 'What happens if students are asked to learn Geography content, specifically population, through SOLE?', *Other Education*, 5 (1), pp.30–54.

Schaefer, C.E. and Kaduson, H.G. (eds) (2006) *Contemporary play therapy: Theory, research, and practice*. London: Guilford Press.

Smith, P.K. (ed.) (2013) 'Play', in *Encyclopedia on early childhood development.* **Available at: www.child-encyclopedia.com/play (accessed 21 June 2017).**

Smith, P.K. and Pelligrini, A. (2013) 'Learning through play', in Smith, K.P. (ed.) *Encyclopedia on early childhood development.* Available at: www.child-encyclopedia.com/play/according-experts/learning-through-play (accessed 21 June 2017).

Stewart, J.B. (2013) 'Looking for a lesson in Google's perks', *New York Times*, 15 March. Available at: www.nytimes.com/2013/03/16/business/at-google-a-place-to-work-and-play.html?_r=0 (accessed 27 October 2016).

Sutton-Smith, B. (1997) *The ambiguity of play.* London: Harvard University Press.

Thomas, A. and Pattison, H. (2007) *How children learn at home.* London: Continuum.

United Nations (1990) *United Nations convention on the rights of the child.* United Nations General Assembly.

Waters, P. (2013) 'Play in education: The role and importance of creative learning', *Guardian*, 27 February. Available at: https://www.theguardian.com/teacher-network/teacher-blog/2013/feb/27/play-education-creative-learning-teachers-schools (accessed 27 October 2016).

Wood, E. (2010) 'Reconceptualising the play–pedagogy relationship: From control to complexity', in Brooker, L. and Edwards, S. (eds) *Engaging play.* **Maidenhead: McGraw-Hill, pp.11–24.**

Yoneyama, S. (1999) *The Japanese high school: Silence and resistance.* London: Routledge.

KEY CONCEPT: PROFESSION

Dave Trotman

Concept origins

In continental Europe, the origins of profession can be traced as far back as the Middle Ages. According to Crook (2008), the professions began to appear as European monarchs turned to the services of physicians and surgeons. At about the same time, the administrative needs of the emerging modern state were met by jurists and bureaucrats, while order was maintained by professional armies. In turn, newly founded universities in Italy and France played their part in shaping the foundations of the so-called 'classical professions' of medicine, **law** and theology (Crook, 2008, pp.11–12). In contrast to these established classical professions, more recent occupations such as **teaching**, nursing and policing have been accorded the term 'semi-professions' (Etzioni, 1969).

Current status and usage

As Whitty (2008) has asserted, the concept of profession is contingent on both time and space. Bottery (2013), for instance, notes that 17 different criteria have been variously ascribed to professional **behaviour** at one time or another. Meanwhile accounts of profession have frequently emphasised what Haug (1973) has called a 'knowledge, service, **autonomy**' model. Typically, this concerns the possession of exclusive knowledge and practice; an ethical concern for clients; and the right to exercise control over admittance to and practice within the profession. Entry to a profession is typically regulated by academic qualification, requisite periods of professional training and/or study and compliance with specified standards of conduct that are either regulated by the profession itself or by an external body.

⏻ In contemporary usage, it is common for the term 'professional' to be applied to a range of occupations and trades. For instance, it would not be unusual to talk about a professional sports man/woman, a professional decorator, a professional musician, etc. In some instances, for a person to be classified as a professional might involve no more than receiving payment for their services, e.g., 'turning professional'. Being *a professional* and *being professional*, however, implies something that extends beyond simply receiving payment for services rendered. Ordinarily, the former suggests a level of skill or ability that is prized within a particular **society**, while the latter implies a set of **behaviour**s, values and qualities. Freidson argues that we should think of profession principally as 'an occupation that has assumed a dominant position in a division of labour so that it gains control over the determination of the substance of its own work' (Freidson, 1970, p.xv). He notes that the distinction between a profession and an occupation is the former's privilege of **autonomy** and self-direction, coupled with the profession's affirmation of its trustworthiness. In this regard, Whitty (2008) notes that the professions of **law** and medicine have benefited from 'licensed autonomy', in which the state bestows on selected professions the authority to regulate their own affairs. In relation to the **teaching** profession in England, this has undergone what some observers regard as an intensive period of *de*-professionalisation. This has involved an erosion of trust in **teacher**s' professional knowledge, **autonomy** and expertise as a consequence of increasing regulation by successive governments (Jeffrey and Woods, 1996; Fitzgerald, 2008).

✿ The emergence of a profession typically involves a range of sociohistorical forces. In Italy, Vicarelli and Spina (2015) note how dentists were once considered 'artisans', with their professionalisation emerging only belatedly in continental Europe, while remaining subservient to a dominant medical profession. Moreover, they observe how dentistry has become subject to increasing routinisation, rationalisation and commodification (Vicarelli and Spina, 2015, p.2). In the UK, Bradford (2005) has noted similar developments in the field of youth work, while Wood (2015) has shown how state intervention has contributed to the reshaping of profession in early **childhood** education. In the province of police education, White and Heslop (2012) highlight the often different philosophical orientations to training and development among public-sector professions. **Teaching**, they assert, is typically associated with **liberal** education and critical thinking, whereas policing is more commonly associated with matters of state control and the constraint of **citizenship**. Nursing, they contend, has focused on the interface between education and professionalism, in contrast with a police service that frames **learning** in terms of task performance and vocational competence (White and Heslop, 2012). As a consequence, interaction between different professional groups can present significant challenges for inter-professional education, with research pointing to the demands of reconciling differences between professional values and practices, conditions of service and training and professional development (Robinson and Cottrell, 2005).

Commenting on **teacher** professionalism in England, Barber (2005) has argued for the existence of four distinct phases of education reform. Beginning in the 1970s with a so-called 'Golden Age' of teacher **autonomy**, he describes this as an era of 'uninformed professionalism'. Barber asserts that it was only after a period of intensive state intervention, involving teachers acquiring appropriate state-approved knowledge and skills, that 'informed professionalism' was to become a reality, with the profession afforded a greater degree of freedom. The assertion that prior to state intervention professional autonomy was uninformed contrasts with ideas of *professionality* being advanced by Hoyle (1972, 1974) at about the same time. According to Hoyle, *professionality* concerns the knowledge, skills and procedures employed by teachers in the process of **teaching**. In a further development of this, he draws a distinction between what he calls 'restricted professionality', in which teaching is framed by immediate interests and imperatives, and the concept of 'extended professionality', involving a commitment beyond the ambit of the classroom and **school** to the influence and support of other institutions and practitioners. Extended professionality, then, involves an ethical and moral dimension of profession that transcends the routine, standardised and mandated version. In recent years, the principles of extended professionality have been given renewed impetus in the form of the 'activist professional'. Grounded in democratic principles, Sachs (2000) has advanced the idea of an activist profession predicated on agreed values, principles and strategies that are debated and negotiated (Sachs, 2000, p.81). In this regard, profession involves an altruistic commitment to collaboration, inter-professional dialogue and joint endeavour.

Questions to consider

1. What does it mean to be professional?
2. What does and what should membership of a profession entail?
3. How can professionalism and profession be safeguarded?
4. How can members of different professional groups learn from each other and work better together?

References (with recommended readings in bold)

Barber, M. (2005) 'Informed professionalism: Realising the potential', *Association of Teachers and Lecturers conference*, London 11 June.

Bottery, M. (2013) *Professionals and policy: Management strategy in a competitive world.* Abingdon: Routledge.

Bradford, S. (2005) 'Modernising youth work: from the universal to the particular and back again', in Harrison, R. and Wise, C. (eds), *Working with young people.* London: Sage, pp.57–69.

Crook, D. (2008) 'Some historical perspectives on professionalism', in Cunningham, B. (ed.) *Exploring professionalism.* London: Institute of Education, Bedford Way Papers, pp.10–27.

Etzioni, A. (1969) *The semi-professions and their organization: Teachers, nurses, social workers.* New York: Free Press.

Fitzgerald, T. (2008) 'The continuing politics of mistrust: Performance management and the erosion of professional work', *Journal of Educational Administration and History*, 40 (2), pp.113–128.

Freidson, E. (1970) *Profession of medicine: A study of the sociology of applied knowledge.* New York: Harper and Row.

Haug, M. (1973) 'Deprofessionalization: An alternative hypothesis for the future', *Sociological Review Monographs*, 20, pp.195–211.

Hoyle, E. (1972) 'Creativity in the school', unpublished paper given at OECD Workshop on Creativity in the School, Estoril, Portugal, reported in Stenhouse, L. (1975) *An Introduction to Curriculum Research and Development.* London: Heinemann.

Hoyle, E. (1974) 'Professionality, professionalism and control in teaching', *London Education Review*, 3 (2), pp.13–19.

Jeffrey, B. and Woods, P. (1996) 'Feeling deprofessionalised: The social construction of emotions during an OFSTED inspection', *Cambridge Journal of Education*, 26 (3) pp.325–343.

Robinson, M. and Cottrell, D. (2005) 'Health professionals in multi-disciplinary and multi-agency teams: Changing professional practice', *Journal of Interprofessional Care*, 19 (6), pp.547–560.

Sachs, J. (2000) 'The activist professional', *Journal of Educational Change*, 1, pp.77–95.

Vicarelli, G. and Spina, E. (2015) 'Professionalization and professionalism: The case of Italian dentistry', *Professions and Professionalism*, 5 (3), pp.1–18.

White, D. and Heslop, B. (2012) 'Educating, legitimising or accessorising? Alternative conceptions of professional training in UK higher education: comparative study of teacher, nurse and police officer educators', *Police Practice and Research*, 13 (4), pp.342–356.

Whitty, G. (2008) 'Changing modes of teacher professionalism: Traditional, managerial, collaborative and democratic',

in Cunningham, B. (ed.) *Exploring professionalism*. London: Institute of Education, Bedford Way Papers, pp.28-49.

Wood, E. (2015) 'De-professionalising or re-professionalising the early childhood workforce in England', BERA Blog: Research Matters, 14 September. Available at: https://www.bera.ac.uk/blog/de-professionalising-or-re-professionalising-the-early-childhood-workforce-in-england (accessed 26 October 2016).

KEY CONCEPT: SCHOOL

John Bayley

Concept origins

Schools across the world are the result of political decisions, which affect structure, **curriculum**, staffing, starting and finishing ages, and systems of accountability. In other words, they are social constructions of a given time and location. Schools have existed in their modern form since approximately the mid-nineteenth century, though their origins appear to be in the ancient Greek *skhole*. These Greek *skhole* were devoted to the appropriate use of leisure time for the aristocracy, in terms of cultural activities, particularly literature, music and gymnastics (Egan, 2008, p.5). According to Bartlett and Burton (2007, p.60), rudimentary education by the Church was gradually succeeded by more widespread schooling in the 1800s, frequently provided by philanthropists. The key date in Britain was the passing of the Education Reform Act, in 1870, which provided for elementary schooling for all, up to the age of thirteen. Globally, schools have taken a variety of forms, but here we are dealing specifically with the emergence of school as a State-devised institution. In that sense, national histories of school differ, but it is broadly agreed that the school can now be found in every country with a significant population and is a force of social **hegemony**, control and **teaching** as **profession**. The rise of the school has come with increasing compulsion to attend and lessening of costs to participate (Nagdy and Roser, 2016).

Current status and usage

There are significant differences between ideas of the purposes of schools (and, therefore, education). In many western countries, the move, in recent years, has been towards competition between schools, greater external accountability via national systems of testing, an increasingly centralised **curriculum**, and the

211

closing or transference of leadership of so-called 'failing' schools. In England, even the term 'school' has, in many cases, given way to 'academy', a move which perhaps denotes a narrowing of purpose, and increasing marketisation. An exception is Finland, a country which performs well in PISA testing, where students do not begin formal schooling until age seven, national testing is by sampling and **teacher assessment**, there are fewer taught hours, little reliance on homework, and the **inclusion** of pupils with **special educational needs** and disabilities is standard in **mainstream** schools (Sahlberg, 2015). A recent market phenomenon is of 'low-fee' private schools catering for the world's poorest parents, who would rather send their children to a school they pay for than the state-provided cost-free school, on account of perceived schooling quality as well as safety issues linked to school attendance (Harber, 2016). A steady rise in **elective home education** around the world seems also to challenge the **hegemony** of the school, but numbers taking this route remain small (Kunzman and Gaither, 2013). Flint and Peim (2012) question our ability to unimagine the school as the key social institution of our times.

The most common practice in Western nations is for schools to be under the control of local authorities. In England, however, the **neoliberal ideology** of the Labour government of 1997–2010 resulted in the introduction of City Academies, directly funded by government, but permitting sponsorship from business, churches and charitable organisations. The ostensible function of these English schools was to improve educational outcomes in so-called 'failing' inner-city areas. This move away from local authority control was enthusiastically extended by the Academies Act, hastily enacted by a newly elected Conservative-Liberal Democrat coalition government in 2010. This provided for any school, not just 'failing' schools (which can now be forced to become academies), to convert to academy status, and for this to be extended to primary schools. This was followed by legislation in 2011, which allowed for the establishment of free schools, whereby businesses, groups of parents, **teachers** and charitable bodies could propose the setting up of a new school. These moves towards greater 'freedoms' for schools have resulted in the diminishing of the role of local authorities, to the point where, as Cunningham (2012, p.122) suggests:'The underlying issue remains, after this relentless sequence of structuring and restructuring, how a service such as primary education mostly controlled and largely funded through national government, can remain democratically accountable in the locality and responsive to local needs.' Such **policy** and **politics** mean changes for **pedagogy**, **profession** and **curriculum**. In other countries, such as the US, similar plans for 'diversification' of school models have meant wide-reaching implications for students, teachers and families, such that school is increasingly market-driven, policy-laden and exposed to political intervention.

Internationally schools have developed in such a way that the voices of pupils are marginal in terms of how the institutions are managed and organised. What mechanisms there are for pupil participation in these areas are generally tokenistic, or have prescribed parameters (e.g., school councils). A very different **ideology** is found in **democratic education** examples, such as Summerhill School. There are some parallels here with the work of Paolo Freire (1921–1997), in Brazil, who saw **neoliberal** concepts of schooling as prescriptive and compliant. He envisaged schools as arenas for 'dialogue, **praxis** and conscientisation' (Aubrey and Riley, 2016, p.130). Ivan Illich (1971) considered de-schooled societies as optimal in the face of social and interpersonal alienation. Unsurprisingly then, schools can play a significant role in bringing disparate communities together as sites of local action for justice, such as in Israel where humanist principles aim to reach out to Palestinian neighbours (Aloni, 2016), or in São Paulo, Brazil, where schools act as sites for 'neighbourhood education' outreach programmes into ghettoised slums. Democratic ideals for school (e.g., Apple, 2000; Fielding and Moss, 2011) do not necessarily reach all (Reay *et al.*, 2008), with some schools being open to charges of violence, where **teachers** take advantage of the vulnerability of students, or interpersonal and **institutional** mores of interaction end in students refusal to enter school (Yoneyama, 1999; Harber, 2004).

Michel Foucault (1926–1984) used Jeremy Bentham's idea of a panopticon (a proposed prison, based upon the central inspection principle) as a blueprint to critique what he considered to be a surveillance **society**. He made few direct references to schools, but his writings (e.g., 1977) have influenced discussions of **power** in schools, if not decisions. For Foucault, schools may be spaces for supervising, hierarchising and rewarding (Piro, 2008). Schools, it may be argued, have increasingly become sites of surveillance, often with external and internal CCTV cameras as the most visible signs, but with high stakes accountability processes (Ofsted), and **performativity** targets as their more insidious manifestations. This may then translate into a high demand for pupil compliance, in terms of school uniform regulations, or an inflexible **behaviour policy**, etc. Of course, many would argue that schools can only function effectively as 'communities' if such demands or 'standards' are in place; that they are, by definition, locations that require a high degree of conformity and security (the supposed justification for which is most provocatively illustrated by a number of well-publicised shootings in US schools—see Lees, 2015). However, whether the often resultant structure of schools (segregation by age, or by ability, artificial groupings into classes, etc.) is the most effective site for **learning** for children and young people remains debatable.

Questions to consider

1. Are schools meant to compensate for **society**?
2. What should be the balance of power in schools between professionals and learners?
3. How useful is a current **diversity** of school models within countries?
4. Should schools be public or private?
5. Who leads/manages/runs/determines the ethos of a school?

References (with recommended readings in bold)

Aloni, N. (2016) 'Humanist schools in the face of conflicting narratives and social upheaval: The case of Israel', in Lees, H.E. and Noddings, N. (eds) *The Palgrave international handbook of alternative education.* London: Palgrave Macmillan, pp.369–384.

Apple, M.W. (2000) 'Away with all teachers: The cultural politics of home schooling', *International Studies in Sociology of Education*, 10 (1), pp.61–80.

Aubrey, K. and Riley, A. (2016) *Understanding and using educational theories.* London: Sage.

Bartlett, S. and Burton, D. (2007) *Introduction to education studies.* London: Sage.

Cunningham, P. (2012) *Politics and the primary teacher.* Abingdon: Routledge.

Egan, K. (2008) *The future of education: Reimagining our schools from the ground up.* New Haven, CT and London: Yale University Press.

Fielding, M. and Moss, P. (2011) *Radical education and the common school: A democratic alternative*. **London: Routledge.**

Flint, K.J. and Peim, N. (2012) *Rethinking the education improvement agenda: A critical philosophical approach*. London: Continuum.

Foucault, M. (1977) *Discipline and punish: The birth of the prison*. London: Penguin.

Harber, C. (2004) *Schooling as violence: How schools harm pupils and societies*. **London: RoutledgeFalmer.**

Harber, C. (2016) 'Is low fee private schooling in developing countries really an "alternative"?', in Lees, H.E. and Noddings, N. (eds) *The Palgrave international handbook of alternative education*. London: Palgrave Macmillan, pp.355–368.

Illich, I. (1971) *Deschooling society*. London: Calder and Boyars.

Kunzman, R. and Gaither, M. (2013) 'Homeschooling: A comprehensive survey of the research', *Other Education*, 2 (1), pp.4–59.

Lees, H.E. (2015) 'School violence', in Dubnick, M.J. and Bearfield, D. (eds) *Encyclopedia of public administration and public policy*, 3rd edn. New York: Taylor & Francis.

Piro, J. (2008) 'Foucault and the architecture of surveillance: Creating regimes of power in schools, shrines, and society', *Educational Studies*, 44 (1), pp. 30–46. Available at: http://dx.doi.org/10.1080/00131940802225036 (accessed 28 November 2016).

Nagdy, M. and Roser, M. (2016) *Primary education*. Available at: https://ourworldindata.org/primary-education-and-schools (accessed 28 November 2016).

Reay, D., Crozier, G., James, D., Hollingworth, S., Williams, K., Jamieson, F. and Beedell, P. (2008) 'Re-invigorating democracy?: White middle class identities and comprehensive schooling', *The Sociological Review*, 56 (2), pp.238–255.

Sahlberg, P. (2015) *Finnish lessons 2.0*. **New York: Teachers College Press.**

Yoneyama, S. (1999) *The Japanese high school: Silence and resistance*. London: Routledge.

KEY CONCEPT: SPECIAL EDUCATIONAL NEEDS

Clare Bright

Concept origins

The introduction in the UK of the term 'special educational need' (SEN) is widely attributed to the Warnock Report of 1978. The primary aims of the report were to promote a positive approach to the educational development of children with special needs and to recognise that children with such needs should have the educational goals of independence, enjoyment and understanding in common with all children, irrespective of their abilities or disabilities. This also marked a general shift from a negative medical model of **disability**, in which a person is seen as having individual physiological or **cognitive** limits and 'defects', to that of a social model, where it is more widely recognised that **society** is responsible for including or excluding people with disabilities (Farrell, 2012). The Warnock committee questioned the need to educate children in special **school**s and recognised the entitlement of children with SEN to an education in **mainstream** settings, thus attempting to minimise segregation by promoting the locational, social and functional integration of children with SEN into an education with other children (Warnock, 1978).

Current status and usage

Since the term SEN was proposed by Warnock, it became the dominant shorthand term used in education, despite there being widespread acknowledgement of the problems in referring to a single category label. Ekins suggested that there was complacency in the use of the term and it had lost its real meaning (Ekins, 2015, p.28). In England, the introduction of the Special Educational Needs and **Disability** Code of Practice in 2015 (hereafter SEND; DfE, 2015) included guidance relating to disabled children and young people, as well as those with SEN. It defines a

SEN as a **learning** difficulty or disability which calls for special educational provision. It confirms that someone has a learning difficulty or disability if they have:

> significantly greater difficulty in learning than the majority of others of the same age, or a disability which prevents or hinders him or her from making use of facilities of a kind generally provided for others of the same age in **mainstream school**s or post–16 institutions.
>
> (DfE, 2015, p.285)

The Code of Practice sets out four broad areas of need: Communication and interaction; Cognition and learning; Social, emotional and mental health difficulties; and Sensory and/or physical needs. The Code also recognises that many children and young people who have SEN may have a disability under the **Equality** Act 2010—that is 'a physical or mental impairment which has a long-term and substantial adverse effect on their ability to carry out normal day-to-day activities'.

 In England, the needs of pupils with SEN or **disability** are protected through statutory legislation in the form of the Code of Practice for SEND and the Disability **Equality** Duty (contained within the Equality Act 2010). This places specific duties on **school**s to improve outcomes for pupils, enabling them to achieve their best, become confident individuals, have fulfilling lives and ensuring successful transition into adulthood. This requires schools to take positive steps to the removal of the barriers for those with a disability—known as the duty to make reasonable adjustments. Schools are required to designate a **teacher** to coordinate SEND provision (The Special Educational Needs Coordinator, SENCo) and to inform parents when they are making special educational provision for a child (DfE, 2015, p.92). All schools are legally required to have a clear approach to identifying and responding to SEND. The Code of Practice places responsibility on teachers for the progress and development of all the pupils in their **class** stating that 'high quality **teaching**, differentiated for individual pupils, is the first step in responding to pupils who have or may have SEN' (DfE, 2015, p.99). Additional provision for pupils identified as requiring SEND support should be delivered through a four-part cycle of Assess, Plan, Do, Review—known as a graduated approach. Factors such as the category of need, the pupil's interests, ability and level of maturity will determine the strategies required to best support the pupil, such as the use of assistive technologies, deployment of additional support staff, adjustments to the physical environment, additional resources, differentiated tasks and interventions from outside agencies.

Reporting on parental confidence in SEN provision in England, the Lamb Inquiry of 2009 made 51 recommendations; an indication that the system at the time was poorly conceived and provision inconsistent. Legislation has since been designed to address many of the shortcomings, including ensuring that pupils participate in making decisions about their provision, enabling more effective multi-agency working of the services around the child through improved communication and consultation with the **family** and more 'joined-up' decision making. Effective provision for pupils with SEND requires collaboration between **teacher**s, support staff, the SENCo, the pupil and their family. Lamb has noted that the deployment of **teaching** assistants to support pupils with SEN can lead to pupils becoming dependent on adult support, reduce opportunities for independent **learning**, and research suggests that 'there is a clear relationship between support from teaching assistants and lower attainment and slower rates of progress' (Lamb, 2009, p.28). Russell *et al.* (2013, p.52) have argued that the most vulnerable pupils need more, not less, time with the school's most skilled and qualified teachers. More complex needs may require support from agencies external to the **school** setting, such as an educational psychologist, physical and sensory services or mental health services. Historically, children with disabilities and their families have experienced barriers in accessing these services, because of the complexities of multi-agency working and the challenges inherent in defining roles and responsibilities, meeting competing priorities, allocating funding and resources and communicating effectively (Hodkinson, 2016, p.139).

Inconsistencies in the use of the term SEN has been reported in England by the Office for Standards in Education (Ofsted, 2010): they found that those in the **profession** often ascribed this label to children requiring better **teaching** or **pastoral welfare** support, which, therefore, gave rise to wide variations in the numbers of pupils specified as SEN (Hodkinson, 2016, p.13). The definition of SEN is also problematic in that it is based on the recognition of difference. Norwich (2008), for instance, describes the core dilemma as whether or not to recognise and respond to difference. Frederickson and Cline (2011, p.33) point out that doing so can lead to more effective provision or the risk of **discrimination** and stigma. The ideological frameworks used to inform our understanding, educational practice and provision for pupils with SEN each offer different perspectives but also have their limitations. The psycho-medical model, sometimes viewed as a deficit model, identifies the person with SEN as having individual impairments, judged against developmental and functional norms leading to a diagnosis and a label, in need of a 'cure' (Hodkinson, 2016, p.24). Swain and French suggest that by locating the cause of the difficulties within the individual, it denies disabled people their **human rights**, fails to recognise **diversity** and their lived experiences or personal empowerment (Swain and French, cited in Hodkinson, 2016, p.24). In contrast, the social model offers the view that **disability** is a result of physical, organisational and attitudinal barriers within **society**. The recent development of an 'affirmative model' of disability aims to extend the social model by incorporating the lived experiences of disabled people with the premise that disabled people should have control of their lives (Swain and French, cited in Hodkinson, 2016, p.33).

Questions to consider

1. Why has the language of SEN been described as 'highly contentious' by Ofsted (2010)?
2. How can educational settings facilitate the participation of pupils and their families in making decisions about their provision?
3. How can settings promote independent **learning** for pupils with a range of SEN?
4. What are the benefits to educating children with SEN in **mainstream** settings?
5. Is it ever preferable for children with SEN to be educated in special **school**s? Why?

References (with recommended readings in bold)

DfE (2015) *Special educational needs and disability code of practice: 0–25 years.* London: Department for Education.

Ekins, A. (2015) *The changing face of special educational needs*, 2nd edn. London: Routledge.

Equality Act (2010) London: HMSO. Available at: www.legislation. gov.uk/ukpga/2010/15/pdfs/ukpga_20100015_en (accessed 27 October 2016).

Farrell, M. (2012) *Educating special children*, 2nd edn. London: David Fulton.

Frederickson, N. and Cline, T. (2011) *Special educational needs: Inclusion and diversity*. Buckingham: Open University Press.

Hodkinson, A. (2016) *Key issues in special educational needs and inclusion*. London: Sage.

Lamb, B. (2009) *SEN and parental confidence*. Nottingham: DCSF.

Norwich, B. (2008) 'Dilemmas of difference, inclusion and disability: international perspectives on placement', *European Journal of Special Needs Education*, 23 (4), pp.287–304.

Ofsted (2010) *The special educational needs and disability review: A statement is not enough*. Office for Standards in Education, Children's Services and Skills. London: Ofsted Publications.

Russell A., Webster, R. and Blatchford, P. (2013) *Maximising the impact of teaching assistants*. Abingdon: Routledge.

Warnock, M. (1978) *Special educational needs: Report of the committee of enquiry into the education of handicapped children and young people*. London: HMSO.

KEY CONCEPT: TECHNOLOGY

Steve Dixon and Richard Sanders

Concept origins

From papyrus, the abacus, chalk and slate, the printing press, radio, television, and more recent developments in computing and the internet, the use of technology in education is nothing new. Following Heidegger's definition of technology as 'a man-made means to an end established by man' (1977), technology has been utilised in education for thousands of years. Whether you are reading this text via a tablet device or a printed book, *both* are technologies. Each of these technologies also has an interrelated chronology. In what she calls 'socio-technological shifts', Harasim (2012) considers this chronology to have profound cultural, political, economic and educational implications and, hence, cannot be considered to be value-free.

Current status and usage

What we understand by technology in contemporary usage has, over the last 20 years, rapidly evolved from analogue to digital devices, requiring development of both hardware and software. In educational settings in the developed world, the use of technology is now the staple of both **teaching** and **curriculum**. In a worldwide market estimated at $5 trillion per annum (Selwyn, 2014), this can be seen in the use of tablets, interactive whiteboards and **learning** software in primary and elementary **school**s, to **Flipped Learning** practices, Virtual Learning Environments, **MOOCs** and **web 2.0** software at secondary and university level. As a consequence, '**e-learning**' is an established term in the educational lexicon. In England, successive governments have portrayed technology in education as a force for good (Livingstone, 2004), in which technology skills are seen as anytime/anywhere learning that can connect with technology uses in the home (Buckingham, 2007). Work by Sugata Mitra and colleagues (e.g., 2005) along similar lines of the **power** of technology to **teach** in any space has evolved out of relatively 'school-less' environments.

Discussions around educational technology typically highlight a distinction between an idealistic view of how technologies *could* be used in education—called 'affordances'—and the realities of how they are *actually* used. This distinction also includes a comparison between home and educational use, where some observers claim the existence of a 'digital divide' or 'digital disconnect' between **school** and the popular **culture** of children's lives outside of education (Buckingham, 2007; Selwyn, 2011). An additional age-related divide has also been popularised by Prensky's characterisation of 'digital natives' and 'digital immigrants' (2001), involving a supposedly common-sense perception that young people are fully immersed spontaneous users of digital technology, which has, in turn, radically changed the way that they learn. This view of the relationship between young people, technology and education has led some researchers to question the **technological determinism** of attempts to promote technological solutions in search of a problem—a so-called 'Trojan Mouse' approach (Selwyn, 2014). In addition, as Buckingham (2007) notes, business interests in the promotion of technology have frequently resulted in a narrow decontextualised focus on ICT skills within education, such as use of Microsoft Office applications. This is despite recent **policy** shifts in English education from Information Communication Technology to Computer Studies, to include, in particular, a new emphasis on coding (Williamson, 2016).

In the UK, government interest in technology has commonly focused on skills acquisition in preference to the more critical dimensions of learner development and the potential of education technology to empower the learner within digital domains. At the same time, protectionist **discourses** around young people's use of technology and social media have also proliferated. These have been centring on the idea of media technologies causing (or facilitating) harm, as opposed to more measured approaches of assisting the development of critical thinking, enabling the personal **assessment**s of risk and the taking of appropriate measures for personal safety (Byron, 2008; Cassidy et al., 2013). While protectionist discourses have focused on the importance of 'Content, Contact and Conduct' (Byron, 2008; Livingstone, 2009), as Cassidy et al. have highlighted, young people often prefer support and advice from adults rather than approaches that are punitive in nature (2013, p.17). In the province of critical digital literacy, Buckingham points out that the interpersonal contexts of encounters as well as 'broader social and economic process that determine how texts are produced and circulated' are also necessary for meaningful education in the digital realm (2007, p.149). This is extended further when we consider the idea of 'transliteracies', where participation in organised and informal education enables transition across traditional and digital domains. Facer (2012) argues that a technological future requires a rethinking of educational interactions to enable young people to have appropriate, rather than alienated, **voice** and for education, broadly conceived as part of social functioning, to make the most of technology.

Interest in the **power** of technology to liberate **learning** beyond the confines of traditional schooling has led to parallels being drawn between the opportunities created by new technological developments and earlier educational ideas advanced in such areas as the 'de-schooling' movement (Illich, 1972) and democratisation and **life-long learning** (Freire, 1970). For proponents of technological affordances, new learning models such as online collaborative learning (Harasim, 2012)—involving forms of mediated collaborative learning and knowledge building through problem solving—and connectivism (Siemens, 2005)—which emphasises the importance of social and cultural contexts—offer contemporary responses to ways in which learning, education and technology may be configured. Following Papert's (1999) view that technology provides new opportunities of engagement for children with different learning and **cognitive styles**, these responses offer theoretical alternatives to realise the claimed transformative opportunities of technology. Certainly, technologies now play a wide range of roles in educational provision, such as tutoring systems, learning aids, online resources, cognitive tools and administrative functions. While these approaches provide a renewed emphasis on the role of technology within learning, how alternative these are to existing **social constructivist** pedagogies remains unclear (Livingstone, 2012). Ultimately, the need for theoretical tools, such as those used to explain social reproduction and stratification, are likely to prove as necessary in problematising technological realities in education as much as the deployment of technologies themselves.

Questions to consider

1. Is technology ethically neutral?
2. Can technology change the **learning** and **teaching** process?
3. What does it mean to be digitally literate in contemporary education?
4. What particular technologies provide meaningful affordances for education?
5. How can the digital divide between technology use at home and **school** be addressed?

References (with recommended readings in bold)

Buckingham, D. (2007) *Beyond technology; Children's learning in an age of digital culture.* Cambridge: Polity.

Byron, T. (2008) *Safer children in a digital world: The report of the Byron review.* Available at: http://webarchive.nationalarchives.gov.uk/20090703110952/http://www.dfes.gov.uk/byronreview/pdfs/Final%20Report%20Bookmarked.pdf (accessed 10 March 2016).

Cassidy, W., Faucher, C., and Jackson, M. (2013) 'Cyberbullying among youth: A comprehensive review of current international research and its implications and application to policy and practice', *School Psychology International,* 34 (6), pp.1–38.

Facer, K. (2012) 'Taking the 21st century seriously: Young people, education and socio-technical futures', *Oxford Review of Education,* 38, pp.97–113.

Freire, P. (1970) *Pedagogy of the oppressed.* Harmondsworth: Penguin.

Harasim, L. (2012) *Learning theory and online technologies.* London: Routledge.

Heidegger, M. (1977) *The question concerning technology and other essays.* New York: Harper Torchbooks. Title essay available at: http://simondon.ocular-witness.com/wp-content/uploads/2008/05/question_concerning_technology.pdf (accessed 10 March 2016).

Illich, I. (1972) *Deschooling society.* New York: Marion Boyar.

Livingstone, S. (2004) 'Media literacy and the challenge of new information and communication technologies', *The Communication Review,* 7 (1), pp.3–14.

Livingstone, S. (2009) *Children and the internet.* Cambridge: Polity.

Livingstone, S. (2012) 'Critical reflections on the benefits of ICT in education', *Oxford Review of Education,* 38 (1), pp.9–24.

Mitra, S., Dangwal R., Chatterjee, S., Jha, S., Bisht, R.S. and Kapur, P. (2005) 'Acquisition of computer literacy on shared public computers: Children and the "Hole in the wall"', *Australasian Journal of Educational Technology*, 21, pp.407–426. Available at: www.hole-in-the-wall.com/docs/Paper08.pdf (accessed 26 October 2016).

Papert, S. (1999) 'Introduction: What is logo? Who needs it?', in *Logo philosophy and implementation*. Montreal: Logo Computer Systems, pp.iv–xvi. Available at: www.microworlds.com/support/logo-philosophy-papert.html (accessed 10 March 2016).

Prensky, M. (2001) 'Digital natives, digital immigrants', *On the Horizon*, 9 (5), pp.1–6. Available at: www.albertomattiacci.it/docs/did/Digital_Natives_Digital_Immigrants.pdf (accessed 10 March 2016).

Selwyn, N. (2011) *Education and technology: Key issues and debates*. London: Continuum.

Selwyn, N. (2014) *Distrusting educational technology: Critical questions for changing times*. Abingdon: Routledge.

Siemens, G. (2005) 'Connectivism: a learning theory for the digital age', *International Journal of Instructional Technology & Distance Learning*, 2 (1). Available at: www.itdl.org/Journal/Jan_05/article01.htm (accessed 26 October 2016).

Williamson, B. (2016) 'Political computational thinking: policy networks, digital governance and "learning to code"', *Critical Policy Studies*, 10 (1), pp.39–58.

KEY CONCEPT: UNSCHOOLING

Helen E. Lees

Concept origins

Unschooling could be said to have emerged out of Ivan Illich's concept of **deschooling** in *Deschooling society* (1971). This seminal, although ultimately unheeded book called for schools to be de-funded and instead 'convivial' institutions to emerge as the norm where people learn in their own way, at their own pace, using '<u>**learning**</u> webs'. Illich later re-considered these views towards a need for less of a destruction of **schooling** itself and more towards a new sense of loving each other (Bruno-Jofré and Zaldívar, 2012). Holt was the first to coin the term 'unschooling' as an idea (1964). He agreed with Illich's original notion of a deschooled <u>**society**</u>, but had a different take on the socio-political conditions of the reality of deschooling. Holt saw the future Illich called for as best expressed through **autonomously** styled <u>**elective home education**</u> and wrote a number of books on this, as well as establishing the *Growing Without Schooling* magazine (1977–2001). These resources for rethinking education unpacked the concept of unschooling not as a political or social change movement, but as educational daily practice. Clearly the idea of a non-schooled regime is a common part of informal learning of any kind. It is also linked to thorough-going <u>**democratic education.**</u>

Current status and usage

Unschooling as a term is becoming increasingly well known, with the global rise in numbers and profile of <u>**elective home education**</u>. The difference between un- and deschooling is possibly the stage at which it occurs: unschooling is the home education style as practice (**autonomous**) and deschooling can be seen as the initial 'detox' process after leaving school attendance (getting used to the freedoms of unschooling). The terms are, however, interchangeably used (e.g., McKee, 2002). The journey of home educating for many practitioners involves degrees of unschooled **learning**—especially as the practice matures and relaxes into the lack of pressures, constraints and expectations of being at home. The concept includes ideas around letting go, trust, discovery, curiosity, freedom, facilitation and a value for long-term and in-depth involvement in any curricula interest rather than short-term goals for immediate gain. We do not know how many unschoolers/deschoolers (past and present) there are exactly 'but the number appears to be growing at a fast pace' (Gray and Riley, 2015, p.9). Forms of unschooled approaches are being translated into **mainstream school** projects such as that outlined by Rix and McElwee (2016) in conducting **teaching** through an internet 'big questions' project, in line with Mitra's unschooling-infused 'hole in the wall' project (Mitra, *et al.*, 2005).

A definition of unschooling is 'When pressed, I define unschooling as allowing children as much freedom to learn in the world as their parents can comfortably bear' (Pat Farenga, in Holt and Farenga, 2003). This is an appropriate definition perhaps: unschooling is often seen by novitiates as scary and needing a leap of faith to follow (Dowty, 2000; Khimasia, 2015). Most people have been to **school** where they learnt to associate education with a raft of limited possibilities, such as only **learning** if and when taught, or learning to a schedule, or in certain kinds of locations such as a classroom. When the freedoms and what seems to be risk of unschooled-style **elective home education** are first experienced, it can be disconcerting for parents who, in terms of education **law**—although national laws vary—must themselves bear the brunt of any possible failure in their educational strategy, or deliberate lack of this, towards the development of preparing and fitting a child for a contributory role in **society**. This fear of failure is possibly most felt in respect to reading competence. In unschooled elective home education, it is not unusual for children to not be able to read until quite late—say, for instance, age 8 or 10—on account of never having been deliberately 'schooled' in reading skills or forced to practice reading. The curious thing is that unschooled children pick up reading by themselves and to their parents' eyes seem suddenly and mysteriously to be able to read advanced materials when the parents thought them illiterate (Thomas and Pattison, 2007; Pattison, 2016). Learning happens *differently* through unschooling than through the **didactic** approach of the school, research suggests. How and why is still being determined. It may not be the usual kind of **cognitive**-based answers which emerge; **attachment**, love, the spirit, choice, **complexity theory** and other matters may be playing an important and decisive role.

There are a number of benefits outlined from practitioners' self-reporting about unschooled life. Popular among teenagers who are or have been unschooled is the idea of forming oneself according to individual interests (Llewellyn, 1998). Reports from unschooled youngsters in research studies discuss appreciation for the ways in which the freedoms involved lead to a 'sense of self' that is secure and well-rounded by these youngsters' own estimations (Sheffer, 1995). Perhaps part of the positivity is that life is not being compartmentalised into the public and private domains of the **school** and the home: 'In unschooling families, children are in charge of their own education and are expected to "learn through living" rather than to think of **learning** as something distinct from life itself' (Gray and Riley, 2015, p.9). Other studies have described unschooling as a lifestyle choice involving an alternative humanity, utilising sustainability and careful, slow living to experience life well. They have also emphasised lower levels of household income (see Gray and Riley, 2015). This resonates with unschooling families who spoke of their existential decision to leave **schooling** for unschooled **elective home education** as life-changing and away from 'that system' (Neuman and Avriam, 2003; Lees, 2011).

Unschooling is a radical educational form. It is hard to grasp as a concept, because it is so different from a **schooling** approach involving timetables and protocols of **behaviour** and **learning**—our common concept of education. Nevertheless, once understood in its basic tenets of degrees of freedom to self-regulate and self-determine, learning the concept acts to allow **education studies** students to reconfigure their perspective on and concept of what education 'itself' is and can be. This is a fundamental issue in and of educational philosophy and returns us to foundations and 'father figures' of philosophy of education with their patriarchal suggestions that initiation from another is key to the 'educated person' (Peters, 1966), or that 'the process' of education is in the hands of **teacher**s (Peters, 1967). Indeed, as a resource for thinking—if not enacting actual lived practice—unschooling and its **deschooling** phase are important in relation to **power**, **society**, **law**, a **democratic education** and the idea of interpersonal, social and personal freedom.

Questions to consider

1. How might children suffer or benefit from unschooling?
2. How can unschooling be judged to have succeeded as an educational pathway?
3. What kind of **family** does unschooling as method or style require?
4. What is the future of unschooling?
5. Should unschooling be regulated and is this possible?

References (with recommended readings in bold)

Block, A.A. (1997) *I'm 'only' bleeding: Education as the practice of violence against children*. New York: Peter Lang Publishing.

Bruno-Jofré, R. and Zaldívar, J.I. (2012) 'Ivan Illich's late critique of deschooling society: "I was largely barking up the wrong tree"', *Educational Theory*, 62 (5), pp.573–592.

Dowty, T. (2000) *Free range education: How home education works*. Stroud: Hawthorn Press.

Gray, P. and Riley, G. (2015) 'Grown unschoolers' evaluations of their unschooling experiences: Report I on a survey of 75 unschooled adults', *Other Education*, 4(2), 8–32.

Holt, J. (1964) *How children fail*. Harmondsworth: Penguin.

Holt, J. (1967) *How children learn*. New York: Pitman.

Holt, J. and Farenga, P. (2003) *Teach your own: The John Holt book of homeschooling*. Cambridge, MA: Perseus Publishing.

Illich, I. (1971) *Deschooling society*. London: Calder and Boyars.

Khimasia, A. (2015) 'Caesurae in home education: Losing control, gaining perspective', *Other Education*, 4 (1), pp.57–60.

Lees, H.E. (2011) 'The gateless gate of home education discovery: What happens to the self of adults upon discovery of the possibility and possibilities of an educational alternative?', unpublished PhD thesis, University of Birmingham, Birmingham, UK. Available at: http://etheses.bham.ac.uk/1570 (accessed 26 October 2016).

Llewellyn, G. (1998) *The teenage liberation handbook: How to quit school and get a real life and education*. Eugene, OR: Lowry House.

McKee, A. (2002) *Homeschooling our children, unschooling ourselves*. Madison, WI: Bittersweet House.

Mitra, S., Dangwal, R., Chatterjee, S., Jha, S., Bisht, R.S. and Kapur, P. (2005) 'Acquisition of computer literacy on shared public computers: Children and the "Hole in the wall"', *Australasian Journal of*

Educational Technology, 21, pp.407–426. Available at: www.hole-in-the-wall.com/docs/Paper08.pdf (accessed 26 October 2016).

Neuman, A. and Avriam, A. (2003) 'Homeschooling as a fundamental change in lifestyle', *Evaluation and Research in Education*, 17 (2–3), pp.132–143.

Pattison, H. (2016) *Rethinking learning to read*. Shrewsbury: Educational Heretics Press.

Peters, R.S. (1966) 'Education as initiation', in Curren, R. (ed.) *Philosophy of education: An anthology*. Oxford: Wiley-Blackwell, 2007, pp.55–66.

Peters, R.S. (1967) 'What is an educational process?', in Peters, R.S. (ed.) *The concept of education*. London: Routledge and Kegan Paul.

Rix, S. and McElwee, S. (2016) 'What happens if students are asked to learn Geography content, specifically population, through SOLE?', *Other Education*, 5 (1), pp.30–54.

Sheffer, S. (1995) *A sense of self: Listening to home schooled adolescent girls*. Portsmouth, NH: Boynton/Cook Publishers.

Thomas, A. and Pattison, H. (2007) *How children learn at home*. London: Continuum.

POWER

KEY CONCEPT: CLASS

Graham Brotherton

Concept origins

The idea that people can be classified according to their social status has existed in some form in most societies throughout history; examples include the feudal system across medieval Europe and the caste system in India. However, contemporary sociological thinking about class has its roots in the work of Marx and Weber and their attempts to explain social status in the context of industrialisation during the 19th century. Marx saw class as primarily an issue of economic inequality and the **power** differences which stem from this. Weber saw class as not solely economic but also linked to other ideas, such as social status and both of these ways of thinking about class have continued to be influential.

Current status and usage

Within sociology generally and the sociology of education in particular, class remains a contested issue. There is much work which still uses ideas about class developed from the work of Marx and Weber, but there are others who cast doubt on its continued relevance. The influential German sociologist Ulrich Beck (2004) described class as a form of analysis that had outlived its analytical usefulness. Others argue strongly that class remains one of the most useful ways of exploring educational inequalities (e.g., Dorling, 2014).

For Marx and others in the Marxist tradition, class is inextricably linked to the possession of economic resources (see **capitalism**). The relationship between the capitalist class who control economic resources and the working class who have to work for capitalists is an inherently conflictual one, as it is in the interests of workers to seek a fairer allocation of resources and in the interests of capitalists to deny this. For Marxists this is not an even struggle, with the resources of the state—including the resource of the education system—actively supporting the capitalist class. An alternative perspective on class can be found in the work of Weber, who suggests that as well as economic factors, we need also to think about the role of status and **power**, as social status and power can come from factors other than simply economic ones, e.g., **family** background. There is a considerable body of research in the sociology of education (for instance, in the work of Ball, Reay or Devine—see below), which does suggest that social class plays a significant role in educational experiences in terms of 'achievements' and that working class children do on average less well than middle class ones. The Royal **Society** of Arts conducted a survey of the literature in 2010, and their report begins by saying 'Social class remains the strongest predictor of educational achievement in the UK, where the social class gap for educational achievement is one of the most significant in the developed world' (Perry and Francis, 2010, p.2).

One of the most influential attempts to apply Marxist ideas to education can be found in the work of Bowles and Gintis and their study *Schooling in capitalist America* (1976). Bowles and Gintis argue that both the nature of the **curriculum** and the way that **school**s are organised are designed to prepare children for their allocated role as either a worker or a member of the capitalist class: children experience school very differently according to their social background, and there is 'correspondence' between school experience and a child's perceived future role. Working-class children experience more of the disciplinary and controlling elements of education and middle-class children more of the supportive and developmental elements. The work of Bowles and Gintis has been criticised for being overly deterministic and of overstating the link between education and work. A number of theorists such as Willis and Giroux have highlighted the way in which working-class pupils create oppositional sub-**culture**s in response, in order to resist the imposition of dominant ideas about the 'value' of education, e.g., the 'lad' culture in Willis's famous study *Learning to labor* (1977) of a school in the 1970s. It can be argued that in some senses this is now a historical document, as the 'lads' were part of a working-class culture where plentiful labouring jobs made opposition to school a realistic position. However, more recent studies, such as Jackson (2006), highlight the fact that children of both **sexes** continue to adopt apparently oppositional attitudes at school and this does have a class dimension.

In recent years, the idea that class still plays a central role both in the context of education and more widely has been challenged (e.g., by Beck, 2004). The suggestion is that we now live in a 'classless' **society** and that opportunities are now more evenly available. Merit or ability become the basis of **selection** rather than social class, and the role of education is therefore to ensure that every child, regardless of background, achieves their potential (see **equality**). Beck suggests that ideas about class reflect the world as it was in the 19th century, when Marx and Weber were writing, rather than the modern world where we live in more individualised ways and have a much less developed sense of class **identity**. Class is therefore a 'zombie' category: dead in terms of its usefulness for analysis, but still hanging around in sociological textbooks. This view has been challenged, perhaps most notably by Reay (2006), who develops a compelling argument about the centrality of class. It is important to note that Beck is not arguing that inequalities have declined or ceased to exist, but is suggesting that class is now less useful as a way of explaining educational or other forms of inequality and that therefore we need more complex ways of thinking about these issues. One influential strand of thinking which seeks to maintain the notion of class as a central element of experience while acknowledging that it is one of a range of factors, is the concept of **'intersectionality'**. This idea, which originated in black feminism but has been applied more widely, originates in the work of Crenshaw (1989). It highlights that oppression is not simply related to a specific dimension of experience or **identity** (e.g., class, **gender**, **ethnicity**, **race**, **disability**, **sexuality**), but is about the relationship between these dimensions of difference: the world is experienced very differently by white, middle-class, heterosexual males from black, working-class gay women. The notion of 'intersectionality' has been increasingly used in education research. This occurred initially in the US but more recently in the UK and has highlighted the complex interplay between different factors and the ways in which this interplay can have both positive and negative implications.

Questions to consider

1. Did your social class affect your own experience of education?
2. Is class still a useful concept in thinking about how people experience education?

3. Is it useful to link class to other possible dimensions of advantage/disadvantage through taking an intersectional approach?
4. Who notices class and how does that affect education?
5. What creates class?

References (with recommended readings in bold)

Ball, S.J. (2013) *The education debate*, **2nd edn. Bristol: Policy Press.**

Beck, U. (2004) *Ulrich Beck—Johannes Willms: Conversations with Ulrich Beck*. London: Polity Press.

Bowles, S. and Gintis, S. (1976) *Schooling in capitalist America: Educational reform and the contradictions of economic life*. New York: Routledge and Kegan Paul.

Crenshaw, K. (1989) 'Demarginalizing the intersection of race and sex: A black feminist critique of antidiscrimination doctrine, feminist theory, and antiracist politics', *University of Chicago Legal Forum*, 1989, 139–67.

Devine, F. (2004) *Class practices: How parents help their children get good jobs*. Cambridge: Cambridge University Press.

Dorling, D. (2014) *Inequality and the 1%*. London: Verso.

Giroux, H. (2012) *Disposable youth*. **New York: Routledge.**

Jackson, C. (2006) *Lads and ladettes in school: Gender and a fear of failure*. Maidenhead: Open University Press.

Perry, E. and Francis, B. (2010) *The social class gap for educational achievement: A review of the literature*. London: Royal Society of Arts. Available at: https://www.thersa.org/discover/publications-and-articles/reports/the-social-class-gap-for-educational-achievement-a-review-of-the-literature (accessed 9 December 2015).

Reay, D. (2006) 'The zombie stalking English schools: Social class and educational inequality', *British Journal of Educational Studies*, **54 (3), pp.288–307.**

Willis, P. (1977) *Learning to labor*. New York: Columbia University Press.

KEY CONCEPT: COLONIALISM

Roger Willoughby

Concept origins

The etymological origins of the word 'colonialism' stem from the Latin *colonia*, which refers to a farm or settlement and related particularly to Roman citizens who settled in conquered territories. Defined by Loomba (2015, p.20) as 'the conquest and control of other people's land and goods', colonialism has been a widespread and recurrent feature of world history, being a prominent characteristic of the Roman, Mongol, Aztec, Inca, Ottoman and Chinese empires among others before the age of modern European colonisation began in the 16th century. By the 1930s, over 84 per cent of the world's land surface was or had been subject to colonisation (Loomba, 2015). Forming a colonial settlement inevitably impacts on indigenous populations, reconfiguring local communities through a wide variety of practices. The latter might include military conquest, mass violence, genocide, trade, expropriation and theft, dehumanisation and marginalisation, slavery, **racism**, patriarchal, and—not least—cultural and educational practices (Ashcroft *et al.*, 2006, 2013). European imperialist colonisation was characterised by, among other things, its extensive exploitation of indigenous resources and population as labour and its use of colonies as captive markets for goods and services.

Current status and usage

As an academic discipline, colonial and **postcolonial** studies are a new, growing and somewhat heterogeneous field (Young, 2003; Ashcroft *et al.*, 2006; Andreotti, 2011, 2015). We do not live in a *post*-colonial world: the colonial and postcolonial intertwine, with on-going dependency between the margins and the centre, neocolonial or postcolonial regimes retaining the marks of colonial dynamics and **identity**. Contemporary **globalisation** reinforces this, with **imperialism** as an economic—rather than a political—system continuing to dominate Third World markets. As both a source of raw materials and customers, capitalism continues to seek to safeguard its own so-called 'legitimate interests' (Fanon, 1961; Olsson, 2014), rendering it complicit in the latent and sometimes overt violence of supposedly postcolonial contexts. With education historically intertwined with the exertion of colonial control (Gramsci, 1971; Viswanathan, 1992; Andreotti, 2011; AbuHilal and Abu-Shomar, 2014), contemporary education often continues to obscure and perpetuate colonial legacies (Dei, 2010; Dei and Simmons, 2010). Here, **teacher** and taught become proxies for the colonial master and subject, recapitulating their relational **power** dynamics in educational curricula and practices, not only overseas but in domestic contexts. Education, thus, continues to be dominated by the living legacies of these on-going histories, with postcolonial problems, such as alienation (Fanon, 1952), **race**, and **racism** (Gilroy, 1987; Mac an Ghaill, 1988; Pajaczkowska and Young, 1992), continuing to negatively impact on educational experience and attainment. In the post-9/11 world, contemporary anxieties around the Muslim other are another iteration of this. Given all this, it is unsurprising that traditional education itself has come to be questioned as a colonising **discourse** (Dei and Simmons, 2010; Hoerder, 2014).

Colonialism impacts on all areas of a colonised people's life, with the colonial agenda being implemented and maintained through both force and propaganda. Drawing heavily on Gramsci's (1971) ideas, Viswanathan (1992, p.167) argued that: 'cultural domination operates by **consent**, indeed often preceding conquest by force ... Consent of the governed is secured primarily through the moral and intellectual suasion'. Submission of colonised peoples is thus substantially achieved through the use of propaganda and mind control: generating a conviction that the colonisers are, not just militarily, but economically, morally and intellectually superior and that they are best suited to govern. As an inevitable part of such **identity politics**, this propaganda process (in promoting the colonisers) demotes and distorts the identity, abilities and **culture** of the colonised. Taking colonial rule in India as one example of this process, the introduction of an English **curriculum** formed a key mechanism of the **ideology** (Althusser, 1971).

The Charter Act of 1813 had placed responsibility for native education on the East India Company, while the 1835 English Education Act made the study of English language and literature compulsory. Such study fostered a cultural ideal and encouraged individualism, undermining group solidarity. This claimed moral, intellectual and cultural superiority was held out as being benevolently available through the Anglicised Indian education system, successful participation in which would allow the colonised population to emulate, equate themselves to, and supposedly 'meritocratically' compete with the colonial rulers (Walsh, 1983; Viswanathan, 1992). Neo-Marxist academics in particular have criticised such ideology as a type of **hegemony** (Gramsci, 1971; Hoerder, 2014) that supports the **power** of a select few, while limiting opportunities for the vast majority.

⚙ In the influential work of Edward Said (1995), the term Orientalism is used to refer to negative stereotype prejudices towards the East. Said variously defines Orientalism 'as a set of constraints on and limitations of thought' (1995, p.42), or 'as a kind of Western projection onto and will to govern over the Orient' (1995, p.95), such that 'the Orient that appears in Orientalism, then, is a system of representations framed by a whole set of forces that brought the Orient into Western **learning**, Western consciousness, and later, Western Empire' (1995, pp.202–203). It is thus an example of dehumanisation, a necessary process in the colonial enterprise as it offers pseudo-justification for the actions of the coloniser, as well as reducing their moral engagement. As Césaire (1950, p.21) pithily remarked: 'colonisation = thingification'. Such constructions of supposed knowledge, following Foucault, highlight the **power** exerted by the West, aided in this process by various intellectuals, educational and cultural institutions. The relevance of these ideas to contemporary education is substantial. Two major reasons will be highlighted here. First, with **globalisation**, mass migration and **multiculturalism**, the populations education serves have become heterogeneous, hybrid and complex. **Postcolonial culture**s are no longer remote and renegotiation of traditional positions and identities is needed on an on-going basis. **Race** and **racism** (as artefacts of colonisation) negatively impact on the educational experience, learning journeys and outcomes of students with postcolonial heritages. Second, the mechanisms, processes and consequences of colonialism usefully illuminate the analogous processes that constrain educational freedom and possibilities. Patriarchy and regulatory practices, for example, disempower students, rendering them subaltern, while demanding their compliance. Colonial and postcolonial theory offers ways to further address such challenges (Gilroy, 1987; Andreotti, 2011; Andreotti and Souza, 2012; AbuHilal and Abu-Shomar, 2014).

Within a colonial system, colonised people can struggle to sustain their **identity** and self-esteem. This stems from their subjugated state, their loss of agency, their lack of recognition, and multiple other indignities suffered as a colonised people. Drawing on Hegel (1807; Kojève, 1934–35), Marx and **psychoanalysis**, Frantz Fanon (1952; Gardner, 1996) suggested one common attempted solution to this problem: the colonised group (and particularly its elites) internalises and unconsciously partly identifies with the typically white coloniser. The native self is devalued in this process. A superficial self-esteem can then be maintained through alliance and subservient lieutenancy with the 'ideal'; the internal coloniser. This false consciousness entails a degree of alienation, though addressing this gives rise to fears not only about social chaos but also about the individual's mental equilibrium. Active collaboration with the colonial **power**, particularly by participation in its administrative institutions including education, offers colonial peoples a position of some perceived value. The cost, however, is high. Such engagement compromises the colonised subject (and the colonised **society**), relegating them to a lower ranked or subaltern status (Gramsci, 1971; Guha, 1982; Spivak, 1985). While Fanon (1952) depicted this adoption of the coloniser's mores as a 'white mask', the allied notions of ambivalence and mimicry have been importantly discussed by Bhabha (1994). Mimicry is perhaps the most subversive here, Bhabha suggests, as it is not far removed from mockery and contains elements of menace, both of which challenge the coloniser's pretensions and disrupt their authority. Bhabha extends such arguments using the contested notion of hybridity to emphasise the interdependence of coloniser and colonised groups, challenging notions of racial purity and promoting **diversity** in the process. While educational encounters in colonial contexts operated to extend **hegemony** through persuasion, and power is being exercised in very similar ways within **postcolonial** setups, domestic educational **policy** and **praxis** too often conspire to create contemporary colonial subjects in the classroom. While challenged by **alternative education**, decolonisation in **school**s and wider society has a considerable way to go (Dei and Simmons, 2010; Andreotti, 2011, 2015).

Questions to consider

1. How does colonialism shape your **identity** and that of your local community?
2. Do colonial legacies only impact on Black Asian and Minority **Ethnic** (BAME) students in education?
3. How does colonialism differentially impact on females and males and how is this reflected in education?
4. How was and is the **curriculum** shaped by colonialism?
5. How might you critique the **globalisation** of education from the perspective of colonialism?

References (with recommended readings in bold)

AbuHilal, F. and Abu-Shomar, A. (2014) 'On pedagogy and resistance: Unravelling the post-colonial politics in the literature classroom', *Realis*, 4 (2), pp.176–192.

Althusser, L. (1971) 'Ideology and ideological state apparatus', in Althusser, L. (ed.) *Lenin and philosophy and other essays*. New York: Monthly Review Press.

Andreotti, V. (2011) *Actionable postcolonial theory in education*. New York: Palgrave Macmillan.

Andreotti, V. (2015) 'Postcolonial perspectives in research on higher education for sustainable development', in Barth, M., Michelsen, G., Rieckmann, M. and Thomas, I. (eds) *Routledge handbook of higher education for sustainable development*. Abingdon: Routledge, pp.194–206.

Andreotti, V. and Souza, L. (2012) *Postcolonial perspectives on global citizenship education*. New York: Routledge.

Ashcroft, B., Griffiths, G. and Tiffin, H. (eds) (2006) *The post-colonial studies reader*, 2nd edn. London: Routledge.

Ashcroft, B., Griffiths, G. and Tiffin, H. (eds) (2013) *Postcolonial studies: The key concepts*, 3rd edn. Abingdon: Routledge.

Bhabha, H.K. (1994) *The location of culture*. Abingdon: Routledge.

Césaire, A. (1950) *Discourse on colonialism*. New York: Monthly Review Press, 1972.

Dei, G.J.S. (ed.) (2010) *Fanon and the counterinsurgency of education*. Rotterdam: Sense Publishers.

Dei, G.J.S. and Simmons, M. (eds) (2010) *Fanon and education: Thinking through pedagogical possibilities*, 2nd edn. New York: Peter Lang.

Fanon, F. (1952) *Black skin white masks*. London: Pluto Press, 1986.

Fanon, F. (1961) *The wretched of the earth*. London: Penguin Classics, 2001.

Gardner, F. (1996) 'The colonial inheritance in theory and practice', *Psychoanalytic Psychotherapy*, 13, pp.135–149.

Gilroy, P. (1987) *There ain't no black in the Union Jack: The cultural politics of race and nation*. Abingdon: Routledge Classics, 2002.

Gramsci, A. (1971) *Selections from the prison notebooks of Antonio Gramsci*. Translated and edited by Q. Hoare and G. Norwell-Smith. London: Lawrence & Wishart.

Guha, R. (ed.) (1982) *Subaltern studies 1: Writings on South Asian history and society*, 7 vols. Delhi: Oxford University Press.

Hegel, G.W.F. (1807). *The phenomenology of spirit*. Translated by A.V. Miller. London: Oxford University Press, 1977.

Hoerder, D. (2014) 'Education for a transcultural life-world or for a hegemonic nation? Schooling in the British empire, in France, and in Canada, 1830s–2000s', *Studia Migracyjne—Przeglad Polonijny*, 40 (3), pp.17–32.

Kojève, A. (1934-35). *Introduction to the reading of Hegel*. Translated by J.H. Nichols. Ithaca, NY: Cornell University Press, 1969.

Loomba, A. (2015) *Colonialism/postcolonialism*, 3rd edn. London: Routledge.

Mac an Ghaill, M. (1988) *Young, gifted and black: Student–teacher relations in the schooling of black youth*. Milton Keynes: Open University Press.

Olsson, G.H. (2014) *Concerning violence: Nine scenes from the anti-imperialistic self-defense* (on DVD). Stockholm: Story AB.

Pajaczkowska, C. and Young, L. (1992) 'Racism, representation, psychoanalysis', in Donald, J. and Rattansi, A. (eds) *Race, culture and difference*. London: Sage.

Said, E. (1995) *Orientalism: Western conceptions of the East*. Harmondsworth: Penguin.

Spivak, G.C. (1985) 'Can the subaltern speak? Speculations on widow sacrifice', *Wedge*, 7/8, pp.120–130.

Viswanathan, G. (1992) 'The beginnings of English literary study in British India', in Donald, J. and Rattansi, A. (eds) *Race, culture and difference*. London: Sage, pp.149–165.

Walsh, J.E. (1983) *Growing up in British India: Indian autobiographers on childhood and education under the Raj*. New York: Holmes and Meier.

Young, R.J.C. (2003) *Postcolonialism: A very short introduction*. Oxford: Oxford University Press.

KEY CONCEPT: EQUALITY

Graham Brotherton

Concept origins

The idea of equality has a long and complex history. It has roots in a number of different areas including philosophy, **politics** and faith traditions. The history of the idea also incorporates a history of struggle; from the anti-slavery movements of the 18th and 19th centuries, through trade unions, women's rights campaigners such as the suffragettes, and later campaigns for equal rights in the context of **disability** or **sexuality**. Modern notions of equality can be traced back to the emergence of the **discourse** of **human rights** in the aftermath of the Second World War, with its emphasis on formal and legal approaches to equality.

Current status and usage

Equality is often defined in relation to other key concepts such as **diversity** and **inclusion.** It also has a specific meaning in English **law** from the 2010 Equality Act. This long-fought-for act makes it illegal to treat someone less favourably on the basis of age, **disability**, **gender** reassignment, marriage and civil partnership, pregnancy and maternity, **race**, religion or belief, sex or sexual orientation (Equality and **Human Rights** Commission, 2014). There is, however, a danger that this can lead to a narrow focus on the avoidance of **discrimination** rather than a more positive approach on trying to develop equality through genuinely inclusive practice. Acknowledging this conundrum can lead to a more positive definition of equality, emphasising the need to ensure fair and equal treatment of all people, regardless of background, and which recognises other sorts of inequality not addressed in the legislation, such as socio-economic background.

⏻ Equality can be thought of as having several interrelated dimensions and it is helpful to separate these out. While in its most general sense it is about equal treatment, there are at least three components of this: equality of access; equality of opportunity; and equality of outcome. In the context of education, this could be thought of as access to provision issues, fair treatment concerns and whether once in a setting all flourish, or not. Leaving aside at this point some of the difficulties, such as what a good **school** might mean or what sort of definition we might use for **achievement**, it is helpful to think about the implications of considering equality in these different ways. As suggested above, much of the emphasis in recent years has been on issues of access with an emphasis on 'improving' existing schools and creating 'better' alternatives. This is promoted through a combination of a tight inspection regime and new initiatives for diverse provision, e.g., through Free Schools. Equality is therefore seen as mainly a question of access, and it is assumed that opportunity and outcome naturally follow on from this.

⚙ A different perspective on equality can be found in the work of a number of authors such as Dorling (2014), Marmot (2010), and Pickett and Wilkinson (2010). These have focused not so much on equality per se, but on the damaging effects of a lack of equality: inequality. Such authors highlight inequality across a number of different dimensions, including educational attainment as measured by test scores, physical and mental health, and social mobility, with societies that are more equal being able do better in terms of health, social mobility, etc. In this context, equality is defined in economic terms as income inequality: more equal societies by definition have narrower gaps between those who have and those who have not (or have less). It is, though, evident that economic inequality is linked to other forms of inequality through social networks, etc. (see **capitalism**). It is important to note that in England and Wales, economic inequalities were originally included in the 2010 Equality Act, but after the 2010 general election, the sections that related to economic inequalities were not enacted. For Dorling (2014), and the other authors referred to above, the only path to fairer and more equal societies is by addressing existing structural inequalities through a broad range of approaches to tackle poverty and exclusion in **society**. Access to a 'good' education is part of this, but cannot work in isolation.

⠸ Any sophisticated understanding of equality needs to recognise that it is a complex and contested area. Equality in the absolute sense may not be possible, but we do need to consider how much inequality we are prepared to tolerate. Some of the most interesting attempts to think about this come from the area of development economics and the work of Sen (2010) and Nussbaum (2013) who each propose slightly different versions of something called the 'capabilities approach'. This approach emphasises what people are able to do or be, the *'actual opportunities a person has'* (Sen, 2010; my italics), rather than just focusing on material inequalities on the one hand and formal processes and outcomes on the other. Equality in this context demands that we consider whether a child or young person has access to all of the resources they need—social, cultural and material. It also requires recognition that barriers which might not always be considered, such as physical, linguistic, or reputational barriers, need addressing through thinking about whether education is in the right geographical places and whether their buildings encourage access. Does education reflect fully the linguistic needs of particular communities in terms of both languages and the structure of communication? Are all students equally valued, regardless of **class** or cultural background? If not, what strategies or attitudes can change this? In thus reflecting we are enabled to move beyond accounts of inequality/equality focusing simply on a single category of explanation, e.g., poverty, **disability**, **ethnicity**. This allows us to develop explanations that acknowledge resources are differentially located in relation to a number of dimensions: e.g., equality might mean very different things to a white, middle-class, non-disabled woman in relation to a black, working-class, disabled man.

Questions to consider

1. How much inequality is acceptable and who decides this?
2. Can education create greater equality and if so how?
3. Can the capabilities approach help us to work effectively with young people?
4. Who decides what is equal or not?
5. Where does equality and inequality come from?

References (with recommended readings in bold)

Dorling, D. (2014) *Inequality and the 1%*. London: Verso.
Equality and Human Rights Commission (2014) *What equality law means for you as an education provider—further and higher education.*

Available at: www.equalityhumanrights.com/sites/default/files/what_equality_law_means_for_you_as_an_education_provider_further_and_higher_education.pdf (accessed 22 April 2016).

Marmot, M. (2010) *Fair society, healthy lives: strategic review of health inequalities in England post 2010.* The Marmot Review. London: Institute of Health Equity. Available at: www.instituteofhealthequity.org/projects/fair-society-healthy-lives-the-marmot-review (accessed 25 November 2015).

Nussbaum, M. (2013) *Creating capabilities: The human development approach*. Cambridge, MA: Harvard University Press.

Pickett, K. and Wilkinson, R. (2010) *The spirit level: Why equality is better for everyone*. London: Penguin.

Sen, A. (2010) *The idea of justice.* London: Penguin.

KEY CONCEPT: HEGEMONY

Dan Whisker

Concept origins

'Hegemony' means the dominant set of ideas in a **society**. The word has its roots in the Ancient Greek word for 'leader', and was used to talk about the way that one city-state (such as Athens) could dominate others through military and political **power**. Since then, its meaning has evolved and, in recent times, found a place in thinking about education and society. The Italian communist Antonio Gramsci (1971), while imprisoned in the 1930s by Mussolini's fascist government, used the word to write about how rival social classes could persuade other groups to accept their leadership (Jones, 2007). He defined hegemony as 'The "spontaneous" **consent** given by the great masses of the population to the general direction imposed on social life by the dominant fundamental group' (Gramsci, 1971, p.12). Of course, he thought that this 'consent' wasn't really 'spontaneous' at all, but was carefully built by propaganda, **culture** and education to produce a version of 'common sense' which protected the ruling **class**. Crucially, he thought of **politics** as a 'war of ideas' which no side could ever completely win (Gramsci, 1971, pp.229–239). Domination by one set of ideas (hegemony) is always incomplete.

Current status and usage

As a Marxist, Gramsci was mainly interested in **class** struggle— in particular, in why some parts of the Italian working class had supported a fascist government which protected the rich. Since the liberation movements of the 1960s, the idea of hegemony has been used to think about dominant ideas of **gender**, **race**, **sexuality**, **disability** and other kinds of oppression, as well as social class. Because hegemonic (for this we could substitute 'common') interpretations of gender or **ethnicity** (or anything else) feel like common *sense*, they are incredibly powerful in shaping the reality of people's lives. Once, not so long ago, it was 'common sense' in British **school**s that boys should study maths, science and woodwork, while girls studied domestic science and typing, with little in the way of 'hard' academic subjects. We can call such ideas expressions of 'gender hegemony' (see Connell, 1987, 1995; Budgeon, 2014), and see how incomplete that hegemony is: what seems like common sense in one time and place seems like prejudice from other perspectives.

To explain how hegemony might work in practice, Smith (2012, p.57) uses the example of three employees on a factory production line. All three do the same job, but interpret their situation very differently. The first is a socialist and sees herself as an oppressed member of the working **class**. The second takes a more common-sense view and sees herself as decent and hard-working, but something of a failure for not making more of her life. The third is a born-again Christian who experiences hardships as God 'testing her faith'. If the owner of the factory asked the workers to accept a pay cut in order to cope with a recession, we can see that some of these views would make life easier for the owner and some would make it harder. Similarly, if a child was given detention for constantly arguing with her **teachers** about the content of lessons, teachers and **school** leaders would find it much easier to deal with a parent who believed in the '*hegemonic*' or common-sense idea that teachers **teach** and students listen, than a parent with '*counter-hegemonic*' views, who defends their child's right to argue with teachers. There are several related *hegemonic* ideas about education which might work in a similar way to help schools function smoothly: the idea that some children are clever and some stupid; the idea that formal qualifications are a good measure of education; the idea that children should attend scheduled lessons whether they want to or not.

As well as hegemonic ideas *about* **school**, there are also hegemonic ideas promoted *through* school. A history **curriculum** can **play** an important role in determining how people *imagine* the national community which they live in (Nash *et al* 1986; Anderson 1991; Taylor and Guyver, 2012). German history lessons, for example, now address the reality of the Holocaust, and encourage students to reflect on the nation's historical responsibility. In Turkey, the **law** forbids anyone—history **teachers** included—from referring to the Ottoman Empire's treatment of the Armenians as 'genocide' (though most non-Turkish historians recognise it as such). This difference will have significant influence on the common-sense (hegemonic) ideas which most people have about their nation's history, its values, and what these mean for its political life today. It could be that having a law to suppress one interpretation of history actually shows a *less complete hegemony* than a situation where certain facts are simply ignored. Every history teacher in Turkey has to hold the phrase 'genocide of the Armenians' in their head at some point, and take great **care** not to say it out loud. In contrast, there is no rule preventing teachers in British '**citizenship**' lessons from discussing the tens of millions of Indians killed by the British Empire's deliberate **policy** of starvation in the 1870s (Davis, 2001) or the 100,000 killed in British concentration camps in Kenya in the 1950s (Elkins, 2005). If these topics don't come into classroom discussion, it is perhaps because teachers don't know about them, or perhaps because it is simply common sense that it would not be appropriate to **teach** British children about them. Ignorance of the facts is a kind of hegemonic silencing also. This is why education offers such a powerful response as a weapon against the totalitarian tendencies of hegemony in full swing.

Gramsci calls small battles over ideas a 'war of position' (1971, pp.229–239). There are political consequences for how anyone (you sitting reading this book *right now*, colleagues you might work with, students you might **teach**) thinks about who they are, how they live and what they do and why. Laclau and Mouffe (1986) argue that because we all carry several different identities, the war of ideas depends on building *counter-hegemonic* alliances between groups with different identities but shared interests. For example, some strands of feminism have historically excluded black women, and weakened themselves by not recognising that black women faced extra forms of oppression because they were black, while some parts of the black liberation movement ignored women's oppression, again excluding black women, but this time because they were women (see hooks, 1981; Hill Collins, 2000). Feminists and other liberation movements have worked hard to overcome this divisiveness in recent years (see Hill-Collins and Bilge, 2016), but **identity** differences still often serve to tie particular groups into a *hegemonic coalition*. This works in favour of the powerful, as when poor white voters are persuaded that **ethnic** minorities or migrants rather than wealthy elites are the source of their economic and national problems (Frank, 2007). Ultimately, hegemony in **school**s connects beliefs about the purpose, content and value of formal schooling to the whole social system; to advanced global **capitalism**. Someone asks: 'What is education for?' And common sense answers: 'Education is to get a good job and become a productive member of **society**.' Hidden inside that answer are a hundred hardly-spoken ideas about ownership and profit; the moral value of wage labour; the purpose of human life and the limits of what is politically possible. There are always other answers to these questions; different, fairer and truer ideas. The British Prime Minister Margaret Thatcher used the phrase 'There is no alternative' throughout her career (1945–2004), but the idea of hegemony teaches us that this is never true. As the motto of the World Social Forum says: 'Another World is Possible.'

Questions to consider

1. If **politics** is a war of ideas, what are the weapons?
2. Is common sense always political?
3. Is hegemony a political tool to gain or keep **power** or an evolution of **society** trying to make sense of life?
4. Do **school**s work with, against or in spite of hegemony?
5. Is there one 'counter-hegemony' or many?

References (with recommended readings in bold)

Anderson, B. (1991) *Imagined communities: Reflections on the origin and spread of nationalism*. London: Verso.

Budgeon, S. (2014) 'The dynamics of gender hegemony: Femininities, masculinities and social change', *Sociology*, 48 (2), pp. 317–334.

Connell, R.W. (1987) *Gender and power*. Cambridge: Polity Press.

Connell, R.W. (1995) *Masculinities*. Cambridge: Polity Press.

Davis, M. (2001) *Late Victorian holocausts: El Niño famines and the making of the Third World*. London: Verso.

Elkins, C. (2005) *Britain's gulag: The brutal end of empire in Kenya*. London: Jonathan Cape.

Frank, T. (2007) *What's the matter with Kansas?: How conservatives won the heart of America*. New York: Henry Holt and Company.

Gramsci, A. (1971) *Selections from the prison notebooks of Antonio Gramsci*. Translated and edited by Quintin Hoare and Geoffrey Norwell-Smith. London: Lawrence & Wishart.

Hill-Collins, P. (2000) *Black feminist thought: Knowledge, consciousness, and the politics of empowerment*, 2nd edn. New York: Routledge.

Hill-Collins, P. and Bilge, S. (2016) *Intersectionality.* London: John Wiley and Sons.

hooks, B. (1981) *Ain't I a woman: Black women and feminism.* Brooklyn: South End Press.

Jones, S. (2007) *Antonio Gramsci: Routledge critical thinkers.* London: Routledge.

Laclau, E. and Mouffe, C. (1986) *Hegemony and socialist strategy: Towards a radical democratic politics.* London: Verso.

Nash, G.B., Crabtree, C. and Dunn, R.E. (1997) *History on trial: Culture wars and the teaching of the past.* New York: Knopf.

Smith, A.M. (2012) *Laclau and Mouffe: The radical democratic imaginary.* London: Routledge.

Taylor, T. and Guyver, R. (2012) *History wars and the classroom: Global perspectives.* Charlotte, NC: Information Age Publishing.

Thatcher, M. (1945–2004) *Speeches, interviews and other statements.* Available at: www.margaretthatcher.org/speeches (accessed 26 October 2016).

KEY CONCEPT: LAW

Helen E. Lees

Concept origins

Law concerning education is a recent phenomenon, comparatively speaking. It was not until 1870 that nation states in Europe began to take notice of the impact of making **school** attendance compulsory and controlling populations through schooling. This began with the Prussians discovering that a schooled populace produced a more efficient army and made them militarily successful. This 'win' for the idea of schooling caught on and inspired other countries around this time to see the benefit of schooled, obedient children as useful for national needs. Such regulation came of course in the context of other forms of 'discipline' as Foucault outlines in his social commentaries and histories (1976, 1977a, 1977b). In the US, compulsory education law began in 1642 in the Massachusetts Bay Colony, with puritan doctrine at that time being moral and upright. It was not until 1918, however, that all US states had passed legislation regarding school attendance. In the Third World, education **law** is a concept still in its infancy. Some might argue that its arrival is driven by a western **ideology** of schooling for all and their organisational inventions such as the OECD. Law, however, as linked to **human rights** agendas since the Declaration of Human Rights, is serving to protect children from abusive practices such as forced child labour.

Current status and usage

Increasingly, education law is a tool of nations to meet their national goals of market place competition success: manipulating education, by law, to capture 'skills' development and create a work-ready populace. The extension of the UK **school** leaving age to 18 is perhaps an example of this. Other countries such as Brazil also wrestle with laws around school leaving age and

what this does to their populace, **society** and **culture**. No law in
education, it seems, is benign or value-free, although laws connected to **safeguarding** aim to protect. These are also contentious and controversial in scope, nature and **power**. Social laws
also affect education: the issue of gun control in the US is one
example where the law interacts with educational settings and
realities, too often with tragic consequences, such as the Colum-
bine massacre (see Lees, 2015). Topics of commonly emerging
interest in education connected to the law are school attendance, school leaving age, points of fairness linked to **race**, **gender**, safety and **diversity**. In a **neoliberal** age, where the law is
being increasingly used for capitalist ends, such as marketisation
of school provision (Harvey, 2005), education is not immune.
The only area where the reach of the law seems to protect rather
than disturb is in a legal and constitutionally embedded (in the
UK at least) right to **elective home education**, as is found in
English-speaking countries, in particular.

Each nation-state has its own specific set of laws relating to education.
As an increasingly general rule, seeming compulsory school attend-
ance is common among them. 'Seeming', because **school** attendance
is not commonly compulsory in law at all. In Germany it is, since
Hitler made laws to this effect in 1939, which have not altered since in
their intolerance of (home) educating beyond or without the school.
In Sweden and Spain, for example, laws have tightened around school
attendance to the extent that not attending a school is very difficult.
In English-speaking countries, children do not have to attend school.
In the UK, the responsibility in law for education rests with the legal
parents/guardians of a child and it is they who have the legal responsibility to ensure a child is educated in an 'efficient, full time' manner
to fit them to take a future role in the community of their **family** or
another one if they so choose. In the UK, not attending school involves
never registering a child for schooling or deregistering them with a
simple letter to the headteacher. The right to education in law does
not exist in the UK; if it did, the state would be liable for any failure
to provide that right and what the right is or what constitutes failure
is open to legal challenge: in other words, the state does not grant the
right to education to avoid trouble with the law, but it does provide
education and legally stipulate it must occur by school attendance or

otherwise (Lees and Nicholson, 2016). Thus we see the relationship of national law to education is both tricky as well as necessarily open on account of a lack of definition of education.

⚙ The law intervenes in education where it appears a child is at risk of harm. This is principally a matter of **safeguarding** rather than education and is the remit of a nation's social services system. Education plays its part in providing 'sight of the child' through **school** attendance and various legal **power**s can be evoked through schools raising alarms. Schools in England have responsibilities to act according to the Equality Act 2010 to avoid discrimination on the basis of **gender**, **race** and other protected characteristics (Wolfe, 2013). Thus, a **relationship** between a school and the law is often in place to attempt to protect children from harm. Unfortunately, some national systems of this relationship do not work effectively enough and children are at times abused by some **teachers** (Harber, 2004). Certain elements in some nations' curricula are made subject of statutory (legal) obligations on schools. At the time of writing, whether sex education will be a legal requirement is being debated in England. In the US, a minute of **silence** at the start of the school day has been the subject of legal rancour over its status as religious silence (thereby going against a secular schooling policy) or not (Masters, 2001), with court cases being fought over the issue. The right of the Amish to stop 'compulsory' schooling at the age of 14 was a legal case brought in 1972 (Yoder versus the state) highlighting issues of **society,** power and child **voice** (McAvoy, 2012). Where the law of the land does determine the entire **curriculum**, this could be seen as 'suspect', for, historically, this has usually been the situation in totalitarian states such as Nazi Germany, Mussolini's Italy, Mao's China, Communist Cuba and Communist Russia. In this sense, it is possible to say that education and the law should only mix for the sake of ensuring protection, **equality** and justice for all. Given the power of education in society for various outcomes, such a belief could be called naive. It is also dangerous, as it positions the law as wholly benign: a contestable claim.

˙ɪ̣ The law of education could be seen in a non-legalistic way. We could consider laws of education to be such things as fairness, good **teaching**, freedom, **voice**, interesting curricula and so on. We could also evoke Lacan in talking of the Law: in brief, of convention and its force to stipulate what is allowable. Education uses Lacanian 'Master **discourses**' to manage itself in ways similar to legalistic speech. Furthermore, education could be said to claim consistency of form and manners of practice (see, e.g., **school**) in ways similar to the claims of Law, as Lacan identified it (Murray, 1999).

Questions to consider

1. Should legal **power**s interfere in education?
2. Is the law useful to protect children and parents against **school**s?
3. What happens if a country changes their educational laws?
4. How does law interact and create education?
5. Who has more power—education systems or the (Lacanian) Law?

References (with recommended readings in bold)

Foucault, M. (1976) *The birth of the clinic.* London: Tavistock Publications.

Foucault, M. (1977a) *Discipline and punish: The birth of the prison.* Translated by A. Sheridan. Harmondsworth: Penguin.

Foucault, M. (1977b) *The order of things.* Abingdon: Routledge.

Harber, C. (2004) *Schooling as violence: How schools harm pupils and societies.* London: RoutledgeFalmer.

Harvey, D. (2005) *A brief history of neoliberalism.* Oxford: Oxford University Press.

Lees, H.E. (2015) 'School violence', in Dubnick, M.J. and Bearfield, D. (eds) *Encyclopedia of public administration and public policy*, 3rd edn. New York: Taylor & Francis.

Lees, H.E. and Nicholson, F. (2016) 'Home education in the UK', in Gaither, M. (ed.) *Wiley handbook of home education.* New York: Wiley, pp.303–328.

McAvoy, P. (2012) '"There are no housewives on *Star Trek*": A reexamination of exit rights for the children of insular fundamentalist parents', *Educational Theory*, 62 (5), pp.535–552.

Masters, B.A. (2001) 'Minute of silence in schools is upheld: Federal judges rule law is not unconstitutional', *Washington Post*, 25 July.

Murray, M. (1999) 'Lacan and the law', *Angelaki*, 4 (1), pp.55–70.

Wolfe, D. (2013) 'Schools: The legal structures, the accidents of history and the legacies of timing and circumstance', *Education Law Journal*, 14 (2), pp.100–113.

KEY CONCEPT: POLICY

Iain Jones

Concept origins

The origins, or etymology, of 'policy' reveals various and multiple meanings. In the Greek philosophy of Plato's *Republic*, policy concerned notions of **citizenship**, while in the Middle Ages the term related to matters of government, the organisation of **politics** and public administration. Medieval definitions offer differing views of policy as either prudent **behaviour** or craft and cunning. In contrast, in late-15th-century Europe, the term policy became associated with polish and elegance (*Oxford English Dictionary*, 1989). Hence, the history of the concept is one of multiple and contested meanings.

Current status and usage

Policy is one of those terms that regularly makes an appearance in the study of education—commonly in three different guises. First, linked to how practices in an institution are aligned, organised, recorded and operationalised. In a **school** this might, for instance, relate to the management of **behaviour**, **inclusion** and attendance, or in administrative terms, employment, pay and promotions policies. Hence, an organisation is likely to have any number of written policies designed to ensure adherence to and practice of agreed protocols; what Ball (2013) describes as 'little p' policies. In the second use of the term, policy has an explicitly political connection in that its 'big P' meaning concerns that which is legislated and mandated by government. Requiring statutory adherence and implementation, big P policies include such things as **safeguarding**, 'Prevent' (an anti-terrorism protocol in England) or **equality** policy. A third contemporary use of the term is described by Dunn as 'an unrealized need, value or opportunity for improvement through public action' (Dunn, 2016, p.5). This last sense is a concept of policy as developmental. With regard to its current status and usage, the concept of policy in the study of education is most frequently encountered in relation to Ball's (2013) 'big P' use and Dunn's 'unrealised need'.

⏻ To begin to understand and apply the concept of policy, the task necessarily involves increasing levels of interpretation and critical analysis. An initial way of approaching this is summarised by Bell and Stevenson (2006, p.15) in their critique of what they call a *rational* model of policy development. Involving six stages of policy formation in a *linear* process, this begins with the identification of a policy problem, e.g., poor levels of participation in post-compulsory education among boys. Then, in a reformulation of the policy, opinions are gathered and specific options identified (this might involve consulting expert professionals, young people and other interested parties). To follow, policy options and possibilities are formally made public (e.g., funding dedicated post-16 provision for boys and girls, recruiting and training specialist mentors for disaffected boys). Then, following discussion, and further debate, these alternatives are shaped into proposals. These proposals may be combined to increase support for them with the aim of building consensus among interested groups. Later, in a process of legitimisation, a group of policy makers identify and select a policy and seek support for it. Finally, policy implementation relies on administrative procedures that enable agreed policy to be put into practice. Despite the simplicity of Bell and Stevenson's model, which offers superficial attractiveness, the model ignores the dual problems of **politics** and **power** and can therefore, on account of this, be considered unrealistic.

⚙ In contrast to a *rational* model of policy formation, an *interpretive* perspective sees policy as contextual and temporal, in which events and their ideological foundations (shaped by debates, shifts and trends within **society**) are made subject to close interpretation. Crucially, in contrast to a rational view of policy as clear and fixed, an interpretive perspective sees policy as partial, incomplete and unstable (Yanow, 2015). In this interpretive approach, an understanding of the inter-**relationships** between different levels of governance (the national, local and **institutional**) is pivotal to making sense of policy as an 'education state' (Hodgson and Spours, 2006). This interpretation of the education state invites us to consider how policy is formulated and shaped by interactions between processes of influence, the production of policy texts and practice, what Bowe *et al.* (1992) call a 'policy triangle'. In contrast to the *rational* policy problem, e.g., poor levels of participation in post-compulsory education among boys and a search for a correct formulation of policy, interpretive perspectives involve *multiple interpretations*, based on various experiences and perceptions of that problem (e.g., should the focus of policy formation also embrace the successful participation of young women in post-compulsory education?). Furthermore, it invites us to consider: What is policy? How can it be interpreted? Why does this matter at local and institutional as well as national levels? In reality, as Ball (2003) has persuasively observed, national policies go through a recurring process of being made and re-made locally and institutionally. Hence, policy 'texts' are essentially translated abstractions of national policy into specific contextualised roles and relationships.

A third approach to policy involves *critical* policy analysis. While sharing an interest in how policy is interpreted, a *critical* view of policy emphasises the role of **power.** In her analysis of this policy lineage, Ozga (2000) considers policy texts in relation to questions about their source, scope and patterns. In the first of these, she argues that policy texts are significant in the messages they convey about their source— what are the origins of the policy? How does it relate to other local, national and international policies? (e.g., how do policies on **safe-guarding** or Prevent align with other political concerns around child protection and terrorism, or education and training for young people in light of international PISA test results?). Hence, the scope of a policy concerns its aims, the framing of debate and how it represents those involved and those excluded who are either not named or are marginalised. Then there are the patterns of each text to consider: What does it build on?; What is continuing or changing?; What **institutional** or organisational changes or developments does the policy text refer to? (Ozga, 2000, p.95). An example of this in the UK is the resurgence of interest in selective Grammar **School** education and the forced 'academisation' modelling of schools which fail inspection reports and are therefore deemed in need of 'saving'. Extending the process of analysis further, Bacchi (2000) not only focuses on the source, scope and pattern of a 'policy problem', but also the 'problematisation' process (Bacchi, 2012), arguing that 'problems' are 'created' and 'shaped'. Consequently, the interest of theorists who focus on policy-as-**discourse** is not only on the 'policy problem', but on how policy 'works' for good or for bad.

Questions to consider

1. What are the strengths and weaknesses of each perspective for the analysis of policy?
2. Why do these interpretations matter and who do they matter for?
3. How could you analyse a policy text?
4. Why is it important to compare and contrast different interpretations of a policy text?

References (with recommended readings in bold)

Bacchi, C. (2000) 'Policy as discourse: What does it mean? Where does it get us?', *Discourse: Studies in the Cultural Politics of Education*, 21 (1), pp.45–57.

Bacchi, C. (2012) 'Introducing the "What's the problem represented to be?" approach', in Bletsas, A. and Beasley, C. (eds) *Engaging with Carol Bacchi: Strategic interventions and exchanges*. Adelaide: University of Adelaide Press, pp.21–24.

Ball, S.J. (2003) 'The teacher's soul and the terrors of performativity', *Journal of Education Policy*, 18 (2), pp.215–228.

Ball, S.J. (2013) *The education debate*, 2nd edn. Bristol: Policy Press.

Bell, L. and Stevenson, H. (2006) *Education policy: Process, themes and impact*. Abingdon: Routledge.

Bowe, R., Ball, S.J. and Gold, A. (1992) *Reforming education and changing schools: Case studies in policy sociology*. Abingdon: Routledge.

Dunn, W.M. (2016) *Public policy analysis*, 5th edn. Abingdon: Routledge.

Hodgson, A. and Spours, K. (2006) 'An analytical framework for policy engagement: The contested case of 14–19 reform in England', *Journal of Education Policy*, 21 (6), pp.679–696.

Oxford English Dictionary (1989) Oxford: Clarendon Press.

Ozga, J. (2000) *Policy research in educational settings*. Buckingham: Open University Press.

Yanow, D. (2015) 'Making sense of policy practices: Interpretation and meaning', in Fischer, F., Torgerson, D., Orsini, M. and Durnova, A. (eds) *Handbook of critical policy studies*. Cheltenham: Edward Elgar, pp.401–421.

KEY CONCEPT: POLITICS

Iain Jones

Concept origins

From the ancient Greek Πολιτικά, Politika, meaning 'affairs of the cities', the origins of the concept can be found in the Ancient Greek philosophy of Socrates, Plato and Aristotle. According to Lane (2014), political theorising at this time concerned arguments about the 'good' of politics, who could participate in politics and why they should do so. The use of argument was considered an important 'tool' in the framing of civic discourses for ideological and material control. In essence, the principal concern of politics at this stage can be regarded as relating to **power** and a desire for a just organisation in line with what was seen at the time as the righteous order of things. Hence, the imperative for politics was the idea of **social justice** and **equality** (of a limited kind for the demos elites who were free men) and divine rights from and relations with the Greek gods.

Current status and usage

In modern usage, politics concerns matters of organisation, action and governance at national and local levels. This can include government, local authorities, trade unions, student bodies, charities and lobbyists and, in a digital networked age, the media and social media as political actors and agents. Political systems are, in turn, subject to national differences as a consequence of their unique histories, cultures, and values. While governance in politics implies a sense of stability and order, Mouffe (2005) considers dissent to be a core element in political negotiation. A key message with regard to this is that the personal is indeed political (Hanisch, 1969), which relates to democratic principles of **equality**, participation and voice. With specific regard to education, policy then becomes pivotal in the relationship between politics and **school** as a key setting for educational activity. As Apple (1993, p.222) asserts, politics and education are found entwined in the **curriculum** materials of educational delivery; as a consequence, education is 'deeply implicated in the politics of culture'.

⏻ One way of developing our political thinking in education can be to consider the descriptions of the historical milestones in national educational **policy**, their legislative milestones and related policy developments. A powerful example of this in England can be found in the 1944 Education Act. Its outcomes can be described as a universal system of secondary education involving three types of **school** (grammar, secondary modern and technical) and **assessment** in the form of the 11+ examination. Although the Act established free secondary education in England and Wales for children up to age 15, a contrasting interpretation is that it represented a 'class-divided vision of education' based on different schools, for different children with different 'types of mind' (Ball, 2013a, p.74). Ball observes that 'the history of English education is then very much a history of social class, and the 1944 Act did little to interrupt that history' (Ball, 2013b, p.8). Similarly, Jones emphasises that the 1944 Act 'was blurred, contradicted and compromised' (Jones, 2003, p.16) by a combination of post-war economic crisis and the vested interests of private schools and churches. Hence, in this political reading of England's 1944 Act, we see the continuation of a diverse and fragmented, rather than universal or uniform, system of schools. Moreover, this was not just an Education Act but emphatically *a political act*—informed by a political ideology of segregation enacted through the lives of children and their families whose life chances were then profoundly affected. Hence, when it comes to education 'the personal is political' (Hanisch, 1969) and the political is personal.

⚙ A second method of reading education as political is in the analysis of **neoconservative** and **neoliberal** critiques of this post-war settlement, where these two strands can be combined into a 'popular politics of education' (Jones, 2003, p.105). A neoconservative vision of social cohesion and national **identity** is coupled with a neoliberal emphasis on the market, parental choice, **selection** and government targets. The different elements of New Right educational **policy** produce practices that are made obvious, common sense and 'true' (Gramsci, 1971; Ball, 2013a, p.7). Privatisation, marketisation and commodification are all terms that can be readily aligned with a neoliberal politics of education, involving such things as the privatisation of school inspection (Ofsted), promoting competition between schools and universities in the form of league tables and the trading of educational services. Meanwhile, neoconservative interests are served by a preoccupation with school selection, 'radicalisation' and 'British values'. These ideological and explicitly political positions not only represent a set of beliefs, attitudes and opinions, they are also a basis for action for both the New Right and those with a different vision of education. This then has a profound effect on matters of **identity**-values, **race**, multiculture and cultural pluralism.

In a third example, we can use the work of Couldry (2010) to interpret the **relationships** between the concept of '**voice**' and **politics** and ask how these relate to education. Couldry's argument extends beyond institutional democratic politics to include a *belief* in politics—and education—as being not only about the equitable allocation of goods and services, but also about values. Couldry asserts that the *values* of **neoliberalism** not only reduce education to the market practices described above, but also create an 'embedding' or normalisation of practice that then materialises in the everyday processes of education in which **teachers** and students interact. Couldry argues that in attempting to imagine a post-neoliberal politics, a number of fundamental challenges have to be confronted (2010, p.139); these include whose voices are excluded and included in an educational system and what space is given to them. Echoing the arguments for **pedagogy** for liberatory practice, education as cultural action and the creation of learning webs advanced by Paulo Freire (1972) and Ivan Illich (1976), Couldry's observations have powerful implications for debating the ways in which new **technology**, for instance, enable politics and educational possibilities to emerge in the future (see **adult education** and **alternative education**). In this sense, the political is pedagogical.

Questions to consider

1. Why are controversial issues political?
2. What are the connections between a political issue and education?
3. Why and for whom does politics in education matter?
4. What other parts of your life are shaped by politics and does this have importance for you?

References (with recommended readings in bold)

Apple, M.W. (1993) 'The politics of official knowledge: Does a national curriculum make sense?', *Teachers College Record*, 95 (2), pp.222–241.

Ball, S.J. (2013a) *The education debate***, 2nd edn. Bristol: Policy Press.**

Ball, S.J. (2013b) *Education, justice and democracy: The struggle over ignorance and opportunity*. London: Centre for Labour and Social Studies.

Couldry, N. (2010) *Why voice matters: Culture and politics after neo-liberalism***. London: Sage.**

Freire, P. (1972) *Pedagogy of the oppressed*. Harmondsworth: Penguin.

Gramsci, A. (1971) *Selections from the prison notebooks of Antonio Gramsci*. Translated and edited by Q. Hoare and G. Norwell-Smith. London: Lawrence & Wishart.

Hanisch, C. (1969) 'The personal is political', in Firestone, S. and Koedt, A. (eds) *Notes from the second year: Women's liberation*. New York: Redstockings, 1970, pp.204–205. Available at: www.carolhanisch.org/CHwritings/PIP.html (accessed 29 November 2016).

Illich, I. (1976) *De-schooling society*. London: Penguin.

Jones, K. (2003) *Education in Britain: 1944 to the present***. Cambridge: Polity Press.**

Lane, M. (2014) 'Ancient political philosophy', *The Stanford encyclopaedia of philosophy* (Winter 2014 Edition). Available at: http://plato.stanford.edu/archives/win2014/entries/ancient-political (accessed 26 October 2016).

Mouffe, C. (2005) *On the political*. Abingdon: Routledge.

KEY CONCEPT: POWER

Dan Whisker

Concept origins

Power refers to the ability of a person, institution or social system to accomplish their ends—often by influencing the **behaviour** of others. Thinkers have debated the origins and nature of power for many centuries: Is it something which is earned or won? Does it belong to individuals or is it an impersonal social force? Does power only come through strength, or can it come from qualities like gentleness, or love? The ancient Chinese author Confucius (1979) thought that power derived from the personal virtue of a ruler, while his near-contemporary Lao-Tzu thought that power came from aligning oneself with the natural order. Others, such as Kauṭilya (1915), an Indian politician of the 3rd century BC, or the 16th-century Italian theorist Machiavelli (2005), placed greater emphasis on the practical tools of state-craft—including espionage, manipulation and warfare. In recent times, power has continued to fascinate politicians and theorists alike, from Mao Tse-Tung's assertion that 'Political power grows out of the barrel of a gun' (1966, p.61) to Henry Kissinger's 'Power is the ultimate aphrodisiac' (Fallaci, 1977) and the first Baron Acton's belief that 'Power corrupts, and absolute power corrupts absolutely' (Dalberg-Acton, 1887).

Current status and usage

The word 'democracy' derives from the Greek words for people (demos) and power (kratia). Thus a democratic **society** is one characterised by 'people power' or 'rule by the people'. Especially in democratic countries where governments are elected, educational institutions are currently mired with questions about who has power, why and what for. Should **teachers** have the power to decide how and what they **teach** or should governments set standard approaches, and test how well teachers and

> students conform to them? Do parents have power to choose their child's education? Should children have power over what they learn and how? Should business people have the power to design **curriculum**s to produce the kinds of workers they want? These debates have been important in the rise of **elective home education** and **democratic education** as **alternative education** to **mainstream** approaches, but, in essence, power in education is still not linked to **pedagogy** and **voice** for the sake of the child. Instead, it is increasingly involved and utilised in capitalist moves to create **school**s as businesses and teachers as servants to **policy** makers' agendas, rather than their own vocation and educational sense or **profession**.

Many people think of power as an issue of **politics**, not of education, as if we could draw a clear line between them. *Where* we draw this line will affect how we speak about power. For example, we might say that a president, prime minister or party was 'in power' or 'out of power'. It would feel strange to describe a headteacher in the same way. We might instead say that they were 'in post' (or not), 'employed' (or not) and so on. This usage recalls the sociologist Max Weber's ideas about 'authority' (1978). He says that in the modern world bureaucratic-rational authority has replaced older, less predictable forms of traditional and charismatic authority. Thus a headteacher's power is circumscribed by the **school** rules and national **law**s, which define the role and responsibilities of a headteacher; a head's power belongs to their job, not to them as a person.

It is relatively easy to look at a classroom, or a staffroom, or a **society**, and to identify who is more powerful, and who is less. It is harder to say what power *is*. The political theorist Steven Lukes (2005) argues that there are 'three faces of power': (1) the *behavioural*; (2) the *agenda setting*; and (3) the *ideological*. Let's apply this model to a **school** council. Imagine that the students have power (1) to affect the behaviour of the school in some way, such as voting whether to paint the corridors green or yellow, or even to shape the school day, by choosing two short breaks or one long one. In this situation, the **teacher** 'in charge' of running the school council might still exercise *agenda setting* power (2), by choosing the issues which the school council should address, or by asking questions in a particular way; by setting the agenda. The choice to vote for one long break or two short breaks implicitly excludes other possibilities—three short breaks, two long breaks etc. Another example of this kind of power is the ability of class teachers to subtly steer the process of choosing members of the school council by suggesting to certain students that they volunteer. Lukes's third form of power, the *ideological* (3) is even more hidden. It could be found in what he calls 'preference shaping'. By allowing some types of students to feel that the school council was 'not for them', schools could avoid ever having to exercise their '*agenda setting*' power at all. Similarly, this *ideological* power governs the kinds of issues which people—teachers as well as students—can imagine being issues at all. For example, the idea that a school council might ever vote to make lessons optional, is so far outside the boundaries of normal discussions of educational **policy** that neither students nor teachers might ever imagine it as a possibility. Paolo Freire (1972) argues that the very *structure* of school **teaching** reproduces this kind of ideological power which works against students, reflecting and enacting the unequal power **relationships** in the wider society.

The French sociologist Michel Foucault suggests that power is present in all human **relationships**. He argues that rather than being possessed by individuals, the power of bureaucrats or experts is embedded in the very knowledge which we use to understand ourselves and our world, and thus it 'is everywhere; not because it embraces everything, but because it comes from everywhere' (Foucault, 1998, p.93). He suggests that ultimately, there is no way to abolish power relations in human societies; that any regime of political **ideology** or expert knowledge will be experienced as illegitimate by some of those within its field of influence. He proposes not a universal revolution but a 'hyper-and pessimistic activism' (Foucault, 2000, p.256) of local struggles within specific institutions or regimes where 'there is always something to do' (*ibid*.). The media theorist Henry Jenkins (Jenkins and Carpentier, 2013; Jenkins *et al*., 2013) suggests that new **technologies** like **MOOC**s (massive open online courses), **learning** apps and online skill exchanges might help new forms of people power through more democratic forms of learning outside the **school** system, in the vein of Ivan Illich's (1971) call for a **deschooling** of **society**. Essentially we can say power is dynamic: James C. Scott writes about the 'weapons of the weak' (1985, 1989, 1990); the ways that peasants and poor agricultural workers use ' … such acts as foot-dragging' (1989 p.34) to subvert their masters' plans, or to take revenge on them. Forms of sabotage are routine occurrences in many schools (see, for example, Hurst, 1991; Marsh *et al*., 1978).

Questions to consider

1. How were power imbued relations enforced in your **school** or college?
2. What is power used for in education?
3. Is it right that adults should exercise power over children?
4. How do we know if someone's power over us is legitimate?
5. Is a **society** without power possible and would you want to live in such a society?

References (with recommended readings in bold)

Confucius (1979) *The Analects*. Translated by D.C. Lau. London: Penguin.

Dalberg-Acton, J. (1887) 'Letter to Archbishop Mandell Creighton', in Figgis, J.N. and Laurence, R.V. (eds) *Historical essays and studies*, London: Macmillan, 1907.

Fallaci, O. (1977) *Interview with history*. New York: Houghton Mifflin.

Foucault, M. (1998) *The history of sexuality, volume 1: The will to knowledge*. London: Penguin.

Foucault, M. (2000) *Ethics: Subjectivity and truth*. London: Penguin.

Freire, P. (1972) *Pedagogy of the oppressed*. London: Sheed and Ward.

Hurst, L. (1991) 'Mr Henry makes a deal', in Burawoy, M. (ed.) *Ethnography unbound: Power and resistance in the modern metropolis*. Berkeley: University of California Press, pp.183-202.

Illich, I. (1971) *Deschooling society*. London: Marion Boyars.

Jenkins, H. and Carpentier, N. (2013) 'Theorizing participatory intensities: A conversation about participation and politics', *Convergence*, 19 (3), pp.265-286.

Jenkins, H., Ford, S. and Green, J. (2013) *Spreadable media: Creating meaning and value in a networked culture*. New York: New York University Press.

Kautilya (1915) *Arthashastra*. Translated by R. Shamasastry. Bangalore: Government Press.

Lukes, S. (2005) *Power: A radical view*. London: Palgrave Macmillan.

Machiavelli, N. (2005) *The Prince*. Translated by Peter Bondanella. Oxford: Oxford University Press.

Mao, T.T. (1966) *Quotations from Mao Tse Tung*. Edited by Lin Piao. Peking: Foreign Language Press.

Marsh, P., Rosser, E. and Harre, R. (1978) *The rules of disorder*. Routledge and Kegan Paul, London.

Scott, J.C. (1985) *Weapons of the weak: Everyday forms of peasant resistance.* New Haven: Yale University Press.

Scott, J.C. (1989) 'Everyday forms of resistance', *Copenhagen Journal of Asian Studies*, 4, pp.33–62.

Scott, J.C. (1990) *Domination and the arts of resistance: Hidden transcripts***. New Haven: Yale University Press.**

Weber, M. (1978) *Economy and society*. Edited by Gunther Roth and Claus Wittich. Berkeley: University of California Press.

KEY CONCEPT: RACE

Parminder Assi

Concept origins

The term 'race' has a biological origin, having been used to distinguish individuals and groups from each other. However, from a biological/genetic perspective, there are almost no substantial distinctions between different human groups. Phenomena such as skin, hair and eye colour, height, and so on, are inherited traits that have varied gradually with human migration across the planet. Thus, both dark and light skin are both genetic mutations, beneficial for survival in different geographical context. Thus, from a scientific perspective there is only one human race (UNESCO, 1978; Sussman, 2016). Despite this, the classification of 'race' has been utilised to treat populations in often negative ways, typically as part of colonial and other exploitative projects across history. 'Race' became a social and political construct to hierarchically categorise groups as 'superior' or 'inferior', in order to benefit some at the expense of others. Such distinctions served to falsely justify **discrimination** (when groups suffered detriments including extreme violence). 'Race' is often used with quotation marks as an acknowledgement that it is not an actual natural phenomenon and its usage may perpetuate racist thinking; however, this portrayal has been contested, as it is seen to serve to diminish the very real experience of discrimination and exploitation suffered (Chakrabarty *et al.*, 2014).

Current status and usage

As a social and cultural category, race is used to identify groups facing differential social and political experience based on their group **identity**. Race and associated terms are thus typically socially and politically charged and their meanings shift across the world, sometimes in very problematic ways that lead to **discrimination** and violence. The term '**ethnic**' refers to a social group identified on the basis of cultural, religious, ancestral or other shared characteristics and traditions; distinctions which are constantly being challenged and redefined (Jaspal and Cinnirella, 2012). **Racism** is described as a process resulting from prejudice (knowing little about a group, but pre-judging on the basis of stereotypes) and holding (and exercising) **power** to affect the lives of others by creating advantage, privilege and unearned social power for some at the expense of others (Allen, 1994). In Britain and elsewhere, some Black Asian and Minority Ethnic (BAME) groups historically or currently defined as 'non-white' (African, Asian, etc.) embrace the term 'black' as a political identity to signify their shared experience of discrimination (Sivanandan, 1989). The term 'race' is highly contested; for example, Bhabha (1994) questions the validity of race, given the increased 'hybridity' or 'racial' mixing brought about by increasing **globalisation** and migration. However, the relevance of the term is seen in how race 'signifies and symbolises social conflicts' (Omi and Winant, 1994, p.55). Examples include discrimination faced by 'mixed heritage' persons who are often defined by their darker skin colour and denied their white heritage; negative reactions to the current migration to Europe of refugees and asylum seekers; and reactions to radicalisation (when groups construct their own identity for the purpose of resistance against exploitation and discrimination: Sivanandan, 1989).

Within education, race has been used to explore differing social experiences and to interrogate practices which serve to disadvantage groups at a personal, structural and **institutional** level. **Racism** in education can be seen in some of the unintended (and intended) consequences of educational policies and practices. Examples include the poor educational provision made for children speaking languages other than particular forms of English and the process of racial **stereotyping** (beliefs such as 'black boys are difficult to control in the classroom') leading to low **teacher expectations** (Andrews, 2013; CRRE, 2016). In a **post-colonial** context, offering all a relevant education for life in the world involves considerable change to a **curriculum**, which, as some observers have noted, still reflects ethnocentric attitudes and values. Some of these values are highly questionable (in terms of democracy, tolerance and social and racial justice) and the on-going debate about issues of race and educational provision continues in England, where non-statutory advice from the Department of Education (2014) is that '**school**s should promote the fundamental British values' (DfE, 2014, p.4).

⚙ Differential educational experiences have been exacerbated by **assimilationist** views (assumptions held that it is desirable for the minority or subordinate group to adjust to the values and norms of the majority or dominant group and to reject the practices associated with their own background as 'inferior'). Unsurprisingly, such experiences often have negative consequences on individual and group **identity**, giving rise to phenomena such as alienation, lowered self-esteem, passing, antagonism, and inter-group tensions (Fanon, 1952). The effect of assimilation (including 'underachievement', and high **school exclusion** rates) led to the Swann Report (Swann, 1985), which identified inequalities resulting from negative in-school interactions, **stereotyping** and low **teacher expectations. Multicultural** approaches (recognising cultural difference and advocating the coexistence of individual qualities) were promoted to counteract these outcomes. However, in 1993, Stephen Lawrence's murder (a black London teenager)—and the subversion of justice that followed—showed that **racism** remained prevalent. The subsequent Macpherson Report (1999) argued for transformative approaches going beyond multiculturalism, and highlighted issues of **power**, justice and inequality often concealed and institutionalised in 'normalised' educational **policy** and practice. This was an important moment in **ethics**. Approaches advocated included the monitoring of incidents and reporting of strategies used to counteract racially motivated crimes.

☺ The **power** to affect the educational experiences and outcomes of race groups is often concealed in practices; for example, **assessment** practices may disadvantage linguistically and culturally diverse individuals and influence beliefs about 'ability' (Gillborn, 2008). Race and **racism** are embedded in the **discourse** and structural forces which supposedly legitimate power hierarchies reproduced by educational **policy** and practices. **Anti-racist** approaches offer a helpful way in which we might delineate race in terms of how it functions and its educational purposes. However, the concept is complex and ideological focus on race relates to the ways in which people perceived to be 'different' are also constructed as 'the Other'. The concept of 'othering' and notions of difference are based on categories that stem from what has been called 'essentialism'; namely, that differences are 'natural', ahistorical and fixed, forming the essential nature of various groups (Said, 2003; Holtz and Wagner, 2009; Hall *et al.*, 2013). This **postcolonial ideology** is reflected in the collective belief systems of predominantly white contexts and is woven into values (Young, 2003). Given the complexity of the concept and that conventional forms of antiracism have struggled to counter racist and exclusionary education policies (Andrews, 2013), Critical Race Theory has been developed to address the UK context (Gillborn, 2008). Here the domination of managerialism, effectiveness and improvement are seen to have de-politicised educational attempts to tackle the structural power base of racism. A more nuanced understanding of race can be seen in views which put emphasis on **intersectionality** (Crenshaw, 1989; Bhopal and Preston, 2012; Carastathis, 2014) and here race (and its intersections with social **class**, **gender**, **sexuality**, etc.) offers a more complex and dynamic understanding of how individuals experience this concept as interaction between social positioning and the everyday practices of social lives.

Questions to consider

1. Why and how often do you encounter discussions around race? If not, why not?
2. How does the concept of race relate to what individuals around you experience and learn?
3. What kinds of research projects on race, **identity** and **culture** can we develop to explore educational experience?
4. Who does race affect in education?
5. What could remove **racism** from education and **society**?

References (with recommended readings in bold)

Allen, T.W. (1994) *The invention of the white race, volume 1: Racial oppression and social control.* London: Verso.

Andrews, K. (2013) *Resisting racism: Race, inequality and the black supplementary school movement.* London: Trentham Books.

Bhabha, H.K. (1994) *The location of culture.* London: Routledge.

Bhopal, K. and Preston, J. (eds) (2012) *Intersectionality and 'race' in education.* London: Routledge.

Carastathis, A. (2014) 'The concept of intersectionality in feminist theory', *Philosophy Compass,* 9, pp.304–314.

CRRE (2016) Centre for Research in Race and Education, University of Birmingham. Available at: www.birmingham.ac.uk/research/activity/education/crre/index.aspx (accessed 27 October 2016).

Chakrabarty, N., Roberts, L. and Preston, J. (eds) (2014) *Critical race theory in England.* Abingdon: Routledge.

Crenshaw, K. (1989) 'Demarginalizing the intersection of race and sex: A black feminist critique of antidiscrimination doctrine, feminist theory and antiracist politics', *The University of Chicago Legal Forum*, 140, pp.139–167.

DfE (2014) *Promoting fundamental British values as part of SMSC in schools: Departmental advice for maintained schools.* London: Department for Education. Available at: www.gov.uk/government/publications/ promoting-fundamental-british-values-through-smsc (accessed 27 October 2016).

Fanon, F. (1952) *Black skin white masks.* Translated by Charles L. Markmann. London: Pluto Press, 1986.

Gillborn, D. (2008) *Racism and education.* **London: Routledge.**

Hall, S., Evans, J. and Nixon, S. (eds) (2013) *Representation: Cultural representations and signifying practices*, 2nd edn. London: Sage.

Holtz, P. and Wagner, W. (2009). 'Essentialism and attribution of monstrosity in racist discourse: Right-wing internet postings about Africans and Jews', *Journal of Community & Applied Social Psychology*, 19 (6), pp.411–425.

Jaspal, R. and Cinnirella, M. (2012) 'The construction of ethnic identity: Insights from identity process theory', *Ethnicities*, 12 (5), pp.503–530.

Macpherson, W. (1999) *The Stephen Lawrence inquiry: Report of an inquiry by Sir William Macpherson of Cluny*, **Cm 4262. London: HMSO. Available at: www.gov.uk/government/uploads/ system/uploads/attachment_data/file/277111/4262.pdf (accessed 27 October 2016).**

Omi, M. and Winant, H. (1994) *Racial formation in the United States: From the 1960s to the 1980s*, 2nd edn. New York: Routledge.

Said, E.W. (2003) *Orientalism: Western conceptions of the orient*, new edn. Penguin Classics: London.

Sivanandan, A. (1989) 'Racism, education and the black child', in Reeves, M. and Hammond, J. (eds) *Looking beyond the frame: Racism, representation and resistance.* Oxford: Third World First, pp.19–24.

Sussman, R.W. (2016) *The myth of race: The troubling persistence of an unscientific idea.* Cambridge, MA: Harvard University Press.

Swann, M. (1985) *Education for all: Report of the committee of inquiry into the education of children from ethnic minority groups.* London: HMSO.

UNESCO (1978) 'Declaration on race and racial prejudice'. Available at: www.unesco.org/webworld/peace_library/UNESCO/ HRIGHTS/107-116.HTM#one (accessed 26 October 2016).

Young, R. (2003) *Postcolonialism: A very short introduction.* Oxford: Oxford University Press.

KEY CONCEPT: SELECTION

Dave Trotman

Concept origins

The origins of educational selection can be readily traced to matters of social position, privilege and affluence (see the Greek origins of **school**—*skhole*) with the concept best considered in relation to ideas of stratification, elitism and (in)**equality**. Plato's *Republic* (380BC) is largely regarded as the touchstone for ideas about the stratification of **society** based on the concept of meritocracy (see **politics** and **assessment**), in which the state sets out to determine the place, utility and social position of each member of its society. The history of educational selection reveals a narrative, not so much about standardisation and equity, but about educational privilege based on parental affluence, a preference for the examination of particular aptitudes, and the possession of particular forms of cultural capital.

Current status and usage

Educational selection is one of the recurrent and controversial themes in UK contexts. While selection courts less controversy in some other international contexts, in the UK its history is closely associated with matters of **class** and inequality. Recent studies of educational selection using data drawn from the OECD's PISA programme reveals the exacerbation of educational inequality, particularly with regard to early age selection (Horn, 2009). Other studies have shown how **school** selection operates in often less visible but equally significant ways, including such things as allowing comprehensive schools a degree of selection based on specialist subjects (West *et al.*, 2007), in-school streaming by ability (Stevens and Vermeerch, 2010), early qualification choices (Horn, 2009, Trotman *et al.*, 2012) and barriers to the access of oversubscribed schools (Hamnett and Butler, 2011).

In the United Kingdom, educational selection is most readily associated with entrance by examination to fee-paying independent **school**s, state-run grammar schools, or admission to university on the basis of post-16 qualifications. In each of these instances, some form of **assessment** is used to determine which applicants are deemed worthy of selection for a particular form of education, qualification or place of study. The issue of selection, however, is contentious and requires us to first respond to some basic initial questions. The first, and most obvious, is why select? A vivid example of one response to this can be found in the post-war reconstruction of England and Wales, where the 1944 Education Act set out to redesign both the school and social system based upon so-called meritocratic principles (see **politics**). In Northern Ireland, the 1947 Education Act followed suit but with an added parallel division based on religious affiliation (Gallagher and Smith, 2000). Crucially, the 1944 Act involved the selection of young people on the basis of a perceived aptitude for future occupational roles. These occupations would be distinguished between such things as the 'classical' professions of **law** and medicine (see **profession**), particular administrative functions, and jobs or trades in manufacturing and other forms of economic production, to which the majority of the secondary-age school populace were destined. Meanwhile, political and military leadership remained by and large the preserve of the public school system. Selection, then, has explicit economic and social aims and leads us to our next two critical questions: when to select and how to select? For the architects of the 1944 Education Act, the question of when was determined to be at the age of 11 at the end of the newly established Primary school phase, and the how, by means of an IQ test in the form of the 11+ examination.

 The pursuit of a selective system of education in the post-war years was not without considerable criticism. First and foremost, critics were quick to point to the exacerbation of a **class** divide in a system where grammar **school** places were 'restricted to a minority by design' (Coldron *et al.*, 2010) and where the majority of pupils would be consigned to what was largely perceived as a second-class education in secondary modern schools. Public disquiet escalated during the 1960s and 1970s around the social inequities of selective education combined with doubts over the reliability of **assessment** by IQ testing (Chitty, 2014, pp.27–28). The challenge to school selection was typified by lobby groups such as the Campaign for the Advancement of State Education. The disquiet and doubts resulted in the gradual dispersal of selective grammar schools in favour of a system of non-selective education, in which secondary schools became comprehensive in their pupil intake: the Comprehensive School was born. Despite the significant **policy** shift in favour of comprehensive ideals, advocacy for selection in state education in the UK continues to be a recurrent theme in the policy rhetoric of the New Right (Chitty, 2014, pp.47–53). Moreover, the selection of young people for specific secondary phase schooling is, as the Organisation for Economic Co-operation and Development (OECD) reports, widely practised in other OECD countries (OECD, 2013). According to their most recent figures, 43 per cent of students from across the OECD are in academically selective schools, with more than 80 per cent recorded as attending selective schools in the Netherlands, Croatia, Hong Kong, China, Japan, Thailand, Serbia, Vietnam, Hungary, Singapore and Bulgaria. Meanwhile, Finland, Spain, Norway, Sweden, Denmark, Greece, Argentina, Poland and Lithuania report fewer than 20 per cent of students enrolled in academically selective schools. This, in turn, reflects broader national educational priorities with regard to matters of social **inclusion**, integration and **citizenship**, competition, and ideas around excellence and choice.

Selective education, by design, then necessarily involves issues of differentiation and stratification, capital and, ultimately, elitism. In the first of these, differentiation and stratification concerns the particular knowledge, curricula, skills and aptitudes that are made the subject of special privilege, i.e., the term 'academic selection' assumes that ability in a first language, **literacy**, numeracy and forms of reasoning are of greater value than say creative, artistic or sporting talents, or environmental, scientific or social awareness. Hence, differentiation and stratification involves hierarchies of subjects or **disciplines**, in which some are prized significantly more than others. Moreover, as studies of school selection and participation have demonstrated, the most pernicious effects of selection relate to the social stratification of excluded minority and socio-cultural groups on the basis, or absence, of their cultural, symbolic and **social capital** (Reay, 2001; Whitty 2001, Gillborn, 2005), e.g., parental occupation and qualifications, geographical location, social **class** and **race** or **ethnicity**. Writ large in the domain of graduate employment, Rivera's (2011) study of the hiring practices among what she calls 'elite professional service employers' in the US reveals an attribution of superior abilities to candidates who had been admitted to so-called 'super-elite' institutions, regardless of their actual graduate performance during their time at university. In addition to this symbolic capital, she also reports a demand among elite employers for evidence of extracurricular accomplishments in which the cultural capital of 'high status, resource-intensive activities' resonates with white, upper-middle-class **culture**. Meanwhile in the UK, studies of <u>**school**</u> choice among white middle-class parents (Crozier *et al.*, 2008) suggest the presence of a more complex weave of moral dilemmas that are, nonetheless, softened by the opportunities and life chances afforded through middle-class social and cultural capital.

Questions to consider

1. Who does selection benefit?
2. In what ways does selection happen?
3. Who is responsible for selection?
4. What are the alternatives to selecting some children in preference to others?
5. What does selection say about the rights of the child and the effects of selection on those not 'selected'?

References (with recommended readings in bold)

Chitty, C. (2014) *Education policy in Britain*, 3rd edn. Basingstoke: Palgrave Macmillan.

Crozier, G., Reay, D., James, D., Jamieson, F., Beedell, P., Hollingworth, S. and Williams, K. (2008) 'White middle class parents, identities, educational choice and the urban comprehensive school: Dilemmas, ambivalence and moral ambiguity', *British Journal of Sociology of Education,* 29 (3), pp.261–272.

Gallagher, T. and Smith, A. (2000) *The effects of the selective system of secondary education in Northern Ireland*. Bangor: Department of Education, Northern Ireland Executive.

Gillborn, D. (2005) 'Education policy as an act of white supremacy: Whiteness, critical race theory and education reform', *Journal of Education Policy*, 20 (4), pp.485–505.

Hamnett, C. and Butler, T. (2011) '"Geography matters": The role distance plays in reproducing educational inequality in east London', *Transactions of the Institute of British Geographers*, 36, pp.479–500.

Horn, D. (2009) 'Age of selection counts: A cross-country analysis of educational institutions', *Educational Research and Evaluation*, 15 (4), pp.343–366.

OECD (2013) *PISA 2012 Results: What makes schools successful? Resources, policies and practices*, vol. 4. Paris: OECD. Available

at: www.oecd.org/pisa/keyfindings/pisa-2012-results-volume-IV.pdf (accessed 29 November 2016).

Plato (380BC) *Republic*. Translated by R. Waterfield. Oxford: Oxford University Press, 2008.

Reay, D. (2001) Finding or losing yourself?: Working-class relationships to education', *Journal of Education Policy*, 16 (4), pp.333–346.

Rivera, L. (2011) 'Ivies, extracurriculars, and exclusion: Elite employers' use of educational credentials', *Research in Social Stratification and Mobility*, 29 (1) pp.71–90.

Stevens, P. and Vermeerch, H. (2010) 'Streaming in Flemish secondary schools: Exploring teachers' perceptions of and adaptations to students in different streams', *Oxford Review of Education,* 36 (3), pp.267–284.

Trotman, D., Martyn, M. and Tucker, S. (2012) 'Young people and risk', *Pastoral Care in Education*, 30 (4), pp.317–329.

West, A., Hind, A. and Pennell, H. (2007) 'School admissions and "selection" in comprehensive schools: Policy and practice, *Oxford Review of Education,* 30 (3), pp.347–369.

Whitty, G. (2001) 'Education, social class and social exclusion', *Journal of Education Policy*, 16 (4), pp.287–295.

KEY CONCEPT: SILENCE

Helen E. Lees

Concept origins

Just as 'Silence ... has been described as "one of the fundamental components in all religions"' (McCumfrey, cited in Landahl, 2011, p.7), so too it is recognised as having an elemental part in education. As might be illustrated in the authority of the **voice** of the **teacher** in the context of the student listening passively, or the issue of many people in one small classroom space or **school** and the organisational management of this, the idea of silence is inherent in educational practice (Landahl, 2011). The history of the idea of silence in schooling has gone through phases, including military control of silence as soundlessness, negative political forms of silencing (e.g., based on **gender** or **race**) to recently, positive silence experiences from techniques of mindfulness and meditation. It is only in the past few decades that specific and continuing academic attention has been made to its pedagogical elements and significance and a concept for silence as **pedagogy** has emerged (Rowe, 1974; Ollin, 2008, 2009; Reda, 2009; Schultz, 2009; Lees, 2012; von Wright, 2012).

Current status and usage

In recent years, a movement for positive silence—or what has been called 'strong silence': 'strong enough to bring forth benefits' (Lees, 2012, p.9)—has highlighted a need in stress-filled schooling for an existential and physical breathing space for mind and body. This is occurring through engagements with experiences of a lack of active **discourse** and is translating itself into a wide panoply of silence techniques and technique-less events, interventions, options and spaces. Silence as a negative or 'weak' concept (not strong enough to be beneficial; *ibid.*) is, despite historical dominance of silences and silencing, still experienced and understood as inevitable forms of oppression, present in schooling through nefarious, unjust modes of organisation and regulation (e.g., Reay, 2012). Silence is a fundamental element of schooling and can be encountered in myriad ways: there is no limit to the manner in which it can be met with as a material and/or presence (Jaworski, 1993, 1997). Recently, its uses in **school**s has been highlighted through trials of mindfulness, which have sought to investigate the potential benefits this might offer children with or without problems, on measures such as neurosis, ADHD or exam readiness (Grosswald *et al.*, 2008; Burke, 2010; Huppert and Johnson, 2010).

 Silence in communication is a key aspect of **school** interactions (Jaworski and Sachdev, 1998). This can be encountered both in the spaces of dialogue and **discourse**, as well as the spaces where no talking is to be found. The way that boys talk to girls or **teachers** to their students has power to create silence either as a pedagogic tool (Ollin, 2008) or as a weak (but powerful) instrument of negation and belittlement. Houston and Kramarae (1991) discussed silencing strategies, such as ridicule or educational presentations using the male epistemological **voice** and way of knowing or forms of sexual harassment in public that keep females silent. Leander (2002) documents boys in a history classroom silencing a girl and after a review of such issues in literature, concludes that most silencing among students is of girls, by boys (p.195). **Race** is an issue here, with whiteness being legitimised via a silencing by white teachers of any topic that creates **dissonance** or impacts upon a comfy, racially unequal status quo (Castagno, 2008). In the classroom, unequal distribution of attention through talk is shown to favour white children (Biggs and Edwards, 1991). Silencing of females and those of colour is not restricted to schooling. In academia, women and perhaps particularly women of colour, are 'presumed incompetent' with consequent **behaviour** from students causing a silencing of their pedagogies and denigration of their **teaching** (Gutiérrez y Muhs *et al.*, 2012; Saul, 2013). Furthermore, **class** is an issue. Even bodies in gesturing and self-presenting without silenced, disciplined form can cause their working-class owners to be marginalised: 'In school, quiet bodies are **learning** bodies' (Henry, 2013, p.14). The lesson here is that *silencing* knows no bounds on the part of the powerful in its pernicious tactics with regard to keeping **power**. Not a word need be spoken.

 Silence as positive and strong for wholesome, loving, community outcomes is another matter altogether. Lees (2012) suggests that only this kind *is* silence, with the weak kinds above being able to be called by other names such as denial, oppression, negation. Silence in this sense is not about noise, for as John Cage pointed out in the 1960s, silence doesn't exist in the noiselessness sense: 'try as we may to make a silence, we cannot' (Cage, 1961, p.8). Techniques of silence in **school**s, such as meditation and mindfulness, suggest long-term positive benefits for children—but only if practised regularly (Huppert and Johnson, 2010). A caveat would be that any kind of silence imposed turns into a negativity: for benefits to emerge the silence must be freely engaged with. In other words, '**teaching**' silence to children in a manner not in line with **democratic education** and **alternative education** principles of individual choice and freedom will not produce the desired pedagogic affect of beneficial outcomes (Lees, 2012). Silence among students where it has not been imposed suggests exciting possibilities for greater interpersonal tolerance of difference (Erricker and Erricker, 2001). Pausing is a particularly interesting use of silence, because it is so simple and needs no costly training or initiation of the willing. Rowe (1974) showed that it aided the students with less confidence and facility with the lesson at hand to speak up. More research on pausing is needed on account of its benefits as well as its cost-free ease of use: we don't know enough. Non-techniqued silence, such as making a quiet space, is a beautiful way to include traumatised children in a classroom (Haskins, 2010).

Silence is a 'slippery' concept (Schwartz, 1996). Educationally, it is hard for some to stomach as an influence in the **school** environment because of its 'hippy' connotations. The rise of mindfulness and meditation, however, in a context of stress and mental illness of children and **teaching** staff, is causing the scientific evidence from uses of silence through such techniques to impact on the volition of **teachers** to get involved. Yet, while the field of such study has 'exploded' academically in recent years (Burke, 2010), persuading busy teachers in a school with pressure-laden student achievement targets to meet to *not* talk or **teach**, to be still, slow down and to, in essence—at least briefly—*not* achieve is a hard sell. Lees (2016) considers that silence has other potentials for school as a democratising force and a social **equality** mechanism: if nobody is speaking, no one is dominating. This level's entry has silences between issues presented to highlight what is not said. So much could be said. But the point is not always to talk in and for education. The idea of chosen, strong silence is presented right here (if you want it).

Questions to consider

1. Is silence relevant in and for today's or tomorrow's education?
2. If there were no forms of silence in **school**s, what would be the result?
3. How can silence be appropriated in ways that do not oppress?
4. Is silence a presence, a material, a utility or something else?
5. Who has the right to silence?

References (with recommended readings in bold)

Biggs, A.P., and Edwards, V. (1991) "'I treat them all the same": Teacher–pupil talk in multiethnic classrooms', *Language and Education*, 5 (3), pp.161–176.

Burke, C.A. (2010) 'Mindfulness-based approaches with children and adolescents: a preliminary review of current research in an emergent field', *Journal of Child and Family Studies*, 19 (2), pp.133–144.

Cage, J. (1961) *Silence: Lectures and writings.* Middletown, CT: Wesleyan University Press.

Castagno, A.E. (2008) "'I don't want to hear that!'": Legitimating whiteness through silence in schools', *Anthropology and Education Quarterly*, 39 (3), pp.314–333.

Erricker, C. and Erricker, J. (eds) (2001) *Meditation in schools: Calmer classrooms.* London: Continuum.

Grosswald, S.J., Stixrud, W.R., Travis, F. and Bateh, M.A. (2008) 'Use of the Transcendental Meditation technique to reduce symptoms of Attention Deficit Hyperactivity Disorder (ADHD) by reducing stress and anxiety: An exploratory study', *Current Issues in Education*, 10 (2). Available at: https://cie.asu.edu/ojs/index.php/cieatasu/article/view/1569.

Gutiérrez y Muhs, G., Flores Niemann, Y., González, C. and Harris, A.P. (eds) (2012) *Presumed incompetent: The intersections of race and class for women in academia.* Boulder, CO: University Press of Colorado.

Haskins, C. (2010) 'Integrating silence practices into the classroom: The value of quiet', *Encounter: Education for Meaning and Social Justice*, 23 (3), pp.15–20.

Henry, S. E. (2013) 'Bodies at home and at school: Toward a theory of embodied social class status', *Educational Theory*, 63 (1), pp.1–16.

Houston, M. and Kramarae, C. (1991) 'Speaking from silence: Methods of silencing and of resistance', *Discourse and Society*, 2, pp.387–399.

Huppert, F.A. and Johnson, D.M. (2010) 'A controlled trial of mindfulness training in schools: The importance of practice for an impact on well-being', *Journal of Positive Psychology*, 5 (4), pp.264–274.

Jaworski, A. (1993) *The power of silence*. London: Sage.

Jaworski, A. (ed.) (1997) *Silence: Interdisciplinary perspectives*. Berlin and New York: Mouton de Gruyter.

Jaworski, A., and Sachdev, I. (1998) 'Beliefs about silence in the classroom, language and education', *Language and Education*, 12 (4), pp.273–292.

Landahl, J. (2011) 'The sound of authority: The rise and fall of the silent school', *Scandia*, 1, pp.1–16.

Leander, K.M. (2002) 'Silencing in classroom interaction: Producing and relating social spaces', *Discourse Processes*, 34 (2), pp.193–235.

Lees, H.E. (2012) *Silence in schools*. **London: Trentham Books.**

Lees, H.E. (2016) 'Choosing silence for equality in and through schooling', *Forum*, 58 (3), 399–406.

Ollin, R. (2008) 'Silent pedagogy and rethinking classroom practice: Structuring teaching through silence rather than talk', *Cambridge Journal of Education*, **38(2), pp.265–280.**

Ollin, R. (2009) '"The silence we create marks out the excellent teacher": A pedagogy of silence in the formal learning environment', unpublished paper presented at The European Conference on Educational Research (ECER), 25–26 September 2009, Vienna, Austria.

Reay, D. (2012) 'What would a socially just education system look like?: Saving the minnows from the pike', *Journal of Education Policy*, 27(5), pp.587–599.

Reda, M.M. (2009) *Between speaking and silence*. New York: State University of New York Press.

Rowe, M.B. (1974) 'Pausing phenomena: Influence on the quality of instruction', *Journal of Psycholinguistic Research*, **3(3), pp.203–224.**

Saul, J. (2013) 'Implicit bias, stereotype threat and women in philosophy', in Jenkins, F. and Hutchison, K. (eds) *Women in philosophy: What needs to change?* Oxford: Oxford University Press.

Schultz, K. (2009) *Rethinking classroom participation: Listening to silent voices*. New York: Teachers College Press.

Schwartz, L. (1996) 'Understanding silence', unpublished PhD thesis, Glasgow University, Glasgow.

von Wright, M. (2012) 'Silence in the asymmetry of educational relations'. In Kristiansen, A. and Hägg, H. (eds) *Attending to silence: Educators and philosophers on the art of listening*. Kristiansand, Norway: Portal.

KEY CONCEPT: SOCIAL CAPITAL

Graham Brotherton

Concept origins

From a sociological perspective, the word capital has its origins as an analytical concept in the work of Karl Marx (1867). For Marx, capital is the sum of resources that a person has access to and is seen predominantly in financial terms (although Marx is very clear that this leads to **power**). The key distinction for Marx was between those whose control of capital enabled them to require others to work for them, the capitalists (or bourgeoisie), and those who needed to work for them because they had no other access to resources—the workers (or proletariat).

Current status and usage

Sociologists since Marx have developed the concept of capital in a number of ways (for an overview see, e.g. Field, 2008; Allan and Catts, 2012); perhaps the most influential version is associated with the work of Pierre Bourdieu, who highlighted that the possession of financial capital brings with it benefits which cannot be expressed in purely financial terms, such as access to particular social networks or the 'best' **school**s and universities. He therefore suggested that capital be broken down into a series of interconnected dimensions; social, cultural and symbolic. Capital is linked to financial status in that other forms of capital are subservient to a system where how much money you have means access to social networks, **culture,** etc., but the inter-**relationships** between the forms of capital are not always transparent. Other social changes, such as the dissolution of the political left, the declining role of the welfare state, austerity policies and the rise of the 1 per cent (Dorling, 2015), have contributed to a growing debate about the implication of the unequal distribution of the various forms of capital. Some suggest that the growth of social media and new forms of virtual organisation present a new way of addressing these social imbalances. This occurs via voicing distaste for the status quo, using democratic voting systems and other means, such as writing for public consumption and communication using **technology** as a democratising and equalising platform for the people. In these contexts, developing the skills for political activism (a form of educational capital) becomes increasingly important.

 Bourdieu's formulation of capital has been one of the most influential ideas in the sociology of education in the past 20 years or so. He suggests that financial capital brings with it access to other, less tangible forms of capital. The first of these—social capital (and Bourdieu uses this term in a quite specific way, which is different to the way it is used by others) is about access to networks. The social networks of those with considerable capital, both personal and **family**, tend to be quite different to those of others and these can be used to gain further advantage. Think for example of internships with prestigious organisations: Who is likely to get access to these? The second form of capital is cultural capital, this relates to the possession of culturally valued attitudes and **behaviour**s. In order to understand what he means by this we need to refer to one of Bourdieu's other key ideas, that of '*habitus*', which relates to our disposition or sense of who we are in the world. We all have a sense of who we are and where we belong, which is a product of our socialisation and includes elements of **class**, **gender**, **culture**, etc. This is not something we are always conscious of, but it affects how we present ourselves in particular contexts. For example, something like attitudes to acceptable 'table manners' is significantly bound up in class and culture and has the potential to make someone who doesn't understand the 'rules' of a particular context—e.g., a very upmarket restaurant—feel ill at ease. Our cultural capital, therefore, has an impact on how we perceive both our role within education and the possibilities available to us, though Bourdieu emphasises this is not to be seen in a narrowly deterministic way. The third form of capital according to Bourdieu is symbolic capital, which can be thought of as prestige or status and the possession of things which demonstrate this—such as a qualification from a 'prestigious' university. Although it can be helpful to think about the three forms of capital as separate for analytical purposes, in practice they are closely interrelated and to some extent interchangeable and interdependent.

⚙ Another attempt to think about the notion of social capital can be found in the work of Robert Putnam (2001). Putnam also sees social capital as being about networks, but his view is more benign than that of Bourdieu, in that he emphasises the role played by trust and reciprocity through the key role played by social capital and the networks it generates in creating communities. For Putnam, communities with high levels of social capital are more cohesive than those without. Putnam's conception of capital has had considerable influence on political thinking around community. In his version of social capital, there are two sorts: bonding and bridging; the former being about the strength of links between existing networks and the latter about creating links between networks through building trust and reciprocity. Crucially, Putman sees a decline in social networks in many communities as people spend less time together. This is encapsulated in the title of his most famous work, *Bowling alone* (2001). Since 2007 **school**s in England have had a statutory duty to promote 'community cohesion', a notion that draws heavily on the idea of being able to create bridging social capital. It is interesting to note, though, that this has taken place in a context where as a result of other aspects of education **policy** it could be seen to be working in the opposite direction. For example, the notion that parents should choose the 'best' school for their child can lead to children going to schools some distance from where they live, and as a result of this, schools are in many cases less 'rooted' in any specific geographic community, in terms of the pupils who attend them, than they were until relatively recently.

⌣ So, is social capital a mechanism for reproducing elites as Bourdieu suggests, or a recipe for social cohesion as Putnam suggests? Can these ideas be related to broader notions of capital? For Bourdieu, you cannot possess social capital if you don't possess the other forms of capital. For Putnam, social capital exists outside the economic realm. Trust and reciprocity are capable of being generated through personal **relationships**, regardless of economic circumstances. It can be argued that the **voluntaristic** forms of social action, which stem from Putnam's conception of social capital, minimise the role of the state as an active social agent. This fits well with the **neoliberal** worldview, in which financial capital is seen as a private good, concentrated with those who 'deserve' it as a result of hard work or effective financial speculation and which they are therefore entitled to keep. As a result of this, interventions which might redistribute capital in its various forms more fairly are deemed to be inappropriate. Such a view has certainly influenced the deliberate attempt to 'rebalance' the relationship between state and civil **society** during recent years as part of the so-called era of austerity. With a smaller state some services are not seen as commercially viable (for example, public libraries) and are instead considered best delivered through the sort of voluntary action which might promote reciprocity and trust. This view links back to the Marxist conception of capital but in mirror image: inequalities in the distribution of the various forms of capital become seen as both necessary and desirable and, perhaps more significantly, are seen as natural and inevitable. Bourdieu captures this well when he suggests 'The most successful ideological effects are those which have no need for words, and ask no more than complicitous **silence**' (Bourdieu, 1977, p.188). For Bourdieu, the triumph of neoliberalism is its success in making the inequalities inherent in the existing economic system hidden and in displacing the worst effects of differential access to the various forms of capital onto those least able to resist.

Questions to consider

1. Do you find Bourdieu's forms of capital helpful as a way of understanding your own experiences?
2. Do you think trust between individuals and groups can be created in order to produce social capital and if so how?
3. Can **school**s or other education settings 'create' social capital?
4. How important is access to the various forms of capital for 'success' in education?
5. Can we avoid forms of capital being divisive between individuals?

References (with recommended readings in bold)

Allan, J. and Catts, R. (eds) (2012) *Social capital, children and young people: implications for practice, policy and research*. Bristol: Policy Press.

Bourdieu, P. (1977) *Outline of a theory of practice*. Cambridge: Cambridge University Press.

Dorling, D. (2015) *Inequality and the 1%*. London: Verso.

Field, J. (2008) *Social capital*, 2nd edn. London: Routledge.

Marx, K. (1867) *Capital: Critique of political economy*, vol. 1. London: Penguin, 1990.

Putnam, R. (2001) *Bowling alone: The collapse and revival of American community*. New York: Simon and Schuster.

KEY CONCEPT: SOCIAL JUSTICE

Iain Jones and Helen E. Lees

Concept origins

Based on the notion of individuals having a common interest in a share of the good life, ideas relating to social justice can be found in Aristotle's conception of justice shared among the community (to an extent) in his work *Politics* (4BC; see Aristotle, 2005). Accordingly, the good in **politics** is closely aligned to justice as promoting the common interest. In writing on the concept of justice, Griffiths (1998) asserts that Aristotle uses it in relation to both distributive justice and the distribution of benefits within a **society**. More recent origins of this concept are found in contemporary work on social justice as about community, **equality** and liberty, advanced in the writing of John Rawls (Swift, 2014). The themes of the individual and the community, and a fair distribution of benefits, remain central to social justice **discourse**.

Current status and usage

It is helpful these days to consider social justice in relation to education in its distributive and relational forms. Gewirtz (1998) asserts that the distributional dimension refers to personal rights and how goods are distributed to individuals in **society**. These fundamental rights include the right to education but also duties in relation to it. Such duties may include those of a student, a **teacher**, parent or carer, but also of institutions themselves—including State institutions. By contrast, the relational dimension of social justice is **holistic**, rather than individualistic. It is essentially concerned with the nature of interconnections and **relationships** between individuals in society—not the goods and services an individual may receive (Gewirtz, 1998, p.471). This emphasis on the relational dimensions of social justice is important because of its connections with other ideas such as 'respect' and 'dignity'. In this regard, recent research on self-esteem linked to social justice highlights feelings of alienation linked to **equality**, and the lack thereof through education (Reay and Wiliam, 1999), suggesting that a socially just education system is one configured entirely differently from the present **mainstream** (Reay, 2012), which works against holistic ideas of the good life for all.

The connections between education and social justice can be understood and described in different ways. For example, one conception compares a **liberal** definition of justice as **equality** of opportunity and the more radical version of justice as equality of outcome. Usually, equality of opportunity is viewed as being dependent upon the existence of equal formal rights, equality of access and equality of participation. However, equality of outcome differs from equality of opportunity as it seeks to ensure an equal distribution of success through direct/external interventions to prevent disadvantage for different groups in **society**. Referring readers to Young's 'five faces of oppression' (1990), Gewirtz emphasises the need to critique multiple relations of disadvantage and oppression that each relate to education. For example, she asks whether educational policies and practices systematically exploit the marginalised, **silence** the already silent 'other', and sustain symbolically violent practices rather than enabling respectful empowering **relationships** (Gewirtz, 1998, p.482).

In a useful example of social justice research, Archer and Yamashita (2003) report on a study of working-**class**, inner-city pupils in a London, UK **school**. This research implicitly *analyses* and *critiques* different dimensions of social justice. Their research was designed to explore how Year 11 pupils (15/16-year-olds), understood and interpreted their futures and whether their right to higher education was one that they imagined. In one sense, the **identity** of each of the young people in this study, reinforced by social and **institutional** factors and educational **policy** that impacted on their school/s and communities, put limits on their right and their aspirations to progress into higher education. Other researchers have built on this study of 'aspiration'. Sellar *et al.* (2011), researching practices in Australia, argue that the notion of 'raising aspiration' may be problematic in terms of social justice. First, there is an assumption that those who do not aspire to higher education have lower aspirations (see also Watts and Bridges,

2004 for a rebuttal of this notion). Instead, Sellar *et al.* reported that the young people in their research may have *different* aspirations. Indeed, while higher education has expanded, it has also fragmented and stratified. Increased demand does not necessarily lead to equitable access. Also, while under-representation in HE may be due to different aspirations, it may also be shaped by a range of interrelated factors, including finance and caring responsibilities. A right to higher education, compared with twin concepts of respect and dignity and further relational dimensions of social justice, can be used to analyse the diverse experiences of those whose transitions from school into the wider world may, or may not, include higher education. Young's 'faces of oppression' further enables us to sensitise our interpretations of their experiences and consider whether anyone ever really listened to what was aspired to in the way of giving and acknowledging **voice** (Fielding, 2004; Trotman *et al*, 2015).

As a concept, social justice is dependent on **politics**: without political **care** for the less advantaged and the marginalised, social justice is impossible. But this view depends on believing that such justice is for all and loses its 'community' meaning of **inclusion** if applied only to those with **power** and wealth. It might be possible for a sense of social justice to involve **exclusion** of the idea of fairness for all, for example; such that only certain groups deserve it while others suffer and for this to not pose any challenge. Can this be just? On the basis of this kind of question rests a great deal of philosophy, theology and politics. With rises in right-wing politics, this question gains weight. Furthermore, social justice demands a vision of people as able to self-express, to be free to lead the life they might choose for themselves rather than capitulate to the demands of leaders, as has occurred in what western standards might deem failed regimes such as Communist Russia or East Germany. In more everyday contexts, conformity to dominant discourses results in restricted lives, which may in turn limit others' perceived opportunities and their (and society's) potential **diversity** (Butler, 1999). This kind of attitude—of people as being required to be a certain 'type'—impacts on numerous communities of people, from **LGBTQ** groups (Walters and Hayes, 1998) to Roma, Gypsy, Traveller groups (Bhopal and Myers, 2009) and beyond. In the **school** setting it is, of course, linked to bullying, a pernicious mainstay of education systems (Walton, 2005). In sum, determining the meaning of social justice as linked to left-wing **politics**—and ensuring the **voice** of the left—is, for some, important on grounds of wishing to avoid violence against others and social justice for every person, not just elites.

Questions to consider

1. How could you apply Young's 'five faces of oppression' (1990) to a description, analysis and interpretation of a contemporary educational issue?
2. What are the connections between social justice and **politics**?
3. What is the relationship between social justice and education?
4. How can we be sure what is socially just?

References (with recommended readings in bold)

Archer, L. and Yamashita, H. (2003) '"Knowing their limits?" Identities, inequalities and inner city school leavers' post-16 aspirations', *Journal of Education Policy*, 18 (1), pp.53–69.

Aristotle (2005) *Aristotle's politics: Critical essays*. Edited by R. Kraut and S. Skultety. Lanham, MD: Rowman and Littlefield Publishers.

Bhopal, K. and Myers, M. (2009) *A pilot study to investigate reasons for elective home education for gypsy and traveller children in Hampshire*. Winchester: Hampshire County Council, Ethnic Minority and Traveller Achievement Service.

Butler, J. (1999) *Gender trouble: Feminism and the subversion of identity*. London: Routledge.

Fielding, M. (2004) 'Transformative approaches to student voice: Theoretical underpinnings, recalcitrant realities', *British Educational Research Journal*, 30 (2), pp.295–311.

Gewirtz, S. (1998) 'Conceptualizing social justice in education: Mapping the territory', *Journal of Education Policy*, 13 (4), pp.469–484.

Griffiths, M. (1998) *Educational research for social justice: Getting off the fence*. Buckingham: Open University Press.

Reay, D. (2012) 'What would a socially just education system look like?: Saving the minnows from the pike', *Journal of Education Policy*, 27 (5), pp.587–599.

Reay, D. and Wiliam, D. (1999) '"I'll be a nothing": Structure, agency and the construction of identity through assessment', *British Educational Research Journal*, 25 (3), pp.343–354.

Sellar, S., Gale, T. and Parker, S. (2011) 'Appreciating aspirations in Australian higher education', *Cambridge Journal of Education*, 41 (1), pp.37–52.

Swift, A. (2014) *Political philosophy: A beginners' guide for students and politicians*, 3rd edn. Cambridge: Polity Press.

Trotman, D., Tucker, S. and Martyn, M. (2015) 'Understanding problematic pupil behaviour: Perceptions of pupils and behaviour coordinators on secondary school exclusion in an English city', *Educational Research*, 57 (3), pp.237–253.

Walters, A.S. and Hayes, D.M. (1998) 'Homophobia within schools: Challenging the culturally sanctioned dismissal of gay students and colleagues', *Journal of Homosexuality*, 35 (2), pp.1–23.

Walton, G. (2005) '"Bullying widespread": A critical analysis of research and public discourse on bullying', *Journal of School Violence*, 4 (1), pp.91–118.

Watts, M. and Bridges, D. (2004) *Whose aspirations? What achievement? An investigation of the life and lifestyle aspirations of 16-19 year olds outside the formal educational system*. Cambridge: Association of Universities in the East of England.

Young, I.M. (1990) *Justice and the politics of difference*. Princeton, NJ: Princeton University Press.

KEY CONCEPT: SOCIETY

Dan Whisker

Concept origins

From the Latin *Socius*—a companion. Society is one of the foundational concepts of the human sciences. It refers to the whole set of **relationships** among a population. The term was first applied to specific associations of individuals (such as the 'Royal Society' of scientists) in the 16th century and its present wider use became common in the 18th-century *Enlightenment* and later among early sociologists such as Auguste Comte (1798–1857) (see Comte, 1975). This usage also has important precursors in earlier academic traditions, such as the Arab scholar Ibn Khaldun's concept of '*aṣabiyyah*', meaning solidarity (Ibn Khaldun, 1377; Dhaouadi, 1990) and Socrates' speculations in the *Republic* (Plato, 380BC) about the importance of citizens' interpersonal dependence as the source of social and political order.

Current status and usage

Concepts of 'society' are not often formally taught in **school**s, apart from (relatively rarely) on sociology courses, and incidentally on vocational courses, such as those related to health and social **care**. More commonly, ideas about society are dealt with through types of a **citizenship curriculum**. The danger of this approach, is that the term can be used in value-laden ways, without giving students and staff the time or the tools to critically examine what is meant by it. The UK National Curriculum for citizenship, for example, says that one of its aims is to 'develop a sound knowledge and understanding of the role of **law** and the justice system in our society and how laws are shaped and enforced' (DfE, 2013), implying that the nation-state is the unit of 'societies', rather than the globe, the city or the community.

> This is debatable, but schools do not typically debate it. It also implicitly excludes at least some international students, migrants and refugee children from the category of 'our society', and possibly a far larger number of students from various **ethnic** and national minorities.

Ideas about how society should be organised, or thought about, always depend on ideas about what society is already like: the kinds of relationship that are important, the kinds of responsibilities that individuals have to one another, the ways in which states should try to shape these. Tensions in education about the concept's use in **school**s reflect wider political debates, such as UK Prime Minister Margaret Thatcher's famous declaration that 'There is no such thing [as society]. There are individual men and women and there are families' (1987) and her successors' characterisations of their ideal societies as 'Classless' (Major, 1991), 'Decent' (Blair, 1995), 'More Equal' (Brown, 2010) and 'Big' (Cameron, 2010). In particular, the political terrain of Western countries over the last 40 years has been characterised by struggles between **neoliberal** and social democratic visions of the relationship between 'the economy' and 'society'— with neoliberals emphasising the importance of free economic activity and social democrats wanting to steer economic activity towards democratically agreed social goals. These political versions of what 'society' means might be reflected in the ways that schools and other educational institutions organise themselves as societies-in-miniature; in the different weight that they give to shared **identity**, individual rights, community feeling, mutual responsibilities, collective or hierarchical decision making and so on. They also draw on much longer-standing debates across the **social science**s about how to understand the overall patterns of interaction among large numbers of people.

The German sociologist Ferdinand Tonnies (1855–1936) introduced a distinction between pre-modern 'communities' (Gemeinschaft) and modern 'societies' (Gesellschaft) (1957). For him, 'communities' were characterised by personal **relationships** and traditional customs, whereas 'societies' depended on impersonal bureaucracy and rational **law**s. Others, such as the French author Emile Durkheim (1858–1917) echo this idea that modernity (including industrialisation, urbanisation, technological change, secularisation, the rise of nation states and so on) radically changes the relationships within human populations (1997).

Durkheim argues that sociology needs to understand the consequences of this change for how **society** is organised and how it can be improved. For much of the 20th century, many authors, such as Talcott Parsons (1977) followed Durkheim's view of society working together, towards shared goals, in a complex system of many different parts—like the organs of a body or the parts of a machine. This view sometimes came to be called '**Functionalism**' (because it looked at how the machine, society, *functioned*). Functionalism has frequently been criticised for covering up the extent of disagreements within societies about the aims and values of a society. For example, Parsons suggested that the 'Educational Revolution' (the invention and spread of formal school-ing) (1977, pp.192–195) had the *function* of helping societies achieve consensus about their goals or 'value generalization'. This was criticised by Bowles and Gintis (1976), Willis (1977) and Bernstein (1971), who all, in different ways, argued that the values transmitted by **school**s are fought over; that the purpose of schooling is to protect the interests of some members of society and to limit the life chances of others.

One problem in thinking about 'society' is the question of bounda-ries; where one 'society' ends and another begins. Popular **discourse** often treats 'society' as synonymous with nation-states: suggesting Brit-ain is one 'society', France is another, Spain is a third, etc. The present world system of nation-states is relatively recent (dating roughly from 1648 in Europe and from the middle of the 20th century in much of the rest of the world), but the idea that human populations are natu-rally organised into countries has become very powerfully ingrained (Anderson, 1991). Early anthropologists often tried to understand 'dif-fusion'—how technologies, practices and ideas travelled from one dis-crete 'society' to another (Kuper, 1988), but nowadays instantaneous mass communication, interdependent economies, large-scale migra-tion and global political institutions make this question obsolete. If we imagine a Malaysian Muslim, drinking Guatemalan coffee, using an iPad built in China and programmed in the US to watch the latest *Star Wars* film, starring John Boyega, a British actor of Nigerian descent, we can see how difficult it is to draw boundaries between one society and another in the real world: what Vertovec calls 'super **diversity**' (2015). Paul Gilroy (2013) points to the positive ways that 'the different translocal solidarities that have been constituted by diaspora, disper-sal and estrangement' can remake our ideas of where societies begin and end—away from closed and jealous models of **race** or nation and towards more open-hearted visions of a society rooted in 'local con-viviality' and 'planetary humanism'.

Questions to consider

1. What society, or societies, do you belong to and how did you become a member?
2. How is a 'society' different from a community, a city, a nation, a tribe, a civilisation?
3. What other, 'different' societies is your society in contact with?
4. What would your ideal society look like?
5. What do and should **school**s **teach** about society?

References (with recommended readings in bold)

Anderson, B. (1991) *Imagined communities: Reflections on the origin and spread of nationalism*. London: Verso.

Bernstein, B. (1971) *Class, codes and control: Theoretical studies towards a sociology of language*. London: Routledge and Kegan Paul.

Blair, T. (1995) *Leader's speech, Brighton 1995*. Available at: www.british-politicalspeech.org/speech-archive.htm?speech=201 (accessed 26 October 2016).

Bowles, S. and Gintis, H. (1976) *Schooling in capitalist America: Educational reform and the contradictions of economic life*. London: Routledge and Kegan Paul.

Brown, G. (2010) *Why the right is wrong*. London: Fabian Society.

Cameron, D. (2010) *Big society speech*. Available at: www.gov.uk/government/speeches/big-society-speech (accessed 26 October 2016).

Comte, A. (1975) *Auguste Comte and positivism: The essential writings*. Edited by Gertrude Lenzer. Piscataway, NJ: Transaction Publishers.

Dhaouadi, M. (1990) 'Ibn Khaldūn: The founding father of eastern sociology', *International Sociology*, 5 (3), pp.319–335.

Durkheim, E. (1997) *The division of labor in society*. **Translated by W.D. Halls. New York: Simon and Schuster.**

DfE (2013) *Statutory guidance: National curriculum in England: Citizenship programmes of study for key stages 3 and 4*. Department for Education. Available at: www.gov.uk/government/publications/national-curriculum-in-england-citizenship-programmes-of-study/national-curriculum-in-england-citizenship-programmes-of-study-for-key-stages-3-and-4 (accessed 26 October 2016).

Gilroy, P. (2013) *Between camps: Nations, cultures and the allure of race*. **London: Routledge.**

Ibn Khaldūn. (1377) *The Muqaddimah: an introduction to history.* Translated by F. Rosenthal. Princeton, NJ: Princeton University Press, 1967.

Kuper, A. (1988) *The invention of primitive society: Transformations of an illusion.* London: Routledge.

Major, J. (1991) *Leader's speech, 1991.* Available at: www.britishpolitical-speech.org/speech-archive.htm?speech=137 (accessed 26 October 2016).

Parsons, T. (1977) *The evolution of societies.* Englewood Cliffs, NJ: Prentice-Hall.

Plato (380BC) *Republic.* Translated by R. Waterfield. Oxford: Oxford University Press, 2008, pp.57–63.

Thatcher, M. (1987) Interview for *Woman's Own.* Available at: www.margaretthatcher.org/document/106689 (accessed 26 October 2016).

Tonnies, F. (1957) *Community and society.* Translated by Charles Price Loomis. North Chelmsford, MA: Courier Corporation.

Vertovec, S. (2015) *Super-diversity.* **London: Routledge.**

Willis, P. (1977) *Learning to labor: How working class kids get working class jobs.* New York: Columbia University Press.

GLOSSARY

Alternative provision (AP): Education that is provided in a setting other than a **mainstream** **school** for students who are at risk of disengaging from school, who may have personal, medical and/or social needs that would benefit from an alternative approach, or who have been suspended or excluded from school. In the UK, Pupil Referral Units or Pupil Reintegration Units (PRUs) come within the remit of AP.

Antiracist/ism: A term that is subject to a wide range of meanings as a consequence of **racism** taking many different forms. The publication of the Macpherson report in 1999, following the inquiry into the murder of London teenager Stephen Lawrence, exposed **institutional** racism in policing, education and the health service. Antiracism, then, seeks to develop dynamic and critical responses to institutionalised processes of **power**, **exclusion** and oppression.

Assimilation/ist: The integration of groups into the dominant **culture**.

Authoritarian/ism: An attitude involving ideas of hierarchy, **power** and domination of others without **consent**. In **school**s, this involves telling students what to do according to school rules and enforcing punishments if rules are not followed according to **teacher** instructions.

Autonomy/autonomous: Freedom to self-determine and choose what occurs. In education, this is often part of **alternative education** and/or **elective home education**, as well as being an integral idea in **democratic education.**

Behaviour/ism/ist: A positivist trend in psychology that developed with Pavlov in the 1890s, and then on through the notable work of Watson, Thorndike, Skinner and others over the ensuing half-century. Sceptical about the imprecision of mental terms, behaviourism sought to redefine psychology as the science of **behaviour** (rather than the science of the mind, as it had been traditionally conceived). Behaviourism thus focused on externally observable and objectively measurable behaviour, investigating how this might be changed (or shaped) by manipulating environmental contingencies. Skinner's radical behaviourism argued that all behaviour was governed by so-called laws of either classical or operant conditioning. Criticism of behaviourism, particularly for its reductionist neglect or outright dismissal of internal mental states and its depiction of learners as passive, came from various quarters. From the 1960s onwards, pure behaviourism declined in popularity, typically becoming hybridised into **cognitive**-behaviourism and allied schools, reflecting the resurgence of interest in mental phenomena. The influence of behaviourism in (especially in traditional or conservative forms of) education has been considerable, particularly in relation to behavioural learning theory and behaviour management.

Capitalism: Involving its chief characteristic of a steadfast adherence to economic markets and competition, the central tenets of capitalism embrace private ownership and the control of the means of production for profit.

Child-centred: Associated with the romantic philosophies and writings of Jean-Jacques Rousseau and Johann Heinrich Pestalozzi, amongst others. Child-centred education honours the agency, interests and **learning** experiences unique to each individual child. 'Discovery learning' and 'facilitators' are terms commonly associated with child-centred education.

Citizenship: In general, this is the idea that a person is a member of a particular country and, furthermore, has a sense of community linked to national and local aspirations for social cohesion. In schooling—particularly in England—this is a statutory National **Curriculum** subject covering **politics**, **law**, **human rights**, community action and national links to global issues.

Cognitive/ism/ist: Influenced by the development of computers during and following the Second World War, cognitivism sought to understand cognition (or thought) through mental models of representational states and processes. Such models typically involved consideration of sensory data, its storage in short- and long-term memory, processes of its transmission, retrieval, and use in action. As an often disparate discipline, it thus drew on psychology, linguistics, artificial **intelligence** and philosophy. Resting heavily on metaphors of (at least) the cognitive aspects of the mind being akin to a computer, cognitivism challenged the preceding emphasis on theories of **behaviourism** to assert that thinking processes mediated the often simplistic stimulus–response **behaviourist** models. The theory emphasised the human subject (the learner in education settings) as an active participant in interpreting and shaping her/his environment. The best-known figure in cognitivism, from an educational perspective, is Jean Piaget (see **learning**), whose development of both a stage theory of cognitive development and a model of schema development has been very influential.

Cognitive styles: Based on the view that how a person might think (involving affect, **behaviour** and cognition) can be seen as preferred style of **learning**.

Complexity theory: Closely associated with chaos theory, complexity theory seeks to both explain and embrace unpredictability in systems and organisation in contrast to the assumed certainties of linear calculations and predictions. Complexity theory has been applied to a range of fields such as economics, environmental sciences, organisational management and education. Crucially, it recognises the importance of fluency in innovation and adaptation in response to unpredicted change.

Constructivism (see also **social constructivism**): As a theory of **learning**, constructivism emphasises human beings as active builders (constructors) of contextualised knowledge and understanding. Such new constructions rest on prior subjective knowledge. The role of the teacher here is as a facilitator, who sustains a learning environment that promotes effective thinking, with knowledge being developed through play, interaction with the environment and with other people. Following Vygotsky and Bruner, one of the facilitator's key tasks is scaffolding a student's learning, temporarily supporting the process while s/he develops competence and expertise. Vygotsky here emphasised the Zone of Proximal Development, the difference between what an individual may be able to learn independently and what they can achieve with the facilitation of a more knowledgeable other. Student ownership of the learning process and outcomes is an important part of the **educational theory** involved, as is the student's ongoing reflexive questioning and gradual refinement of their own learning as they become increasingly expert. Significant theorists in this area, though their ideas differ in important respects, include Lev Vygotsky, Jean Piaget and Jerome Bruner.

Culture: Involving social values, beliefs, **behaviour**s and practices of an identifiable group of people with a shared background and traditions, which influence and characterise members of that group's outlooks and activities.

Deschooling: Widely attributed to the work of academic Ivan Illich in his seminal text *De-schooling society* (1973), deschooling, as the name implies, presses for the de-institutionalisation of education. In the face of the worst excesses of **school** systems, Illich and associates, such as Everett Reimer, argued for informal **learning** without schools, and accreditation based on learning webs activated through community and social networks. It is used as a term by some home educators at the start of a home education journey to stand for a process of detoxification from the effects, impressions and mentality of school attendance.

Didactic/s: In an Anglo-Saxon context, this means **teacher**-centred **teaching** and content-driven delivery. In Continental Europe, didactics refers more to the science of teaching.

Disability: The World Health Organization regards disability as a complex phenomenon involving the interaction between the physical self and society. As an umbrella term covering a range of impairments, activity limitations and restrictions on participation, it is also a contested concept, as recent theoretical developments suggest no one is dis-abled; instead all are 'differently' abled.

Disciplines: Education is a discipline made up of sub-disciplines. These are historically the four of History, Philosophy, Psychology and Sociology. More recently, Economics and Geography have been included. Many **Education Studies** courses are described as **interdisciplinary**. For a good account of the scope of the field and its histories, see work by John Furlong and colleagues and the Quality Assurance Agency's Subject Bench Marks for Education Studies: www.qaa.ac.uk/en/Publications/Documents/SBS-education-studies-15.pdf

Discourses: Communication, discussion or debate that uses symbol systems (e.g. spoken or written language), which typically incorporate value-based (ideological) positions, either explicitly or implicitly. Such narratives or scripts can appear 'common sense', or hegemonic, and can through their persuasive power contribute to the manufacture of consent. Discourses are typically multiple and competing; they demand critical scrutiny to understand or deconstruct them and the field(s) to which they pertain.

Discrimination: Involving the unjust or prejudicial treatment of people based on grounds, among others, of **race**, sex, **gender**, age, **disability**, nationality, political affiliation. See **human rights** and **equality**.

Dissonance: A feeling of disquiet caused by encountering realities or beliefs that fundamentally challenge one's own.

Education: Originally from the Latin *educere*, 'to lead out' and *educare* 'to mould', Education is, however, a dynamic field of contested ideas and competing interests. Hence, what it means to be educated and what counts as a 'good' education are always matters of dispute. Due to the frequency with which this book uses the word education, it is not bolded in the concept entries' text.

Education Studies: In the UK, typically related to undergraduate programmes of study that, while having their origins in **teacher** education, now stands as an **interdisciplinary** field of study in its own right (see **disciplines** of education above). Described by the QAA Bench Marks for Education as: 'concerned with understanding how people develop and learn throughout their lives, and the nature of knowledge and critical engagement with ways of knowing and understanding'.

E-Learning: This is a much debated concept for which you will find many (often conflicting) definitions, including valid arguments that any distinctive definition is underserved, and that it is, in fact, just *learning*. Generally, it is now understood as a portmanteau term covering any learning that is supported or facilitated by the use of **technology**.

Empirical: What can be verified by reference to the material world, through observations and enquiries in and of that world.

Essentialist: For something to be what it is, there are a set of characteristics which are supposedly necessary and immutable. An essentialist view of males and females means they are essentially different. This is, of course, controversial and tends to be particularly problematic when there is a failure to take account of socially constructed aspects of this and when different values are associated with these supposed unchanging characteristics.

Ethnicity/ethnic: A group typically defined on the basis of some cultural characteristic such as language, religion, traditions and cultural practices.

Fascism: When authority is used as a means to dominate others without consent – particularly in systems of government and the manner in which societies are organised. Fascism is characterised by national sentiments, excluding the Other, and is aligned with the extreme right of politics. It uses violence to achieve its means and maintain its hold over its form of order and denigrates democratic processes. An example would be Mussolini's Italy between the two world wars.

Flipped learning: __Learning__ taking place outside the classroom with the classroom used for discussing such learning, instead of 'delivering' it.

Functionalism: A sociological theory, articulated by Emile Durkheim, which emphasised that overall social order depends on the efficient cooperation and functioning of the different constituent parts (or institutions, such as education) of society. Drawing on an analogy with biological organisms, Durkheim argued that each part is necessary and cannot function alone; they are interdependent. The theory had significant precursors, not least Plato, who, in *The Republic*, argues for an essentially functionalist social organisation. Functionalism is often criticised as conservative, as antagonistic to social change, as protecting the interests of the powerful and disempowering the majority: Gramsci's concept of **hegemony** is one particularly useful critical tool in problematising this theory.

Globalisation: Involving the rise of supra-national organisations such as the World Bank, International Monetary Fund, the European Union and the Organisation for Economic Co-operation and Development (OECD) over a declining nation-state. Critics point to the negative effects of globalisation on education, involving the aggressive pursuit of market principles and managerial practices with little regard for national borders or local interests.

Hidden curriculum: What is taught and learnt through indirect means and not expressed as **curriculum** targets or aims.

Holistic: Taking account not just of parts, but of the whole.

Humanities: Academic **disciplines** linked to the arts, religion, language and literature. Focused on human experience.

Human rights: The idea that people—irrespective of anything other than their status as living humans—should be protected from various forms of harm. Emerged from the UN Declaration of Human Rights after the Second World War.

Ideology/ies: The term is generally used to describe a set of ideas that are partial, subject to selective interpretation, or simply prejudicial. Ideology is typically not only concerned with the nature of **society** and the lived life, but, moreover, how society should be. Ideologies can operate at the level of personal conviction and standpoint or involve highly structured systems of thought and belief, such as those found in communism and fascism.

Imperialism: Traditionally defined as relating to the political rule of an empire and hence of colonial possessions, imperialism is a phenomenon originating in the metropolitan *centre*, from which power flows, that leads to domination and control of lands (colonies and peoples) on the *margins* or periphery. Lenin saw **capitalism** as distinguishing modern colonialism from its pre-capitalist precursors and argued that imperialism was a stage in the development of capitalism. Edward Said describes knowledge and power as two cornerstones of imperialism. In this, knowing the other underpins dominance and becomes the means through which indigenous peoples are encouraged to know themselves and their essentially subaltern position (see **colonialism**). Education is thus an instrument of imperialism, fashioning the identities of colonial subjects, regulating their freedom. With political imperialism currently diminishing, analogous processes of domination and subjugation may be discerned in **globalisation**, which involves a form of economic imperialism, in which markets are controlled. Imperial functions arguably continue with education in the domestic situation, the **hidden curriculum** and the influence of **functionalism**, producing what Michel Foucault termed 'docile bodies'.

Institutional: Being of the nature of an environment that functions according to rules and regulations.

Instrumental: In education, objective-led curricula or instruction leading to measurable outcomes for utilitarian purposes. Often in contrast or in opposition to experiential or process-focused curricula and facilitation.

Intelligence: A contested concept with a history of measuring and classifying people based on tests of their supposed intellectual abilities. Both neuro-biological **plasticity** and historical proofs of the occasional incongruences and inaccuracies caused by intelligence testing have problematised and many educationalists would say has discredited the idea that some people are more intelligent than others. It is, however, true that some people can do certain things more quickly or more effectively than others, and therefore can score highly in intelligence tests like those provided by e.g., MENSA. However, intelligence as idea is one that often fails to acknowledge human uniqueness and value for self rather than such narrow abilities.

Interdisciplinary/ity: Involving a range of **disciplines** that inform the subject of interest/study, in which the disciplines are in a reciprocal relationship but maintain their own integrity/**autonomy**, e.g., the study of education can be considered to be an interdisciplinary field of study drawing on the disciplines of psychology of education, philosophy of education and so on.

Intersectionality: The intersection of various social statuses and the inequality and oppression associated with each in combination with others.

Labelling: Associated with the work of American sociologist Howard Becker, and widely critiqued in the **social science**s, labelling seeks to explain the idea of deviance as a social construct in which deviance is created through the act of labelling.

LGBTQ: Abbreviation for those identifying as Lesbian, Gay, Bisexual, Trans or Queer.

Liberal: A major political **ideology** that is distinguished by its emphasis on an individual's civil and political rights, on their personal freedom (including among other things: speech, association, **equality** of opportunity, education and **sexuality**). Criticised by some as a means of justifying free-market **capitalism**, within which the liberal ideal of **autonomous** individualism is depicted as promoting self-interest and consumerism, these particular trends within this political philosophy have since the 1970s been branded as 'neoliberal'. The latter have had a significant influence on school 'reform' policies in the UK and elsewhere, with marketisation, testing, performance pay and competition markedly changing the character of education.

Life-long learning: A set of values linked to the idea of education as worth pursuing whatever one's age—see **adult education**—as well as a 'movement' for continuing post-**school** education for adults. Linked to national notions of work-based employability, as well as efficacy. Connected to the idea of continuing professional development (CPD). It is possible to suggest that the age of the internet has increased the potential and possibility for life-long learning by virtue of easier access to resources of information.

Mainstream: What is most common. Pejoratively used by some educationists aligned with **alternative education** to mean **authoritarian**.

MOOCs: Massive Open Online Courses—often provided by universities as free courses. Retention rates on such courses are low and the **pedagogy** that best works is still under review.

Multicultural/ism: While recognising that **culture** is a contested concept, typically multiculturalism embraces matters of **ethnicity**, **race**, nationality, language and religion. Multiculturalism, moreover, gives particular attention to issues of disadvantage and marginalised identities in relation to dominant **discourses** and political and economic **power**.

Neoconservative: A political trend originating in the US in the 1970s that emphasises democracy, conservatism, national interest, aggressive ('hawkish') foreign policy, and an antipathy to leftist and radical politics. Criticised as a modern form of **imperialism**, in Britain Tony Blair was often depicted as a 'neo-con', particularly in relation to foreign policy. Typically allied to **neoliberal** ideas, neoconservatism is often critiqued as one of the ideological promoters of marketisation, national testing and national curricula in education.

Neoliberal: Originating from political ideas advanced during the post-war settlement as a response to concerns among some political thinkers about encroaching extensions of political **power** in post-war Europe and its threat to personal freedom. Neoliberalism involves the tenets of individual freedom articulated in liberalism but configured with the free market. In the neoliberal state, innovation and wealth creation are mobilised through private enterprise and entrepreneurial initiative is aided by the removal of bureaucratic impediments. In the UK and America, neoliberalism has been most powerfully associated with the **policy** imperatives of Margaret Thatcher and Ronald Reagan, involving privatisation, de-regulation and competition.

Ontotheological: So powerful and all-consuming of our **imagination** that we cannot perceive that the world and its contents could be anything other.

Paradigm: A world-view regarding the positionality and belief system of the thinker or knower.

Plasticity: Brain function that displays flexibility and ability to morph and adapt to circumstance and needs for new **cognitive** skills. The concept has been significantly developed more recently in the work of Catherine Malabou, who points to a 'plastic ontology' entailing a core mutability to being.

Postcolonial: Distinguishing the postcolonial from the colonial is not a straightforward task. Simply designating ex-colonies as postcolonial due to their political independence is tempting, yet too often such states continue to exist in a subaltern status, being economically and culturally dependent. Decolonisation is a slow and uncertain process. Postcolonial as such can be regarded as a process, yet it is also a critical **praxis** examining the effects of colonialism and oppression. It challenges and seeks to deconstruct the hegemonic Western-centric ways of knowing and thus delimiting and objectifying the colonial other.

Praxis (pl. praxes): Often thought of as between theory (abstract ideas) and practice (doing something), *praxis* involves the interplay between thought and action but, moreover, informed judgement about action in a particular situation. In this regard, *praxis* involves matters of informed ethical and morally positioned **behaviour**.

Pupil Referral Units (PRUs): Establishments maintained by a local authority, intended to cater for children and young people who are unable to attend **mainstream school**. Typically, this can be as a consequence of exclusion for persistent poor behaviour, a medical condition, school phobia or as a result of bullying or other circumstances.

Qualifications: Fabricated standards to adjudicate, sift and sort between individuals for work and entry to study. Also helpfully used to prove necessary training and education for complicated jobs requiring specialist skills. The standards involved in qualification achievement are controversial, as are the **exclusion** caused by an increasingly qualifications-driven and -dependent economy.

Qualitative: Involving things such as interviews, questionnaires, narratives and images to interpret meaning and experience.

Quantitative: Involving use of number and statistics to gain new knowledge.

Racism: Defining a group as a **race** and attributing characteristics (negative) to that group.

Randomised controlled trial: <u>Assessment</u> of efficacy of solutions to problems which use groups chosen at random, to see whether positive effects might occur in general and more generally rather than for a specially chosen few. The idea is to avoid bias but also to generalise findings across larger cohorts than the trial utilised. Such trials are controversial for their assumption that one size might fit all.

Relationality: Being in relation to another person or other people. The idea is that this is important and can be done through forms of mutual engagement.

Safeguarding: In the UK, involving actions, process and policies to promote the welfare of children and protection from harm. This can involve multi-agency working where different services come together to align their concerns over a child's welfare with a view to finding solutions. Safeguarding, however, is not a neutral or uncontroversial principle, as it also reflects issues of power and control regulated and advanced through the apparatus of the state.

Schooling: Often thought of as simply the process of being educated through the institution of **<u>school</u>**, or reference to the place of your education. The term 'schooling', however, also refers to processes of control and indoctrination, often through forms of subordination. Hence, schooling can be seen as both a neutral reference to the process of going to school or can regarded as one that involves often powerful **cognitive**, emotional and social legacies that are not always for the good.

Self-fulfilling prophecy: A form of circular causation in which an initially poorly founded claim leads to the consequences that were actually predicted. It thus offers a form of false verification. Deriving from the 1948 work of Robert Merton, it is particularly important in considering the role of **teacher expectations** on outcomes.

Social constructivism (see also **constructivism**): A type of constructivism, social constructivism emphasises social and cooperative/collaborative efforts in learning, within a particular community context. Drawing on Piaget, Vygotsky and Bruner, social constructivism emphasises ways in which learners co-construct knowledge, clarifying ideas through negotiation with others. Human knowledge is thus a socio-cultural construction, a contingent product of engagement and interaction with other people. Vygotsky particularly emphasised that social learning preceded development, that development is socially situated, and the interpersonal pre-dates the intrapsychic.

Social science: An academic domain of forms of science linked to social issues.

Stereotyping: An exaggerated generalisation about a group.

Teach: Involving specific interventions by someone (a **teacher**) to help a person learn something. It requires the teacher to give specific attention to the person's intellectual, emotional and social needs, prior experience and interests in conjunction with an understanding of **learning** processes, contexts and ways of evaluating whether something has been learned.

Teacher: Typically, a professional individual who teaches others set material (curriculum) in a formal educational institutional context (e.g. a school).

Teacher expectations (aka **self-fulfilling prophecy**): The classic study by Rosenthal and Jacobson of 1968 about a 'self-fulfilling prophecy' has shown how the expectations of teachers for pupils can be seen to contribute to achievement. It illustrates how children believed to be 'bright' by their teachers performed well and were seen as having more positive **behaviour** and **motivation** than those described to the teachers as being 'less able'.

Teaching: The act of imparting knowledge, sometimes with techniques used to do so effectively and/or efficiently by employing pedagogic (**pedagogy**) knowledge.

Technocratic: Stresses the merit of technical knowledge or expertise in leadership and governance, often to the neglect of an explicit political or value base. The promotion of such ideas and people can be attractive as a supposedly 'rational' and 'scientific' approach to human problems, yet the results can be anti-democratic and threaten human subjectivity.

Technological determinism: Refers to the reductionist theory that societal and educational change is **technology**-led, rather than (in the case of education) through **pedagogy**. Such a view ignores the educational, social and cultural contexts in which technology is both developed and used.

Tripartite: A system of education introduced in Britain after the Second World War to select children for different forms of secondary education based on the results of IQ tests know as the 11+. This involved three differing types of schooling: secondary modern, technical and grammar **school**s. What school a child went to would affect their long-term life chances, with those selected for grammar schools being most likely to enter a **profession** and earn more over their life course.

Voice: An actual ability or right or a sense of **power** to speak one's mind and take part in collective decision making.

Voluntaristic: Involving the will to act; potentially to volunteer.

Web 2.0: Refers to a supposed second-generation of internet-based services (social networking sites, wikis, communication tools, etc.) that emphasise collaboration and sharing, and allow the user to generate and publish their own content. Mirroring Tim Berners-Lee's original vision of a 'read/write' web, these tools tend to be easy to use and facilitate sociality, changing the way we use the web from a document-delivery system to an application platform.

CONTRIBUTORS

Parminder	**Assi**	Senior Lecturer in Education and Professional Studies, Newman University
John	**Bayley**	Senior Lecturer in Education and Professional Studies, Newman University
Clare	**Bright**	Senior Lecturer in Education and Professional Studies, Newman University
Graham	**Brotherton**	Programme Leader, Working With Children, Young People and Families, Newman University
Steve	**Dixon**	Senior Lecturer in Education and Professional Studies, Newman University
Stephen	**Griffin**	Senior Lecturer in Education and Professional Studies, Newman University
Peter	**Harris**	Senior Lecturer in Youth and Community Studies, Newman University
Gill	**Hughes**	Senior Lecturer, Education, University of Hull
Iain	**Jones**	Senior Lecturer in Education and Professional Studies, Newman University

Helen E.	**Lees**	Reader in Alternative Education Studies, Newman University
Leoarna	**Mathias**	Lecturer, Early Childhood, Education and Care, Newman University
Nick	**Peim**	Senior Lecturer, Education, University of Birmingham
Richard	**Sanders**	Senior Lecturer in Education and Professional Studies, Newman University
Allison	**Tatton**	Senior Lecturer, Early Childhood, Education and Care, Newman University
Dave	**Trotman**	Professor of Education Policy, Newman University
Stanley	**Tucker**	Emiritus Professor, Education and Social Policy, Newman University
Dan	**Whisker**	Lecturer, Working With Children, Young People and Families, Newman University
Roger	**Willoughby**	Senior Lecturer in Education and Professional Studies, Newman University

INDEX